Photoshop®

Design for the Web

Chulyoo Kim

Technical review by Dennis R. Cohen

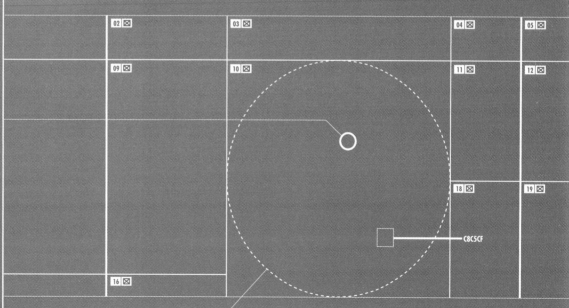

.../DMcDaniel/koolkeith/delasoul/seon/dream/_futura2000-dondi.htm

C8C5CF

Hungry Minds, Inc.

Best-Selling Books • Digital Downloads • e-Books • Answer Networks • e-Newsletters • Branded Web Sites • e-Learning

New York, NY • • Cleveland, OH • • Indianapolis, IN

Photoshop® Design for the Web
Published by:
Hungry Minds, Inc.
909 Third Avenue
New York, NY 10022

Korean language edition originally published in Korea in 2001 by Youngjin.com, Seoul, Korea. All rights reserved. This edition published 2002 by Hungry Minds. Copyright © 2001 by Youngjin.com. English translation ©2002 by Hungry Minds, Inc. All rights reserved. No part of this book, including interior design, cover design, and icons, may be reproduced or transmitted in any form, by any means (electronic, photocopying, recording, or otherwise) without the prior written permission of the publisher.
Library of Congress Control Number: 2001099738
ISBN: 0-7645-3671-0
Printed in the United States of America
10 9 8 7 6 5 4 3 2 1
IK/RZ/QU/QS/IN

Distributed in the United States by Hungry Minds, Inc.
Distributed by CDG Books Canada Inc. for Canada; by Transworld Publishers Limited in the United Kingdom; by IDG Norge Books for Norway; by IDG Sweden Books for Sweden; by IDG Books Australia Publishing Corporation Pty. Ltd. for Australia and New Zealand; by TransQuest Publishers Pte Ltd. for Singapore, Malaysia, Thailand, Indonesia, and Hong Kong; by Gotop Information Inc. for Taiwan; by ICG Muse, Inc. for Japan; by Intersoft for South Africa; by Eyrolles for France; by International Thomson Publishing for Germany, Austria and Switzerland; by Distribuidora Cuspide for Argentina; by LR International for Brazil; by Galileo Libros for Chile; by Ediciones ZETA S.C.R. Ltda. for Peru; by WS Computer Publishing Corporation, Inc., for the Philippines; by Contemporanea de Ediciones for Venezuela; by Express Computer Distributors for the Caribbean and West Indies; by Micronesia Media Distributor, Inc. for Micronesia; by Chips Computadoras S.A. de C.V. for Mexico; by Editorial Norma de Panama S.A. for Panama; by American Bookshops for Finland.

For general information on Hungry Minds' products and services please contact our Customer Care department; within the U.S. at 800-762-2974, outside the U.S. at 317-572-3993 or fax 317-572-4002.

For sales inquiries and resellers information, including discounts, premium and bulk quantity sales and foreign language translations please contact our Customer Care department at 800-434-3422, fax 317-572-4002 or write to Hungry Minds, Inc., Attn: Customer Care department, 10475 Crosspoint Boulevard, Indianapolis, IN 46256.

For information on licensing foreign or domestic rights, please contact our Sub-Rights Customer Care department at 212-884-5000.

For information on using Hungry Minds' products and services in the classroom or for ordering examination copies, please contact our Educational Sales department at 800-434-2086 or fax 317-572-4005.

Please contact our Public Relations department at 212-884-5163 for press review copies or 212-884-5000 for author interviews and other publicity information or fax 212-884-5400.

For authorization to photocopy items for corporate, personal, or educational use, please contact Copyright Clearance Center, 222 Rosewood Drive, Danvers, MA 01923, or fax 978-750-4470.

About the Author

A representative of NOOVO Design, Chulyoo Kim is also a Web design professor in the field of Interior Design at Chung Cheong College. He has designed sites for MetaBiz 'Info114n' B2B, Farbe furniture, Edupia Flash, the occupational education site at SK, and Mokpo City Hall. He is also the author of books on Photoshop 5.5 and ImageReady (Youngjin.com) for Web designers.

Dedication

To all graphic designers:

From the moment that I decided to start writing this book until the moment when I completed the final chapter, I was consumed by an obsessive fear: What could I do to present newer and more modern designs? This fear has caused me to miss many deadlines as I tried to come up with better and innovative designs.

Many people will probably wonder why I was so consumed with design when all I was doing was writing a manual. Well, first of all, eight years has already passed (too short, you think?) since I decided to devote my life to design. However, I have yet to create a design that I consider satisfactory and worthwhile. Now that I think back, this is also what one of my beloved teachers once said. Burdened by this same worry, I find myself reading and studying extensively on my own. Perhaps it's because this common worry of all designers takes priority over their desire to publish a good book? While working on this book, each example, for me, was a long and exhausting process.

It's a given that graphic designers write books that will aid other graphic users. This is because the foundation of creating good graphic designs lies in the understanding of the graphic software. In addition, this is the main reason graphic users pick up these books. I am a Web graphic designer, and the focus of this book was placed on Web graphics. I wrote this book with the hope that readers will find the fun in Web graphics.

While working on this book, I tried to think of what words and expressions I could use to stimulate readers. I wanted readers to feel the urge to create a thing of beauty and follow along with this book as they developed their own unique designs, because I myself am a person who has become drunk on the beauty of graphic design. Don't let learning Photoshop become your goal of reading this book. Instead, open your mind and let this book lead you into the infinite and beautiful world of Web graphic design.

Author's Acknowledgments

To all those who have made me laugh . . .

To my mother, who always has an affectionate and kind word for me. To my father, who has always taught me the value of hard work. To my brother, my sister-in-law, and to my nephew or niece who will come into this world very soon . . . to my entire family, I thank you for the confidence that you have placed in me. I would also like to thank my one true love, Hae-rim Yoon, and the two confidantes who have never left my side, Jae-hong Seong and Jeong-hwan Kim. I also want to thank my respected teacher, Professor Soon-jong Lee and all my pupils at Choong Cheong College and at the learning institute. Last, but not least, I would like to thank Young-mok Lim at Youngjin.com for buying me dinner when I was hungry and for reminding me of the responsibility with which I should write my first book.

Publisher's Acknowledgments

We're proud of this book; please send us your comments through our Online Registration Form located at www.hungryminds.com

Some of the people who helped bring this book to market include the following:

Acquisitions, Editorial, and Media Development

Project Editor: Kelly Ewing

Acquisitions Editor: Tom Heine

Technical Editor: Dennis R. Cohen

Senior Permissions Editor: Carmen Krikorian

Media Development Specialist: Angela Denny

Editorial Manager: Rev Mengle

Media Development Manager: Laura Carpenter

Editorial Assistant: Amanda Foxworth

Art Director: Daniela Richardson

Cover Design: Anthony Bunyan

Production

Project Coordinator: Cindy Phipps

Layout and Graphics: Michael Trent

Proofreader: Sandra Profant

Indexer: Liz Cunningham

Special Help

Hungry Minds Consumer Production: Debbie Stailey, Production Director

Contents

Introduction

One thing that I realized after teaching numerous people about software is that the easiest way to learn is through many examples. Even in my own case, I came to be hooked on graphic design after following a particularly fun example. The recommendation of a friend at school to try drawing dice using the Auto-CAD program has made me the person I am today. I spent a great deal of time absorbed in drawing dice, and then I started trying out other examples and slowly came to try other software.

Even now, I recommend this method to other people. Whether the person is a complete novice or has some experience with the software, I tell them to start looking at a lot of examples. I began writing this book with this basic idea. The various examples in this book, from beginner to advanced, will help you get a handle on the various techniques and tools of Photoshop.

I don't recommend that readers grit their teeth and resolve to study this book from start to finish. Quickly flip through the book, and when you see a particularly interesting example, try it. Then, if you run into something you don't know, find the particular term or technique in the Table of Contents or Index and read up on it. Learn the techniques as you go along. Instead of discovering them by accident, you can learn about them while working on a fun example. You'll master Photoshop before you know it.

The Intermediate User

If you're an intermediate user, you probably can confidently handle Photoshop, but you use only the tools you're familiar with. You understand all the tools, but cannot apply them to graphics. Perhaps you even stubbornly stick to old versions of Photoshop. Learning a few shortcuts will promote your status to that of an advanced user.

This book takes Photoshop apart and teaches you how to effectively use all of its features. Hidden somewhere in the depths of Photoshop 6 are functions and tools that will make your life much easier and your work that much better. I will teach you how to take full advantage of Photoshop.

What's in This Book

Chapter 1 is filled with praise for Photoshop 6. There was so much criticism for the upgrades in the previous version that even Adobe could not have failed to notice. Version 6 takes a giant leap with advanced features and a secure interface. You'll look at these new features in this chapter.

Chapter 2 helps you become familiar with the new features and tools of Photoshop 6 through examples and shows you how to apply these tools in a variety of fun ways.

In Chapter 3, you'll discover how to use Photoshop to create Web graphics. Included are examples collected from an analysis of the image trend in more than 300 actual venture enterprise Web sites, thus providing more realistic and practical examples.

In Chapter 4, you'll find out about ImageReady, a software program created for Web design. Although basic image creation is similar to Photoshop, image optimization and Web application have been added as the chief features in ImageReady. You'll learn how to use ImageReady in Web graphic design.

In Chapter 5, you'll learn how to use Photoshop and ImageReady to create a Web site, as well as discover useful design hints.

In Appendix A, I'll introduce well-designed Web sites and other recommended sites that you can reference. In Appendix B, you'll find out all about the CD-ROM.

::

chapter 1

Photoshop 6:
The New Features of ImageReady 3

This chapter is filled with praise for Photoshop 6. There was so much criticism of the updates in the previous version that even Adobe noticed. This new version, Version 6, takes a giant leap with its advanced features and secure interface. We will look at these new features in this chapter.

The Biggest Change in Photoshop 6

LESSON HIGHLIGHTS

The biggest changes to Photoshop 6 are the dramatically transformed interface, the introduction of vector graphics, and the more powerful Layer Style functions.

The New Options Bar

First of all, the interface has a new tool called the Options Bar. Photoshop, despite its fame, has had the stigma of a difficult and complex interface. The new interface cannot be found in any other Adobe software. In some aspects, users of existing Adobe products may find this new interface quite different from anything they have ever seen.

Adobe based its new Options Bar on the characteristics of the Properties Window in Dreamweaver, which is developed by rival Macromedia. The many subfeatures of the tools in the Toolbox will now appear in this Options Bar, eliminating the need to hunt through numerous palettes, as users had to do in the past.

The Shape Tool for Vector Graphics

The once-rumored merger between Illustrator and Photoshop has materialized in the addition of the Shape Tool and the Text Tool in Photoshop. With the inclusion of the Shape Tool, Photoshop users can now draw and transform basic shapes.

The More Powerful Layer Style Features

Nowhere is there stronger evidence of Photoshop's powerful improvements than in the features of the Layer Style submenu. This submenu includes the features seen in competitive software, yet it's distinct enough to withstand criticism on its own. It's even rumored that half of the time and effort that it took to create the new Photoshop 6 was invested into Layer Style and Preset. Without a doubt, Layer Style is indeed one of the powerful new aspects of Photoshop 6 that has been added by Adobe for the convenience of the user.

Improved Save Features

Even Photoshop's Save feature is more powerful and improved. The new Adjustment Layer and Preset Manager helps you save work in a template while you're creating it. For example, when you use the Adjustment Layer to make color modifications, you can apply frequently used effects, like Hue/Saturation and Brightness/Contrast, while maintaining the original image. By saving the original image and these different effects in fixed templates, working in Photoshop becomes much more convenient for the user.

practice! practice! practice!

Most people agree that the main reason people practice and review programs is so that they can become familiar with its features. However, learning and memorizing all these features may not be worth your time and effort. For example, when using this book, you can look up the task you want to learn in either the Table of Contents or index. As you read about the feature, you'll probably come across other techniques you'll want to learn — all without memorizing a thing!

Lesson 2

The More Effective and Powerful Photoshop 6 Interface

Toolbox Power Upgrade: Options Bar

The unfamiliar bar at the top of the screen is the Options Bar. The Options Bar's organization is unlike anything in previous Adobe products and may seem quite strange to you. In fact, if you're a graphic designer, you may even consider the Options Bar an unwelcome addition because you probably want as much workspace as you can get.

However, after you use the new Options Bar, your criticism may turn to acclaim because it effectively and efficiently holds all the powerful and diverse features of Photoshop 6 in one place.

Palette Well

Options Bar

The Options Bar acts as a submenu to the Toolbox. However, the Options Bar actually contains its own features and is probably better referred to as an extended Toolbox.

The Options Bar allows the user to select and use the submenus that are held within a selected menu in the Toolbox.

Slice Select Tool Options

The Slice Select Tool contains options that allow the user to move between duplicate slices, changing the Auto-Slice to User Slice and activating the Slice Options dialog box.

Gradient Tool Options

This option contains the standard and extended menus of the Gradient Tool.

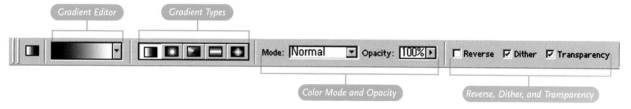

The palettes within the Palette Well

A Palette Well appears on the right side of the Options Bar. This feature is where users can place the palettes they frequently use. To do so, simply drag your desired palettes into the well. Then, place your mouse cursor over the palette in the well to reveal a pop-up menu where your choice can be made.

After you drag your frequently used palettes into the well, simply hide the remaining palettes, and you've created a larger workspace!

Marquee Tool Options

This option contains selection tools and buttons for adding to and removing from selection frames.

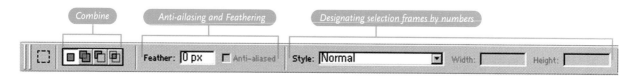

Shape Tool Options

This option lets you create layers and paths using Clipping Paths, apply three variations to general shapes to create Custom Shapes, and assign numbers and other options to the created shapes.

Paint Brush Tool Options

Here, we find the all-new Wet Edges feature.

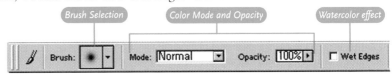

Path Component Select Tool Options

This option contains the Combine button, which is used for combining shapes created using Path. It also contains features used to align two more paths.

Using the Options Bar: An Example

You can select various shapes from the Options Bar, which is displayed by selecting the Custom Shape Tool from the Toolbox.

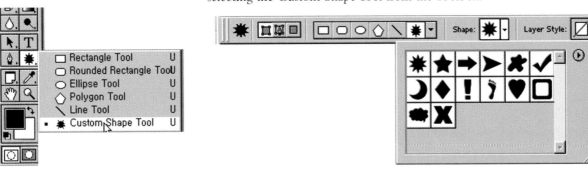

▲ Selecting the Custom Shape Tool from the Toolbox   ▲ The Shape List in the Options Bar

The More Powerful Layer Palette

In Version 6, you can now categorize the layers by folder and color, unlike Version 5.5, where you could control the layer style of the sublayers only by using the Toggle button.

Managing layers using Layer Set

You can now manage layers by using the Layer Sets, much like placing files into folders. The Toggle button on the right allows you to hide/show the sublayers beneath each layer, making it easier to control a greater number of layers.

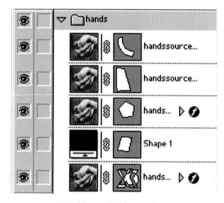

▲ *Sublayers hidden in the Layer Set.*

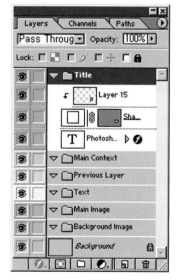

▲ *Layers organized in the Layer Set.*

The color-coded Layer set

Color-coding the Layer Set and each layer makes for easy distinction. We can do this by double-clicking Layer Set and choosing one of six colors from the respective Layer Set Properties dialog box. This color is then assigned to the Layer Set and the layers within the set.

Executing Layer style

In the previous versions, when the layer was double-clicked, a pop-up window appeared, allowing you to make changes to the Layer properties. In Photoshop 6, this feature has been incorporated into the Layer Style button. However, you must be careful when double-clicking this button.

If you double-click the right side of the layer thumbnail by mistake, you have to wait for the Layer Style property window to appear.

Because of this, you can now access Layer by selecting it from the menu that appears by right-clicking the mouse (or Control-clicking on a Macintosh).

Clipping Path and Grouped Layers

One of the main changes to the Layer Palette is the ability to hide or display certain regions. Whereas you used masks in previous versions to control areas within the region, the new Clipping Path and Grouped Layers features let you modify areas of the image without any damage to the original image.

▲ *The Clipping Path, Mask Layer, and Grouped Layer in the Layer Palette.*

The Clipping Path, like the mask, allows you to hide/show portions of the image while allowing you to apply the Layer Style at the same time. In addition, with the Path activated, you can make continuous modifications to the masked region using this convenient and practical tool.

The Broader and More Diverse Layer Effects

Layer Style Palette

Introduced for the first time in Version 5.0, the Layer Style Palette in Photoshop 6 boasts more powerful features. In this palette, you can control the Styles and Blending Options simultaneously, as well as apply many styles.

The Brush Palette has been removed from Version 6.0 because the Brush selection feature is now included in the Options Bar. In Photoshop 6, the Layer Style Palette and the Styles Palette are also two palettes that do the same task. It remains to be seen which one will be removed in the next version.

Style Library

It's said that the people at Adobe invested a lot of time in the creation of the Style Library. The Photoshop 6.0 Style Library contains more than 100 various styles used to create buttons, banners, and titles for Web sites.

As if the pure abundance of styles offered in Photoshop is not enough, the tools that are used with these styles are even more amazing. You can see just how powerful the Style Library is when you look at the various examples in Chapter 3.

LESSON HIGHLIGHTS

No words can adequately express the importance of Layer Style. Layer Style is the major reason Photoshop is more convenient and more enjoyable than ever before. This lesson looks at how small changes to Layer Style can create a more polished piece of work.

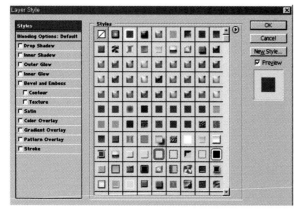

▲ The Styles List window in the Layer Style Palette.

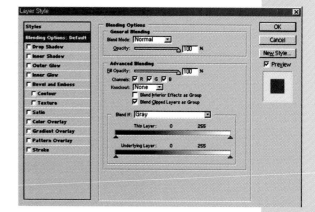

▲ The Blending Options window in the Layer Style Palette.

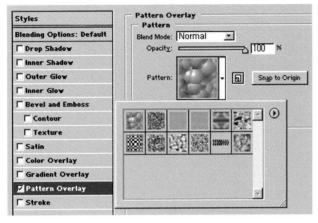

▲ The Pattern window in Pattern Overlay.

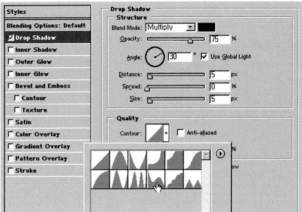

▲ The Contour configuration in Drop Shadow.

Applying Layer Style

The image on the right places glassy, bubble letters on top of a blue grid. The following example demonstrates how the new Layer Style has simplified this once complex process.

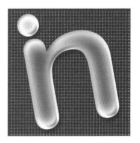

▲ Completed image.

1.

Create a new work window with text and background color layers.

If you want to skip this step, use the sample **Samples⇨Chapter1⇨In.Psd** file on the CD. Make sure that you deselect the Read-only property.

▲ The sample file.

2.

Select the text layer and click the Add A Layer Style button from the Layers Palette.
The Layer Style dialog box appears. This box consists of the Styles List on the left and the corresponding Style options on the right. By clicking a style in the list, you can see what style has been applied.

▲ *Applying Layer Style to the text layer.*

3.

The Layer Style dialog box consists of the Styles List on the left and the corresponding Style options on the right. By clicking a style in the list, you can see what style has been applied.
Click the color selection box and select the color white at an Opacity of 100.

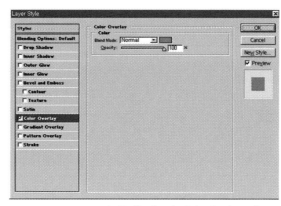

▲ *Configuring the Color Overlay option.*

4.

Apply Bevel and Emboss.
From the list on the left side of the Layer Style dialog box, select Bevel and Emboss. The Style Options window will appear in the space to the right.

The preview thumbnail on the right side of the Layer Style dialog box shows how the combined styles will appear when saved in the Styles Palette.

If the color in the image is the same as that of the Color Overlay, you will not be able to verify the effect. In other words, Photoshop will think that verification is not necessary. In the example, because the color seen in

The Favorites feature in the Open Dialog Box

When another file is opened in Photoshop, it automatically looks first in the same folder from which the previous file was loaded. When loading images from the network, Photoshop will look in the folder where Photoshop is installed. This is where the Favorites feature comes in.

In Windows, click the Favorites button to open the pop-up menu and choose Add to Favorite. Then add the network folder to the Favorites list. Now you can easily access this folder at any time from the Favorites pop-up menu.

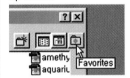

▲ *The Favorites button in the Windows Open dialog box.*

On a Mac, first navigate to the folder you want to access. Then click the Favorites button to open the pop-up menu and choose Add to Favorites, which adds the network folder to the Favorites list. Now this folder can be accessed easily at any time from the Favorites pop-up menu.

the layer image is not included in Style, the Style applied to the blue color and the Style applied to the red color can give two completely different results. In order to prevent these kinds of problems, we included the background color information for the Style itself. I emphasize this point here because it's something many users overlook.

5.

To apply Bevel and Emboss, select that option from the list on the left side of the Layer Style dialog box.
The Style Options window appears in the space to the right.

You can make a selection from the list on the left by simply clicking the checkbox next to the Style name or by clicking the name of the Style itself. You can also use the checkbox to undo a certain Style or to apply the default style.

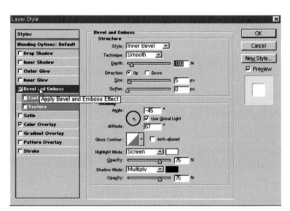

▲ *The Style Options window for Bevel and Emboss.*

6.

To apply Inner Glow, which gives the letters a transparent, glassy effect, select Inner Glow from the list on the left and configure the options on the right.

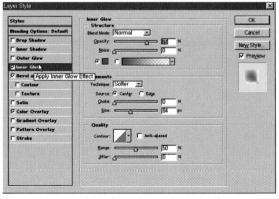

▲ *The Style Options window for Inner Glow.*

7.

To add a very soft shadow, choose the Drop Shadow option.

After applying only three styles, the image is now complete. The transparent, glassy style that you applied to the image is now saved in the Styles Palette.

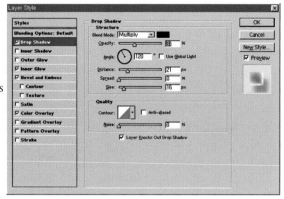

▲ *The Style Options window for Drop Shadow.*

▲ *Your nifty image after applying the Layer Style.*

8.

To save styles in the palette, first activate the layer to which the style was applied and then click the mouse on an empty space in the Styles Palette.

A dialog box appears where you can enter the name for the new style.

9.

Name the style and then click OK.

The style is now added to the list.

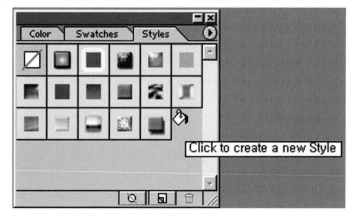

▲ *The new style added to the Styles Palette.*

The use global light option

Global Light refers to the position of the light and is an option that can be applied to all styles. When this option is selected, the position of the light source in all the styles will be the same. It also means that when the position of the light source in one style is changed, the light source will change for all the other styles in the current layer. If you want to give each style a unique light direction, uncheck this option.

10.

To make the background tile image, activate the background color layer by opening the Layer Style dialog box and applying Color Overlay (R:6, G:0, B:255).
You should see a blue color.

11.

Select Bevel and Emboss again from the list on the left and apply it to the image using the default values.

12.

To make the tiles, select Texture from the submenu under Bevel and Emboss and configure Layer Style to complete the image.

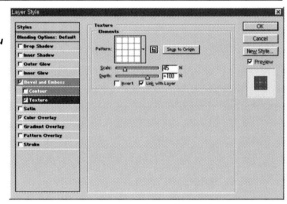

▲ *Configuring the Texture option.*

If you want to verify your results, simply load the file **Samples⇨ Chapter1⇨In-after.Psd** from the supplementary CD-ROM.

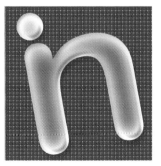

▲ *The completed image.*

The Slice Feature for Image Optimization

The New Slice Tool

The Slice Tool that's in ImageReady has now been added to Photoshop, but with even more options for use with Web graphics. More specifically, Photoshop's submenus now contain features for Slice and Image Optimizing in addition to the Save For Web feature used to create HTML files. These features are also organized in a much simpler way than in ImageReady.

LESSON HIGHLIGHTS

If you're familiar with the Slice Tool in ImageReady 2.0 or later, you should have no problem with the Slice feature in Photoshop. Although Photoshop's Slice is a highly simplified version of the one seen in ImageReady, it is enough to create and optimize Web images using only Photoshop.

◀ *The Slice Option Palette.*

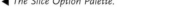

◀ *The Slice Tool Option Bar.*

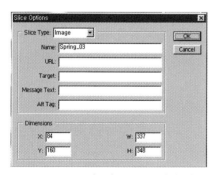

▲ *The Slice Options dialog box.*

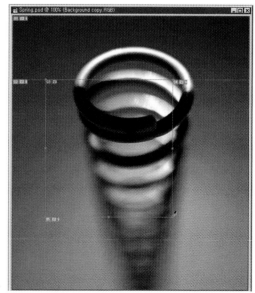

▶ *Slicing the screen using the Slice Tool.*

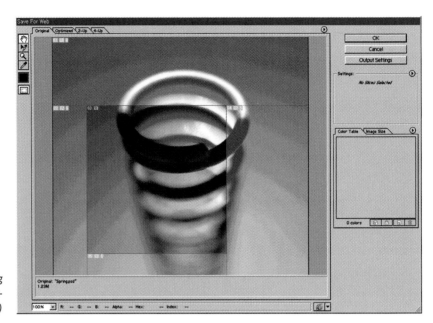

▶ *The control window that appears by choosing Save For Web. (Used to optimize images, preview changes, and configure Slice options.)*

τip

The Slice numbers may make previewing the overall image impossible. You can eliminate this problem by deselecting the Show Slice Numbers option in the Slice tool's Options Bar.

Dynamic Layer-Based Slices

You will now convert the image frame of the layer to a Slice frame. The following technique is an easy way to create a Slice frame:

1.

Select New Layer Based Slice from the Layer menu.

▶
The image where the clipping path is made up of the masked region and only a portion of the image.

▼ *The application of the New Layer Based Slice command to slice the two layers.*

Creating My Own Workspace

Preset Manager

Photoshop 6 has more diverse Preset tools than previous versions. The Preset Manager, located in the Edit menu, allows users to control the several hundred types of brushes, swatches, gradients, patterns, styles, contours, and custom shapes in seven different palettes at the same time. This tool offers a work environment that allows the user to control the many support files located in the Photoshop folder. As a result, you no longer need to go searching throughout your computer's hard disk when you want to change your brush style.

LESSON HIGHLIGHTS

In this lesson, we see how to use the Preset Manager to make many subordinate file types related to Photoshop and how to develop various templates.

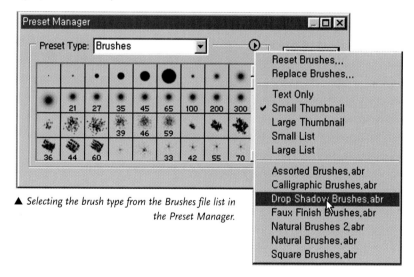

▲ *Selecting the brush type from the Brushes file list in the Preset Manager.*

preset save function

The Save feature in Layer Style and Preset is the most telling sign that Adobe has indeed made revolutionary developments in this upgrade. The fact that users can now develop their own presets and save them as Photoshop tools is a very big development. After its appearance on the Web, the response to open source has been tremendous. This software is being evaluated and modified by many ordinary people and seems as if Adobe did not want to be left out of this phenomenon. Just look at the thousands of free presets that can be found on the Internet!

Paint Shop Pro played a large role in Adobe's decision to put the development of the preset in the user's hands. Hidden by the limelight placed on Photoshop, Paint Shop Pro has always lurked in the shadows. However, in the world of the "Internet Underground," Paint Shop Pro exceeds Photoshop by far. Many brushes, patterns, and tiles can be found on personal Web sites, and JASC, the developers of Paint Shop Pro, offers full support of the infrastructure through its Internet homepage. At the root of all this was the Preset Save Function. Users everywhere will play a big role in the development of sources through the Preset Save Function.

Save Set

You can see the Save Set feature in the Preset Manager dialog box. This feature lets you combine the abundant Photoshop sources or their own source creations and save them in a file.

You can create your own brushes, gradients, patterns, styles, contours, and custom shapes and save them in a folder to create your own unique Photoshop presets. To do so, you just choose either Define Brush, Define Pattern, or Define Shape from the Edit menu or the Save feature in the Styles Palette.

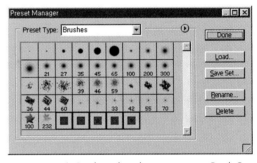

▲ *Brushes selected to create a new Brush Set.*

adjusting presets

The Preset Manager is set up so that it can be adjusted within each Layers Palette. Therefore, if you want to change just one part of the preset, as opposed to the entire preset, you don't have to load the Preset Manager. Instead, you can simply select Preset from the Layers Palette pop-up menu.

Text Modification and Transformation

Text Changes

Photoshop 5.5 used the text creation methods found in Illustrator. However, Version 6 incorporates more effective means of text creation. You now can enter text directly onto the screen and then edit the text by using the sub-features of the Text Tool found in the Options Bar.

However, the greatest change to text creation comes in the form of the Create Warped Text feature.

▲ *Entering text directly onto the screen.*

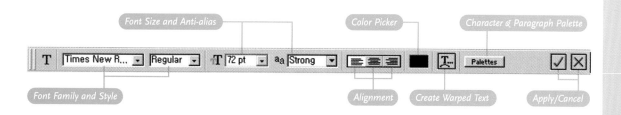

Font Size and Anti-alias

Color Picker

Character & Paragraph Palette

Font Family and Style

Alignment

Create Warped Text

Apply/Cancel

Warped Text

Warped text refers to a line of text that is made to follow the curve of a path. In previous versions, you had to rely on the help of Illustrator to create these same effects, but now you can use Photoshop to achieve similar results. You can find the Warped Text feature in the Options Bar.

Clicking the Create Warped Text button opens the Warp Text dialog box. By selecting the desired shape and applying it to the text, you can distort the text without converting the text layer into a rasterized layer.

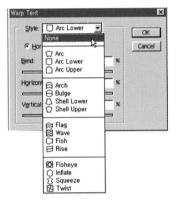

▲ The Warp Text dialog box.

▶ Entering text in the text frame.

You can use the Text Tool to create the text frame where you plan to type the text. Then, working directly in the text frame, you can type the text and change its color, size, and alignment.

▲ Making the text frame.   ▲ Entering and modifying the text within the text frame.

20

Creating a Work Path

In order to change the shape of the text or to add fun graphic elements, simply choose the command Layer⇨Type⇨Create Work Path. After entering the text using the Text Tool, you can create a work path by choosing Layer⇨New Fill Layer to create a colored shape. You then can use the Path and Shape Tools to change the shapes or to add new ones to liven up the image.

▲ *An example of a work path.*   ▲ *An example of modifying the created work path.*

Creating Descriptive Text

1.

Activate the cotton candy text path prepared in the Paths Palette and display it in the work window.

getting ready

Copy **Samples⇨Chapter1⇨ Cottoncandy.Psd** onto the hard disk and, after undoing the Read-Only property, load it into Photoshop.

▲ *Completed image.*

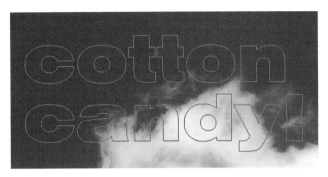

▲ The activated text path.

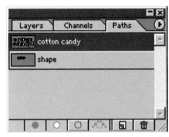

▲ Activating cotton candy in the Paths Palette.

2.

Select Solid Color from the Create New Fill Or Adjustment Layer pop-up menu in the Layers Palette to create a new Clipping Path layer.

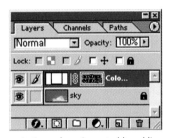

▲ A new layer is created by adding color to the path.

▲ Application of the text path as a clipping path in the new layer.

▲ Adding an Adjustment Layer.

3.

Select the Direct Selection Tool from the Toolbox.

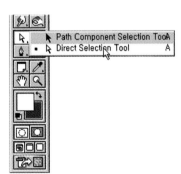

▶ Selecting the Direct Selection Tool from the Toolbox.

4.

Select the internal paths of the letter o and press the Del key to remove.

You can select the respective curve in its entirety by clicking a portion of the path curve while holding down the Alt key.

▲ *Selecting the internal paths of the letter o.*

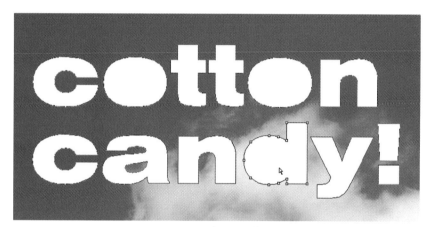

▲ *The internal paths removed from the letters o and d.*

5.

To add shape to the text, first activate the Shape Path in the Paths Palette.

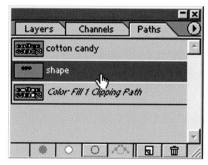

▲ *Activating the Shape Path in the Paths Palette.*

6.

Using the Path Component Selection Tool from the Toolbox, move the Shape path onto the image so that it aligns with the text as shown in the figure.

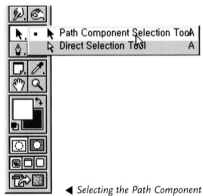

▲ The Shape path moved onto the image.

◄ Selecting the Path Component Selection Tool.

7.

Select all the paths while holding down the Shift key and choose Edit⇨Copy to duplicate them.

8.

Activate Color Fill 1 Clipping Path and use Edit⇨Paste to merge the duplicated Shape paths and the text paths.

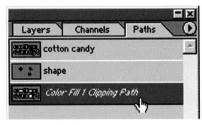

▲ Selecting Color Fill 1 Clipping Path.

▶ Merging the duplicated Shape paths and the text paths.

9.

Select Exclude Overlapping Shape Areas from the Options Bar to remove the Shape paths from the text.

You can verify the completed image by loading **Samples⇨Chapter1⇨ Cottoncandy-after.Psd** from the supplementary CD-ROM.

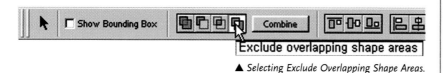

▲ *Selecting Exclude Overlapping Shape Areas.*

▲ *The completed image Cottoncandy-after.Psd.*

> ## Tools for creating text transformations
>
> You can use the many Text Tools in Photoshop to add new life to your old fonts. First of all, in the Character Palette, adjust the Vertically Scale and the Horizontally Scale to create a longer and wider font. Then select Faux Italic and Faux Bold from the pop-up menu at the top right. You can then apply Warp Text and Texts Create Work Path to this font to create more diverse shapes.
>
>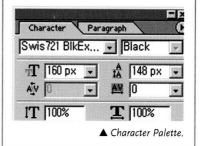
>
> ▲ *Character Palette.*

Lesson 7

Other New Features

LESSON HIGHLIGHTS

In this lesson, you find out about the Liquify and Notes Tools.

A Fun Feature of Photoshop: Liquify

You may be familiar with Kai's Power Goo software program from Metatools, which is similar to Photoshop's Liquify command, located in the Image menu. You can use this program to distort images and pictures that are loaded into it.

You can use the Smudge tool to create an image that appears to have been drawn with water. If you have been frustrated by this tool before, try the following example to see just how fun Liquify can be.

▲ Original image.

▲ The Liquify work window.

▲ After applying the filter.

smudge

Whereas the Liquify command creates a watery distortion, the Smudge tool in the Toolbox creates an image that appears to have been smeared by hand and is very effective for dealing with areas that stand out too much.

Adding Notes to the PSD File: Notes Tool

Say that you want to prevent other people from plagiarizing or copying your work without permission or, as the author, you just want to include a few words about your work. You can do so by adding an Annotation.

When this tool is activated, you can look up the profile, by date or author name, at any time. In addition, you can use the Audio Annotation Tool to record a voice message on the image. However, the downfall is that, because the Notes Tool can only exist on a layer, you can use it only in PSD or PDF formatted files.

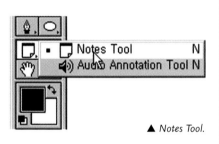

▲ *Notes Tool.*

▲ *Using the Annotation Tool to leave a message on the image.*

Lesson 8

LESSON HIGHLIGHTS

The Image Map Tool in the
Toolbox is a frame configuration tool that you can use to
hyperlink one image to
several pages. You can then
enter this frame as a URL in
the Image Map Palette and
give it hyperlink features.

The New Features of ImageReady 3

Image Map Tool and Slice

The most visible difference in Photoshop 6 is the addition of the Image Map Tool to the Toolbox. This tool and the Slice Tool are both used for the Web.

Additionally, ImageReady 2.0's Image Map (on the Layer Option Palette) has been reborn as the improved Image Map Palette.

The Image Map is used to create several hyperlinks in images that cannot or do not need to be sliced.

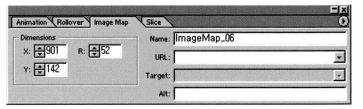

▲ *Image Map Tool.*

what is the image map?

An HTML page contains several frames (rectangular, circular, and polygonal) based on the image pixel information. Image maps are tags that hyperlink these frames to other pages. Rectangular frames are configured based on the top-left and bottom-right coordinate, and circular frames are configured based on the midpoint and the radius. The pixel information used to configure the Image Map frame can be verified through the coordinates in the Info Palette.

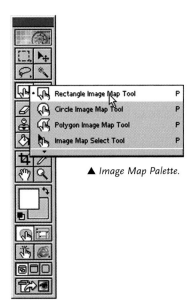

▲ *Image Map Palette.*

Tween

The Tween function, found in a submenu of the Animation Palette, adds effects, such as Fade, between frames to create animation. Although this feature was seen in Version 2.0, Version 3.0 brings Tween to the surface of the palette for easier use.

You can use Tween to create a simple animation. In my sample two-layer animation, I chose the theme of Day and Night and created the images of the moon and the sun by using Photoshop's Custom Shape Tool. I then loaded these images into ImageReady and added animation effects by using the Animation Palette.

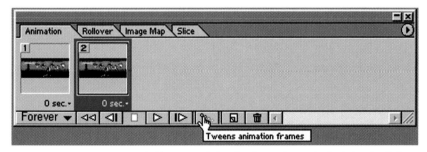

▲ The Tweens Animation Frames button in the Animation Palette.

▲ The two images made in the Layers Palette.

improvement in performance speed

ImageReady contains thumbnail images of the Animation Palette, Rollover Palette, and the Slice Palette. The thumbnails in Photoshop and ImageReady use the system's cache and, therefore, the performance speed of the program will depend on the system. As a result, it may appear that Photoshop outperforms ImageReady.

You can improve the performance speed somewhat by right-clicking (control-clicking on a Mac) the mouse on the thumbnails shown in each palette and then reducing to Small and setting the thumbnails to None in the Layers Palette.

1.

To create the first frame, move the Night layer all the way to the left so that it's hidden from view and then select Duplicate Current Frame from the Animation Palette to create the second frame.

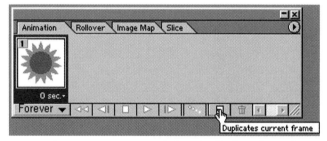

▲ *Executing Duplicate Current Frame.*

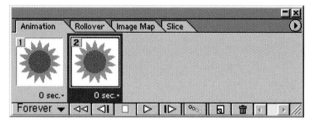

▲ *The duplicated second frame.*

2.

For the second frame, move the Night layer back to its original position.

▲ *Configuring the image for the second frame.*

3.

Execute the Tweens Animation Frames command.

In the Tween dialog box, make sure that Position is the only thing checked under Parameters. You can use Frames To Add to designate the number of frames to add between the two frames.

▲ *Executing Tweens Animation Frames.*

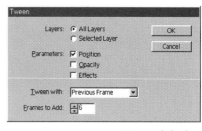

▲ *Tween dialog box.*

Keep in mind that a greater number of frames leads to a smoother animation, but it also increases the file size.

You can verify the result by loading the **Samples⇨Chapter1⇨ Daylight–after.Psd** file from the supplementary CD-ROM.

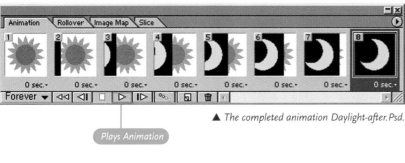

▲ *The completed animation Daylight-after.Psd.*

Plays Animation

▲ *To preview the complete animation, press the Plays Animation button at the bottom of the palette.*

The Preview The Behavior Of The Rollovers Feature

From the bottom of the Rollover Palette, select the Preview The Behavior Of The Rollovers command to add the ability to preview the Rollover that has been applied to the slices.

▲ *The button that enables the Preview The Behavior Of The Rollovers command.*

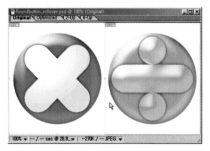

▲ *A normal Slice.*

▲ *You can preview the rollover by placing the mouse cursor over the slice.*

New Layer Based Slice and New Layer Based Image Map Area

You can use these two features, which have been added to the Layer submenu, to convert the image into a slice or an image map. You can apply these features by right-clicking (control-clicking on a Mac) the mouse on the Layer Palette.

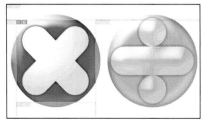

▲ *The result after applying the New Layer Based Slice feature to the image of the X to create a slice frame.*

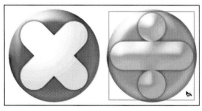

▲ *Use the New Layer Based Image Map Area feature to add an image map to the ÷ image layer.*

::

chapter 2

Photoshop Through Examples

This chapter allows the user to become familiar with the new features and tools of Photoshop 6 through examples and shows you how you can apply them in a variety of fun ways.

An Easy Photo Gallery Homepage: Web Photo Gallery

LESSON HIGHLIGHTS

In this lesson, you look at how to organize the images scattered around on your computers into an image library folder and find out how to use Web Photo Gallery to make an image gallery homepage.

Organizing Images into an Image Gallery Website

I created this homepage by converting various filter images into gallery format. The thumbnails at the bottom show previews of the original images. These thumbnails are hyperlinked to show the original image, in full size, in the middle of the page. The image's relevant information, including file name, author name, and date of creation, also appears.

As one of the Automate features in Photoshop 6, Web Photo Gallery organizes all of the images on your computer and automatically creates a Web page where the images can be searched for by file name and location.

---

the web photo gallery

The Web Photo Gallery shows you a thumbnail preview of images, which are linked to the original images saved in folders, and automatically creates HTML files. Simply choose File⇨Automate⇨ Web Photo Gallery.

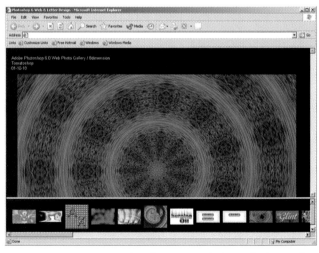

▲ *Web page created using Web Photo Gallery.*

Now you, too, can organize all your massive and bulky image files into a neat and organized gallery.

Executing Web Photo Gallery

First of all, you need to save all the images that you want to place in the gallery in one folder. One thing to note is that you must make two separate folders, one for the source image files and the other for the resulting thumbnail images. To do so, choose File⇨Automate⇨Web Photo Gallery to open the dialog box seen here.

The Four Image Layout Styles of the Web Photo Gallery

You first need to select one of the four layout styles offered by the Web Photo Gallery. In this example, I chose Horizontal Frame. You can change this style after completing the gallery by simply modifying the HTML file that is created.

styles

Used to select how the images will be arranged in the gallery.

options

Used to determine the site name, the size of the original image, the size of the thumbnails, and the color, font, and size of the text.

files

Used to select the location of the source image and the folder where the gallery will be saved.

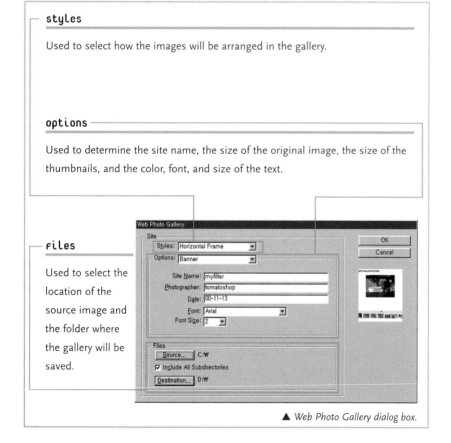

▲ Web Photo Gallery dialog box.

Horizontal Frame

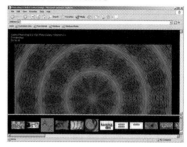

Simple

Vertical Frame

Table

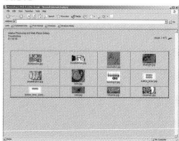

▲ The four layout styles of the Web Photo Gallery.

35

web photo gallery

The Web Photo Gallery can be executed automatically by opening the image in the source folder, adjusting and saving the size of the gallery image (JPG), adjusting and saving the size of the thumbnail image (JPG), and saving the HTML file and button image.

Obviously, the more images that will be saved in the gallery, the more time you must spend making the gallery. However, you can save a lot of time if you use the size of the source image as the size of the original image in the gallery.

Configuring Options

1.

From the Options area, choose Banner to enter the site name, photographer's name, and date of creation that will be inserted at the top left of the gallery page.

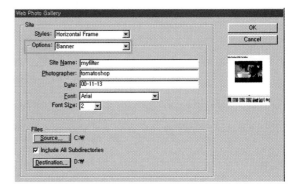

2.

Select Gallery Images in the Options area and then configure the size of the original image that will appear in the center of the page after clicking the respective thumbnail. In order to save time, make sure that the Resize Image option is not selected.

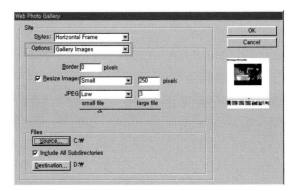

Batch

Batch, a type of Automation feature, automatically applies a specific action to all the images files within the respective folder and saves the results. The required action is created in the Action Palette, not in Web Photo Gallery, and then included in the Batch to be applied to the image. In this way, not only are you able to create unique actions, you're able to apply them to numerous image files at a time.

3.

Next, select Gallery Thumbnails in the Options area and configure the size, caption style, and alignment of the thumbnails.

This is the option that will be applied when Simple or Table is selected.

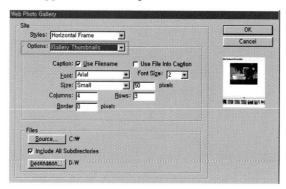

4.

Use the Custom Colors option to determine the color for the background, banner, text, and link that will be applied to the homepage.

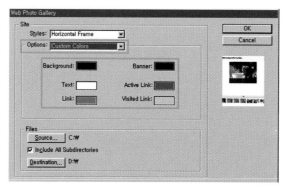

- **Link:** The color of the link when the Web page is first displayed.

- **Active Link:** The color of the link when the text is clicked.

- **Visited Link:** The color of a link that has already been visited.

▲ *In my example, I set the background and banner colors to black and the text color to white.*

The Removal of the GIF89a Export Menu

In Photoshop 6, the Export⇨GIF89a Export feature in the File menu has been removed. This feature made a portion of the GIF image, created using index color, transparent. Beginning with Version 5.5, the method for creating a transparent background was included in the work window, and with the advent of Version 6, this GIF89a Export menu option has been removed.

5.

After configuring the four options, click OK to begin the automatic creation of the gallery.

Once all the images have been saved in the gallery, a browser will appear, and you can verify the results.

When Web Photo Gallery is restarted and the layout style changed, you can click the OK button to compare the four different layout styles to the image generated on the screen.

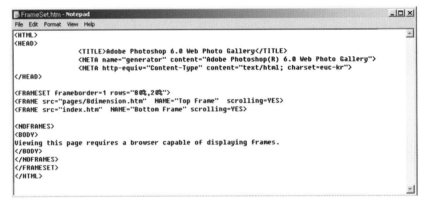

Editing the Source of the Automatically Created HTML File

At times, the completed HTML file will be covered up, depending on the size of the thumbnail image in the browser. You can correct this by modifying the source file. To do so, open the HTML page in the Internet Explorer browser and execute the View menu source.

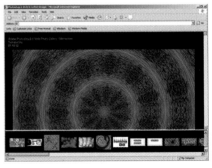

▲ *The source of the HTML Frame created automatically by Web Photo Gallery.*

An Easy Photo Gallery Homepage: Web Photo Gallery

This is the information on the Frameset, which details the arrangement between the source thumbnail page shown in your text editor and the image page. Change <FRAMESET frameborder=1 rows="80%,20%"> to <FRAMESET frameborder=1 border=0 rows="*,120"> and save. You can see that this eliminates the problem of the thumbnail image being hidden by changing the browser and removes the horizontal line that had divided the image from the thumbnails.

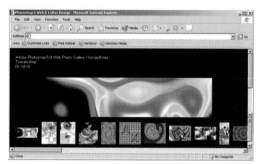

Editing HTML Sources in the Web Photo Gallery

LESSON HIGHLIGHTS

The HTML file, the source for the Web Photo Gallery, exists in the Photoshop folder. The user can create the desired image gallery page by simply modifying this file.

The HTML file, which is made automatically with the creation of the image Web gallery, calls out the sources within the Horizontal Frame, Simple, Table and Vertical Frame folders found in Photoshop Folder➪Presets➪ WebContactSheet.

The source is an HTML file and, therefore, users who have a good understanding of HTML will have no problem modifying these sources to create their own unique image galleries. This lesson will cover how to modify sources and how to apply optimized images to the Web page.

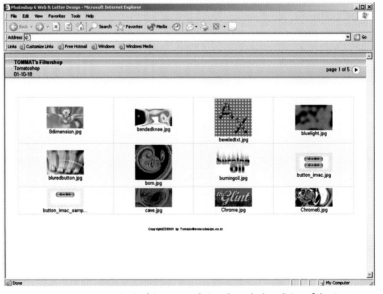

▲ *Applying a new design through the editing of the Preset source.*

Creating a Gallery Page by Editing the Web Photo Gallery HTML Source

Opening Presets⇨WebContactSheet⇨Table in the folder installed in Photoshop, you can see that there are four HTML files (Caption, IndexPage, SubPage, and Thumbnail) and an images folder. If you create a gallery using the Table format, the IndexPage.htm file takes on the role of the index page.

getting ready

From the supplementary CD-ROM, copy **Samples⇨Chapter2⇨ Photogallery.Psd** onto the hard disk and remove the Read-Only property. Then, load it into Photoshop.

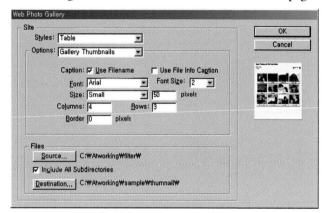

▲ *Configuring the options for the Table form of the Web Photo Gallery.*

Opening IndexPage.htm in the browser, you see that this is a very simple HTML file containing two arrow buttons, Header, Photographer, Date display strings, information on the location of the thumbnails, and a background. Looking at the image route used here, you see that it has loaded and applied four image files from the Images folder (background.jpg, home.gif, previous.gif, and next.gif).

First, replace the four image files with newly created images to see whether the results show up in the page.

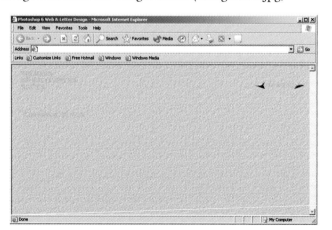

▲ *IndexPage.Htm.*

Slicing the Slice Frame

1.

Open the prepared Photogallery.Psd file and select the Slice Tool from the Toolbox.

▲ *Selecting the Slice Tool.*

2.

In order to slice the background image, you first need to verify how the image pattern was made.

You can see that this page contains long images placed horizontally next to each other. Use the Slice Tool to specify an area on the left side of the background.

The three button images utilize the New Layer Based On Slice function.

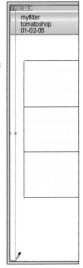

▶ *The slice frame in the background.*

3.

Select the Home layer in the Layers Palette and choose Layer⁺New Layer Based Slice.

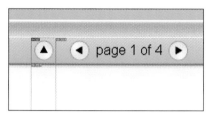

▲ Adding a slice frame to the button.

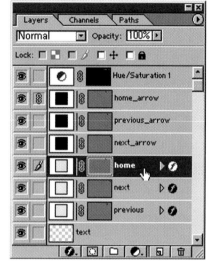

▲ Selecting the Home layer.

4.

In the same way, add the slice frame to the two remaining buttons.

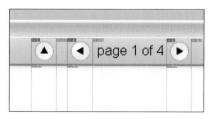

▲ The slice frames added to the three buttons.

Measure Tool

Photoshop 6 contains a Measure Tool that is useful for ensuring exact measurements within the image. The mouse is clicked on the desired starting point and dragged and released at the desired endpoint. You can verify the information regarding this interval in the Options Bar or in the Info Palette.

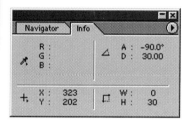

▲ Verifying the information in the Info Palette.

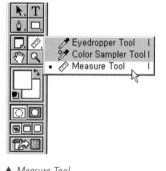

▲ Measure Tool.

creating the background image

The background for the image gallery was created using Gradient Overlay from the Layer Style Palette. Color was added to give the background an uneven and jagged appearance. The color and numbers were applied by double-clicking the Layer Style applied to
the Bar layer to open the Layer Style Palette and by selecting Gradient Editor from the option configuration.

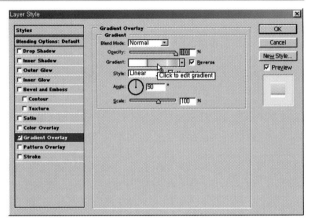

▲ *The Gradient Editor is executed by checking on the gradation box in the Gradient Overlay line in the Layer Style Palette.*

▲ *The gradation in the background image.*

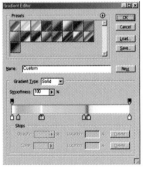

▲ *Application of the Gradient Editor.*

▲ *Double-clicking Gradient Overlay.*

1. The gray area of the gradation will be used for the gallery title, and the rounded, jade-green gradation will be used for the author's name and date. First, to create the gray area, add the gray (R: 183, G: 183, B: 183) Color Stop at Location 5%.

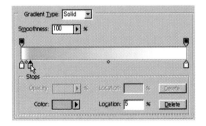

▲ *Addition of the gray Color Stop*

creating the background image

In this added area, from the white area on the right to the midpoint, adjust the gradation so that the left side appears to protrude. (The white on the left represents the highlight, and the gray area represents the shadow due to the protrusion.)

Adjust the position of the Color Midpoint to Location 11%. (This midpoint will be added automatically to all Stops added from this point on.)

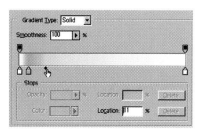

▲ *Adjusting the position of the Color Midpoint.*

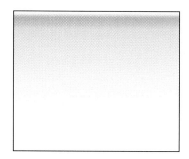

▲ *After application of the gradation.*

2. The highlights in the jade-green bar were expressed by adding three Color Stops.

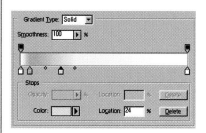

▲ *Gray (R: 219, G: 219, B: 219); Location: 24%.*

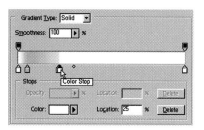

▲ *White; Location: 25%.*

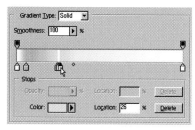

▲ *Jade-green (R: 133, G: 225, B: 222); Location: 26%.*

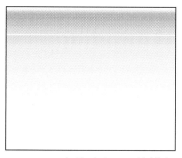

▲ *The jade-green highlight.*

45

creating the background image

3. Finally, you add the Color Stop for the protrusion and the shadow.

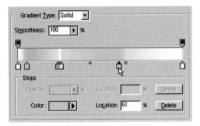

▲ *Jade-green (R: 57, G: 199, B: 197); Location: 61%.*

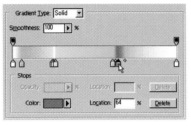

▲ *Dark Gray (R: 126, G: 126; B: 126); Location: 61%.*

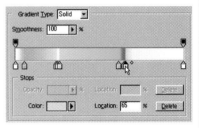

▲ *Light Gray (R: 212, G: 212: B: 212); Location: 61%.*

I created a slightly rounded effect by using only the Gradient Overlay. However, there is one thing you have to remember here. If you want to apply the gradation created here to another image, you must keep in mind the width and the length. As you saw, each Color Stop was distributed by percents. When this gradation is applied to an image of different dimensions, the gradation may appear wider or shorter than it is. Therefore, to achieve the same effects, the gradation should only be applied to images with the same dimensions. (In this example, I created the gradation for an image with the height of 81 pixels. Therefore, to achieve the same results, this gradation should be applied only to images with a height of 81 pixels.)

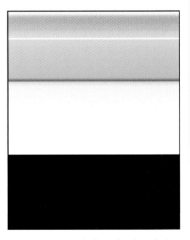

▲ *Completed gradation.*

Configuring Slice Options

1.

Using the Slice Select Tool in the Toolbox, select the 01 slice in the background image.

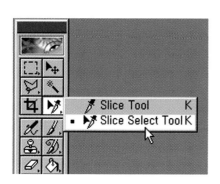

▲ *Slice Select Tool.*

▲ *Selecting slice 01.*

2.

Select Slice Options from the Options Bar to open the dialog box and enter ***background*** *for the Name.*

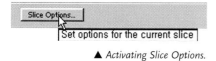

▲ *Activating Slice Options.*

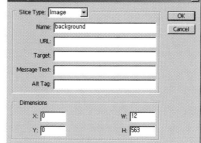

▲ *Entering* ***background*** *for the Name in the dialog box.*

3.

In the same way, enter home, previous, and next for the Names of slices 04, 06, and 09, respectively.

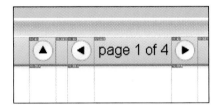

Using Save for Web to Save the Transparent Background Image

1.

First of all, save the button image.
It's difficult to precisely situate the background image and the image above it on a blank HTML page. Also, when the pattern is applied to the background, even a space of 1 pixel will seem extremely large. This is why images that have a separate background use a transparent background image. In addition, transparent backgrounds minimize the number of colors thereby reducing the file size. In this example, you'll save the button with a transparent background.

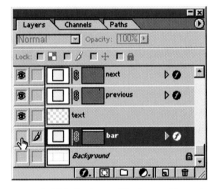

▲ *Hide the bar and background layers in the Layers Palette.*

▲ *The button image has been converted to one with a transparent background.*

2.

Open the Save for Web dialog box by choosing File⇨Save For Web.

3.

Select slice 04 using the Slice Select Tool from the Toolbox. In the Settings option on the right, enter the settings GIF, 32-colors, and No Dither and then apply the transparent background by checking Transparency and setting the Matte Color.

4.

Using the drop-down list (pop-up menu on a Mac) on the right, the Matte color is set to Eyedropper Color in the list that appears.

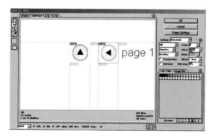

▲ Save For Web dialog box.

As a result, the Matte color should be applied to the borders of the slice image, and the background should be transparent.

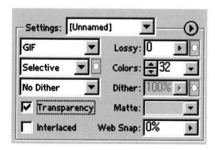

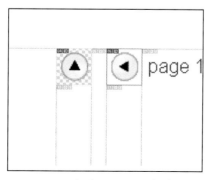

▲ The transparent background.

49

5.

Apply the same settings to the remaining two buttons.

▲ The three optimized buttons.

6.

Hold down the Shift key and select all three slice buttons.

▲ Selecting the three buttons.

7.

Click the OK button at the top right to open the Save Optimized As dialog box and make the settings as shown here.

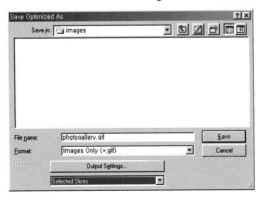

▲ Save Optimized As dialog box (Windows version).

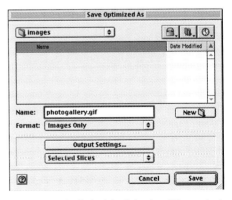

▲ Save Optimized As dialog box (Mac version).

8.

Press the Output Settings button to open the dialog box and deselect Put Images In Folder to prevent the creation of a new folder for the selected image files.

The images should be saved in the Photoshop folder Presets⤵ WebContactSheet⤵Table⤵Images.

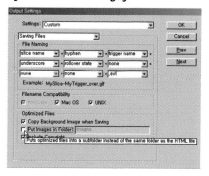

▲ *Configuring Output Settings.*

Saving the Background Image

1.

Return to the image window, unhide the bar and background layers in the Layer Palette, and then open the Save For Web dialog box to optimize the background image.

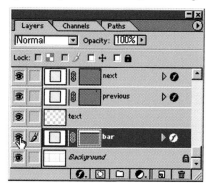

▲ *Adjusting the Layer Visibility.*

2.

Select slice 01 using the Slice Select Tool and select JPEG Medium from the Settings list on the right.

3.

Click the OK button and save the background in the same folder as the images.

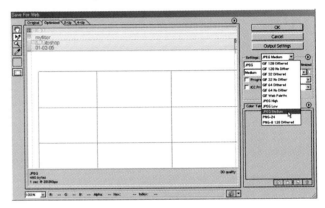

▲ *Optimizing the background image as JPEG Medium.*

Verifying the Exchange

To verify that the images have been replaced properly, choose File⇨ Automate⇨Web Photo Gallery and set the Site Style to Table. Then save the image.

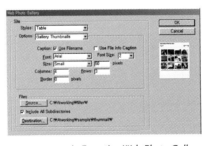

▲ *Executing Web Photo Gallery.*

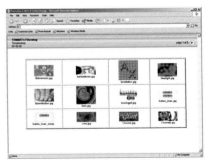

▲ *Verifying the replaced images.*

Modifying the HTML Source and Verifying the Results

Open the source file of the Table Style, IndexPage.Htm, in Memo Pad and change the settings for the font and table.

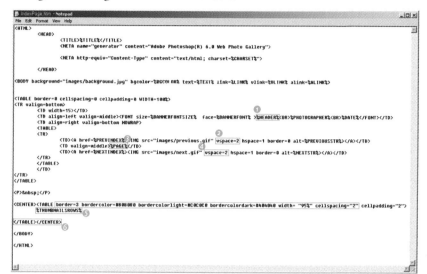

◄ *The IndexPage.Htm source opened in Memo Pad.*

setting changes

1. To display the site name in boldfaced characters, you need to add a boldfaced tag.

   %HEADER%➪%HEADER%

2. Make the following change to remove the empty space above and below the button image:

   vspace=2➪vspace=0

3. To reduce the font size of the page, you need to add a font tag:

   %PAGE%➪<font size=2>%PAGE% </font>

4. Make the following change to apply a background color to the image thumbnail table and to trim the dividing line:

   border=3 bordercolor= #808080 bordercolorlight= #CoCoCo bordercolordark= #404040 width="95%' cellspacing="2"➪border=1 bgcolor=#F2F2F2 bordercolorlight=#CoCoCo bordercolordark+#FFFFFF width="95%" cellspacing="0"

5. To reduce the size of the thumbnail title, you need to add a font tag.

   %THUMBNAILSROWS%➪<font size=2>%THUMBNAILSROWS%</font>

6. Insert the copyright information between </TABLE> and </CENTER>.

<font size=1>Copyright©2002 by ABCDEFGHI<font>

Adding a web photo gallery source

Four folders are within Photoshop's WebContactSheet folder where the photo gallery sources are saved. You can save the HTML page that you modified in a new folder to add a new photo gallery list.

After modification of the source is complete, save the file and return to Web Photo Gallery. Then, after saving the Table Type page, verify the result in the browser.

This current design format will be applied to all future Web Photo Galleries that are created. You can modify the SubPage.Htm, which is linked to the thumbnail, in the same as you did for IndexPage.Htm to obtain the same results.

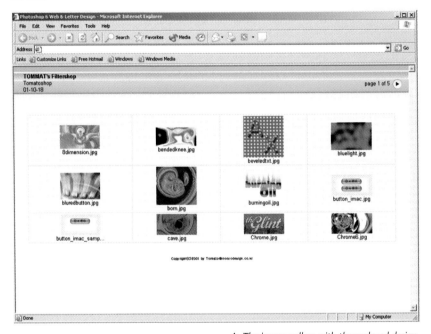

▲ *The image gallery with the replaced design.*

Using the Notes Tool

If you've looked through the Filter menu, you've probably noticed a sub-menu called Digimarc. This submenu contains the Watermark filter that is used to enter author information. Using the Watermark filter, you can add the author name, as well as copyright and author contact information, inconspicuously on the image. Actually, the information isn't really entered into the image, but rather a membership number that is interpreted through the Digimarc site. This number is then used to search and view the relevant image information on the site.

This lesson covers the Notes Tool, which is similar to the Watermark function. Executed directly in the Toolbox, the Notes Tool allows you to add a memo or voice-recorded file to the image.

The Notes Tool Features

Thanks to the spread of the Internet, you can access many images and pictures and can even share them. However, with all this passing and sharing of images, the author and copyright information is soon forgotten. This is a potentially dangerous problem because using an image without knowing to whom it belongs may land you right in the middle of a huge copyright violation.

 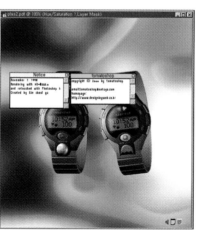

▲ Using the Notes Tool to add a note (shown on the right) to the original image (shown on the left).

However, including the copyright information with the image makes things easier for everyone involved. This is where the Notes Tool comes in. The Notes Tool, found in the Toolbox, allows you to enter the relevant information, in text or voice-recorded format, directly onto the image without damaging the overall appearance. A similar tool is the Filter⟳ Digimarc Filter. The Digimarc filter allows you to verify the copyright information through its site.

Executing the Notes Tool and Entering Information

1.

Select the Notes Tool from the Toolbox.
The Audio Annotation Tool allows you to leave behind a voice recording.

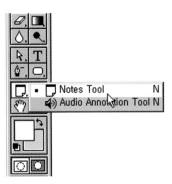

2.

Enter the author's name in the space marked Author in the Options Bar.
Color is used to specify the color of the note and is handy for differentiating between several different notes on one image.

3.

After saving this information, enter the author information.

4.

Using the Exit button at the top right to close the note, and position the icon on the desired spot.

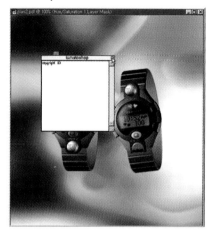

▲ *Entering the contents of a note (left) and positioning the icon (right).*

Verifying the Entered Text

You can verify the entered contents by double-clicking the Note icon. Choosing View⇨Show⇨Annotations allows you to hide/display the icon.

If you save the image file in PDF format, you can apply this note to other files by using the command File⇨Import⇨Annotations. By saving the user information (entered using the Notes Tool) in PDF format, even a computer without Photoshop can view this information through Acrobat Reader, which you can download from the Internet.

▶ *Choosing File⇨ Import⇨Annotations.*

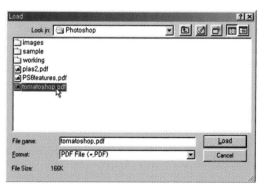

> **The Annotations Menu.**
>
> The command File⇨Import⇨ Annotations is used to load the note saved in a PDF file. In order to store the author information in a fixed format and to import it, the file must be saved in PDF format.

Creating Shapes and Buttons

LESSON HIGHLIGHTS

This lesson is devoted to the wonderful effects you can create using the Layer Style dialog box. You can use Layer Style to create the effects of your imagination. Although the tools in Layer Style are not that different from those seen in previous versions, the presence of the Layer Style dialog box itself, along with its various options, makes Photoshop 6 quite a powerful upgrade.

Here's the function sequence:

1.

Choose Edit⇨Preferences⇨Guides And Grid.

2.

Select the Shape Tool.

3.

Select the Direct Selection Tool.

4.

Select the Path Component Selection Tool.

5.

Select Adjustment Layer.

This lesson is devoted to learning how to use the Shape Tool and how to manipulate it to create the shapes you want. In addition, we also look at how to use the Layer Style dialog box to create buttons easily and conveniently.

Using the Shape Tool

The Shape Tool, along with the Type Tool, is one of the new vector graphic tools in Photoshop. In addition to the basic tools, (the Rectangle Tool, the Rounded Rectangle Tool, the Ellipse Tool, The Polygon Tool, and the Line Tool), the Custom Shape Tool boasts a new Option Palette. You can use this palette to take advantage of a greater array of preset shapes. (Refer to the Photoshop library in Lesson 13.)

The new vector graphic capacity in Photoshop will forever change the way you think about graphic design.

First of all, it is very easy to change the shape of a figure drawn using the Shape Tool. The problem with applying the Anti-Aliasing to change the size of the shape that was seen in the previous version has been solved.

In addition, you can apply a Clipping Path to a portion of the image, without affecting the entire image. This, along with the Adjustment Layer, has been improved to be a more effective and helpful tool.

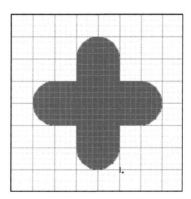

▲ *Drawing the shape using the Rounded Rectangle tool.*

▲ *Shape Tool Options Bar.*

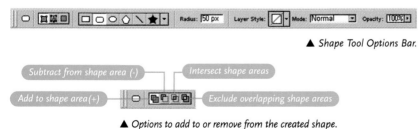

▲ *Options to add to or remove from the created shape.*

Creating Buttons Using the Shape Tool

You'll now create some simple buttons to practice using the Shape Tool.

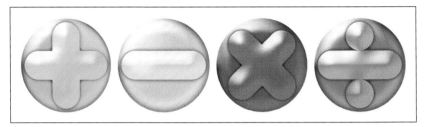

▲ *Completed button images.*

The first thing you need to do is set up the grid:

1.

Make a new 1,000 x 300 work window.

2.

Choose Edit⇨Preferences⇨Guides & Grid to open the dialog box and set the Gridline Every option to 50 and the Subdivisions to 4.

3.

Activate the Snap by selecting View⇨Snap and then execute View⇨Show⇨Grid to display the grid in the work window.

Now, you're ready to make the ellipse.

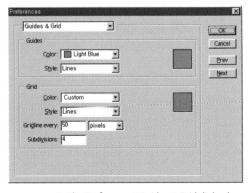

▲ *The Preferences⇨Guides & Grid dialog box.*

1.

Select the Ellipse Tool from the Toolbox.
In order to draw a shape in the new layer, you must first verify that the Create New Shape Layer option is selected in the Options Bar.

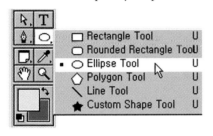

▲ *Selecting Create New Shape Layer in the Options Bar.*

2.

Use the Ellipse Tool to draw a 200 x 200 ellipse.
Verify that a new layer has been created in the Layers Palette.

3.

Use Create New Layer to make a new layer that is filled in with the foreground color and add a Clipping Path mask to this layer.
This Clipping Path mask cuts slices out of the shape without distorting the appearance of the entire image.

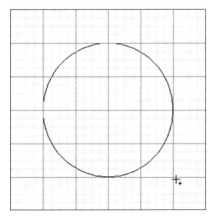

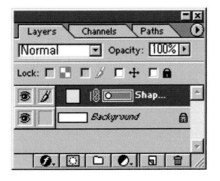

activating the clipping path

activating the clipping path

Activating the Clipping Path before adding a shape allows you to add or remove portions from the shape. Remember, though, that the Clipping Path of the layer must be deactivated before drawing a shape in the new layer.

4.

Select the Direct Selection Tool from the Toolbox.

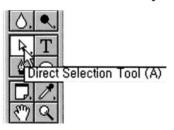

5.

Select the entire image frame and move it while pressing the Alt key to make three additional copies.

Next, you're ready to add shapes.

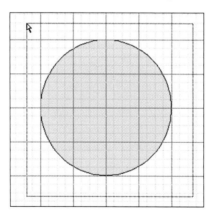

▲ *Selecting the shape using the Direct Selection Tool.*

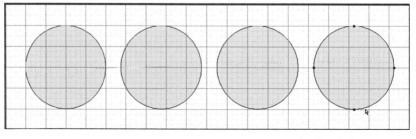

▲ *The three duplicated shapes.*

To add shapes

1.

Switch to the Rounded Rectangle Tool and then, in order to draw a shape in the new layer, deactivate the Clipping Path thumbnail in the Layers Palette.

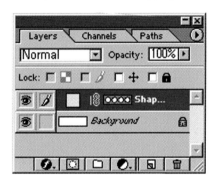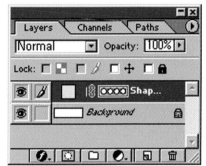

▲ *The activated (left) and deactivated (right) forms of the Clipping Path.*

2.

In the Options Bar of the Rounded Rectangle Tool, set the Radius to a value greater than 30 px.

3.

Draw a + in the first circle on the left.

First, draw in the horizontal shape and then, after activating the Clipping Path, draw in the vertical shape.

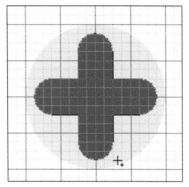

▲ *An example of the Rounded Rectangle Tool.*

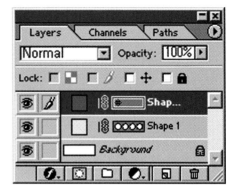

▲ *The new shape layer.*

4.

Draw a - in the second circle.

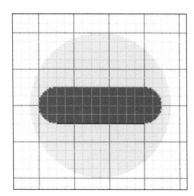

5.

For the third circle, make a copy of the + shape and rotate it to make the x shape.

Because the + shape is a combination of two shapes, you need to use the Path Component Selection Tool before moving and copying it.

Select the shape as you did when you made a copy of the circle. Then drag the mouse to the inner frame of the path while pressing the Alt (Option) key to copy. Rotate the shape 45 degrees to make the x shape.

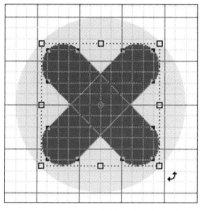

▲ *Rotating the + shape.*

> ## using the path component selection tool
>
> When using the Path Component Selection Tool, checking Show Bounding Box in the Options Bar allows you to apply Free Transform periodically to the Clipping Path or Path.

6.

Make a copy of the - shape and add two dots above and below it to make the final ÷ shape.

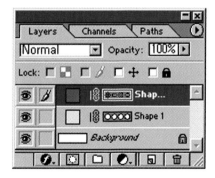

▲ *Several layers combined on one layer page.*

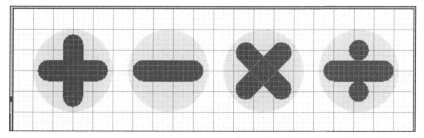

▲ *All the shapes have been added to the circles.*

65

Now you're ready to add styles.

1.

Open the menu using the toggle button at the top right in the Styles Palette and select Glass Buttons.asl as the default style.

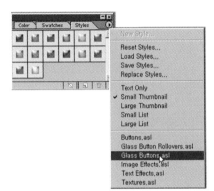

2.

Apply Blue Glass to shapes 1 and 2.

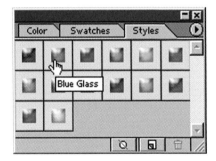

▲ *Applying the Blue Glass style.*

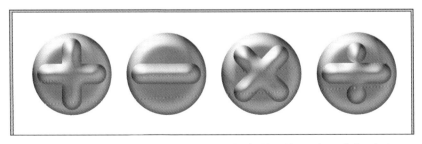

▲ *The Blue Glass style applied to the image.*

3.

Edit the Effects option in the Layer Style Palette to tone down the protrusion of the shapes and to make the buttons more homogenous.

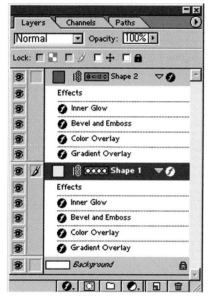

▲ *The Effects applied to the shapes and the rounded background image layer.*

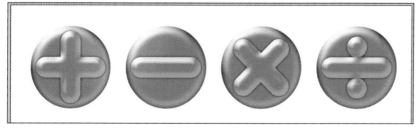

▲ *The result after adjusting the Style option.*

Now you're ready to add color using the Adjustment Layer.

1.

Click the button shaped like an upside-down triangle in the Shape Layer to close the Style Layer.

67

2.

Select the Rectangular Marquee Tool from the Toolbox and select the frame that encompasses the first shape.

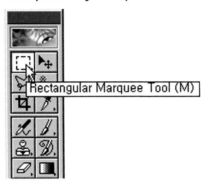

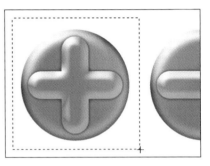

▲ *Selecting the first frame using the Rectangular Marquee Tool.*

3.

Select Create New Fill Or Adjustment Layer from the bottom of the Layers Palette and select Hue/Saturation from the menu that appears.

You can use the Hue adjustment bar to change the color.

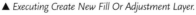

▲ *Executing Create New Fill Or Adjustment Layer.*

▲ *The Hue/Saturation layer added to the Layers Palette.*

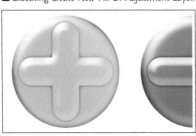

◄ *The Adjustment Layer applied to the first shape.*

4.

Continue to add to the Adjustment Layer to change the color of the remaining buttons.
You can verify the result by loading **Samples⇨Chapter2⇨Easy button-after.Psd** from the supplementary CD-ROM.

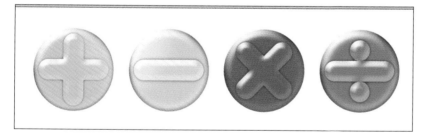

▲ *The completed button images (Easybutton-after.Psd).*

Getting Ready to Make Graphics

Configuring the Preset Manager

When creating Photoshop 6, the people at Adobe invested a lot of time in constructing the library. The result is that users can now create even more diverse and magnificent styles using just the default library.

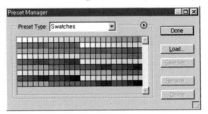

▲ *Preset Manager dialog box.*

Preset Manager

The Preset Manager dialog box contains options for making selections from the Preset Type list and for adding, editing, removing, or saving to a new library.

You can save the presets you made using the Define Pattern and Define Brush in the Edit menu as a new file to create your own unique Photoshop environment.

Adding new presets to the existing library using the Load button or Append command allows you to compare and utilize several presets at a time. However, loading too many libraries at a time will drastically reduce the work speed, so you should take care that you load only the necessary presets.

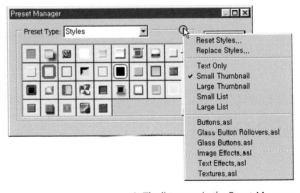

▲ *The list menu in the Preset Manager.*

Creating Your Own Presets

1.

Select Styles from Preset Types and load all the style files in Photoshop by using the Load command.

▲ *Loading a new Style file using the Load command.*

▲ *Loading all the styles.*

three commands for loading presets

If you want to load presets, you can do it in three ways. First, if you're using the Styles Preset, you can use the Reset Styles command. This command is selected from the pop-up menu that appears when you click the arrow button at the top right and is used to load only default styles.

Second, you can use the Replace Styles command. This command replaces the existing preset with the new file.

And, finally, you can load presets by pressing the Load button. This button adds the newly loaded styles to the existing Styles menu.

2.

Remove all the styles that you won't be using from the loaded Style list.

To select all the styles that you want to delete, click them while pressing the Shift key and then click Delete to remove them.

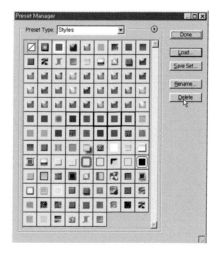

▲ *Removing styles from the Style list.*

purge

The Edit⟹Purge command effectively manages the file size of the image by removing all Undo, History, and Clipboard contents that have been added.

Using Photoshop to create huge, publishable images places a great strain on the memory and the storage disk, which can lead to a drastic reduction in work speed. You can solve this problem somewhat by using the Purge command to empty the buffer and effectively manage the memory.

However, to go to the root of the problem, you need to recover the reserve memory in the storage disk. Stop your work for the time being, save the file, and then reboot the computer to recover adequate memory.

Another effective way to recover the memory is to convert the thumbnail in the Layers Palette to text form and then work on the image in that way.

3.

After you've deleted the unnecessary styles, select all the remaining styles and then click Save Set.

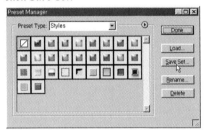

4.

Enter the file name in the Save dialog box and click Save.

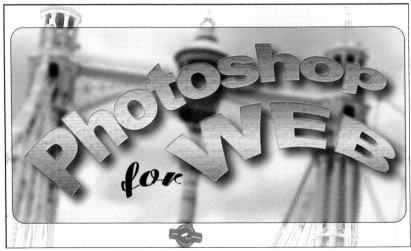

▲ *The typography created using Brushed Metal after changing the Styles Palette to Text Effects.Asl.*

Photoshop 6 Library (Brushes)

Default

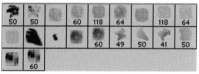

Faux Finish

Natural 2

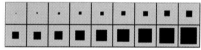

Natural

Calligraphics

Drop Shadow

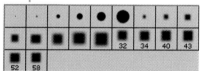

Square

Photoshop 6 Library (Gradients)

Default

Color Harmonies

Color Harmonies 2

Metals

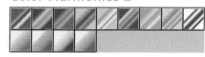

Noise Samples

Pastels

Simple

Special Effects

Spectrums

Photoshop 6 Library (Patterns)

Default

Patterns

Patterns 2

Photoshop 6 Library (Custom Shapes)

Default

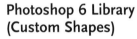

Custom Shapes

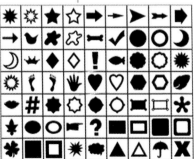

Photoshop 6 Library (Styles)

Default

Buttons

Glass Button Rollovers

Glass Buttons

Image Effects

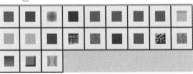

Text Effects

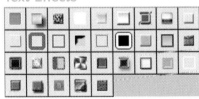

Textures

Optimizing Web Graphics in Photoshop: Save For Web

In this lesson, you'll come to understand the Layer-Based Slice feature and how to use Save For Web to create Web images. In order to understand Save For Web, you must first look at the Slice feature.

Layer-Based Slice

The efficiency of the Slice feature became widely acknowledged through ImageReady. It is a handy tool that lets you save several image formats, such as GIF and JPG, on one image page, while maintaining the PSD format of the active layer.

Photoshop 6 added the feature Layer-Based Slice, and it allows you to configure the active layer elements as slices.

Let's look at how to use this feature through an example.

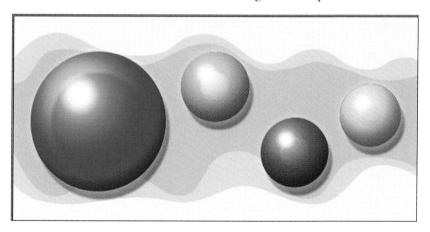

1.

Select the yellow ball layer from the Layers Palette in order to differentiate the yellow ball in the image into one slice. Choose Layer⇨New Layer Based Slice and verify the result.

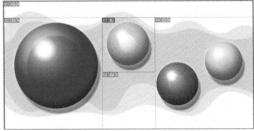

▲ *The yellow ball differentiated into a slice.*

◀ *The activated yellow ball layer.*

2.

Repeat the previous step to apply a slice frame to the remaining balls.

After the frames are configured, the Slice Options feature is used to enter the file name, link, and Alt tag information for each slice.

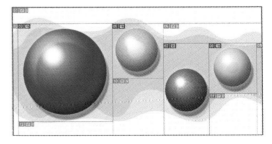

▲ *A slice frame has been added to each ball.*

3.

Select the Slice Select Tool from the Toolbox and select the slice that you want to configure. Then execute Slice Options from the Options Bar.

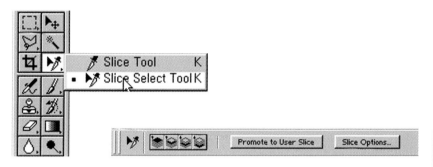

You can enter the file name (Name), link route (URL), target frame (Target), message text (Message Text), and image information (Alt Tag) in the Slice Options dialog box. I entered just the file name here as an example.

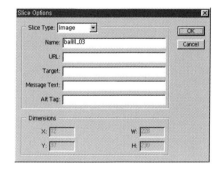

Save For Web

In Photoshop's Toolbox, there is a button called Jump To ImageReady. This button links the two programs for more effective Web design. After setting up the basic slice frame, more detailed work is usually done in ImageReady. This button is for more complex processes such as Image Optimize or Rollover Image. However, for users with a less efficient system, the time it takes to save the image in Photoshop, execute ImageReady, and then load the image may seem like forever.

If you're performing a rather simple operation, you can complete the entire process using Photoshop alone, without the aid of ImageReady. The tools for this process are contained in the Save For Web dialog box.

The Role of the Alt (Option) Key

Copying objects: Copying images, slices, and clipping paths all depend on the Alt (Option) key. Images are copied using Alt (Option) + Move Tool. Slices are copied using Alt (Option) + Slice Select Tool. Clipping paths are copied using Alt (Option) + Path Component Selection Tool.

Configuring a slice from the center: A frame is configured from the center by pressing the Alt (Option) key while using the Slice, Marquee, and Shape Tool. Adding the Shift key to this operation allows a fixed rectangle to be made.

Color extraction: When using the Shape brush and Gradient Tool, the Alt (Option) key is used as a shortcut key for the Eyedropper Tool for color extraction.

Zoom/delete: Using the Alt (Option) key along with the Zoom and Marquee tools enlarges/reduces the screen and removes the newly selected frame from the selection frame.

1.

After entering the basic information in the Slice Options dialog box, execute File⇨Save For Web.
This dialog box lets you control the options for image optimization and for HTML file creation.

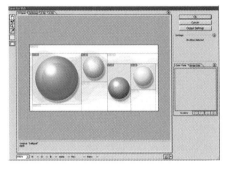

▲ *Save For Web dialog box.*

2.

Click Optimized at the top of the screen to preview the image. Then, select the Slice Select Tool from the toolbar on the left to select the image that will be optimized.

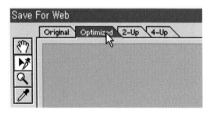

▲ *Selecting the Optimized work window.*

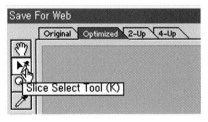

▲ *Selecting the Slice Select Tool.*

3.

Selecting the slice will activate the optimized Option Palette at the right. The Option Palette is where you can control the number of colors in the final image, create a transparent background, and convert to Web-safe colors.

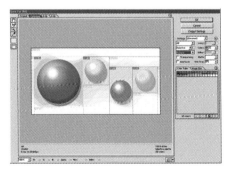

▲ *Making the optimized configurations for the slice.*

save for web's GIF color table

When saving slices in GIF format, the maximum 256 colors in the Color Table allows users to change to Web-safe colors and change, lock, add, or delete selected colors.

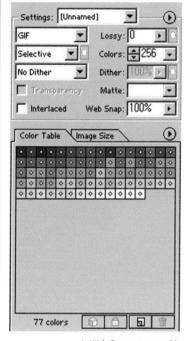

▲ Web Snap set to 100%.

First, after setting Web Snap to 100% (in other words, you convert to complete Web-safe colors), a rounded mark will appear around all the colors. In addition, despite the number entered in Colors, the application of the Web Snap will reveal the information on the number of colors used (77 colors) at the bottom of the palette.

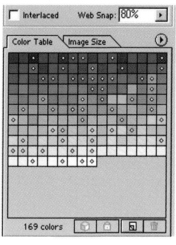

When the same colors are used and the Web Snap is set to 80%, the actual 169 colors that are used will be distributed based on those that are Web-safe colors and those that are not.

You can use the functions at the bottom of the Color Table to convert to Web-safe colors and lock, add, or remove colors. In addition, you can apply a different color from the Color Picker that appears by double-clicking the color itself.

▼ The features at the bottom of the Color Table.

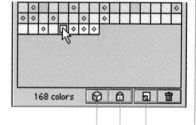

Converts the color to the closest Web-safe color

Prevents the selected color from being deleted due to the application of Web Snap (the Lock Feature)

Add/remove a new color

79

Creating and Applying Web Graphic Pattern Images

LESSON HIGHLIGHTS

In order to create the smallest unit of repeating image patterns, you can usually use Filter :: Other :: Offset. Other features are also included in the Offset option, and they allow you to make precise links in the patterns. The function sequence is as follows:

1. Select the Custom ShapesTool.

2. Choose Layer :: Layer Style.

3. Choose Filter :: Other :: Offset.

4. Choose Edit :: Define Pattern.

5. Choose Edit :: Fill.

In this lesson, you will learn how to create patterned images and how to apply the most effective background effect to the main image.

Patterned images are perfect if you want quick-loading images for your homepage. You can create patterns out of simple images and apply them to your Web sites. The general image pattern is then usually applied as the background for a main image.

▲ *A completed image using a pattern.*

Making a Pattern

1.

Make a new 100 x 100 work window.

2.

To create a precise image size, choose View⇨Show⇨Grid. Then choose Edit⇨ Preferences⇨Guides & Grid and set the Gridline Every to 50 and the Subdivisions to 4. Then choose View⇨Snap.

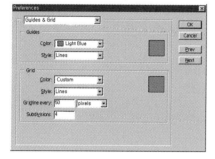

▲ *The Guides & Grid configuration window.*

3.

Select the Custom Shape Tool from the Toolbox and select 5 Point Star from the Shape List in the Options Bar.

To draw a shape in the new layer, first make sure that Create New Shape Layer is activated in the Options Bar.

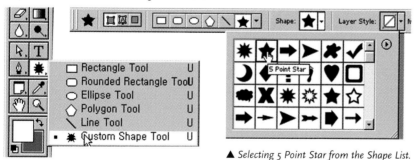

▲ *Selecting the Custom Shape Tool.*

▲ *Selecting 5 Point Star from the Shape List.*

▲ *Selecting the shape in the Option Palette.*

81

4.

Set the foreground color to yellow (R: 255, G: 216, B: 0) in the Toolbox and then, while holding down the Shift key, create a shape that fills the entire work window.
The Shift key lets you draw precise rectangles.

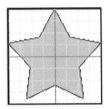

Using Layer Style

To add dimension to the star, you need to use Layer Style.

In this example, you'll initiate the Layer Style by clicking the Add A Layer Style button located at the bottom of the Layers Palette.

▲ *Clicking Add A Layer Style.*

1.

Use Gradient Overlay to add highlights.

Select Gradient Overlay from Styles. Click the color bar at the right to adjust the color. Adjust the color bar in the Gradient Editor to create the gradient seen here.

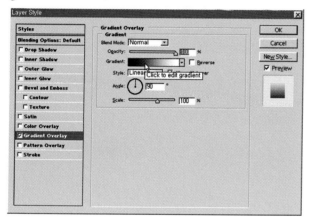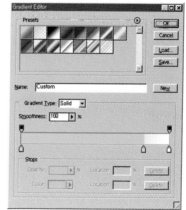

▲ *Configuring the Gradient Overlay option.*

After editing the gradient, click Reverse, located next to the gradient color bar, to complete the creation of the highlight.

You can adjust the position of the highlight directly on the image using the mouse.

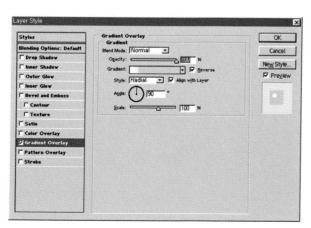

2.

Apply Bevel and Emboss.
Bevel and Emboss is used to add dimension and depth to the image.
Increase the size in the option configuration to add dimension and
set the color of the Shadow Mode to yellow (R: 255, G: 216, B: 0).

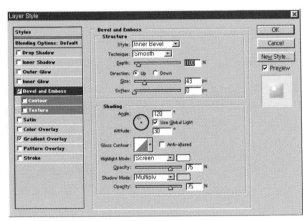

3.

Apply Color Overlay.
Color Overlay is used to intensify and brighten the image's overall color.
This option also prevents the style from being changed by the background
color when it's saved and loaded into the image.

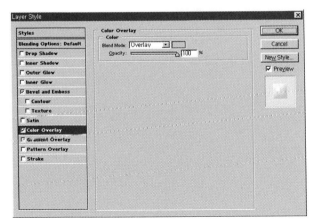

4.

Apply Inner Glow.

Finally, to create a distinct outline of the image, you apply Inner Glow. Select Gradient from the option configuration to create a soft and smooth outline.

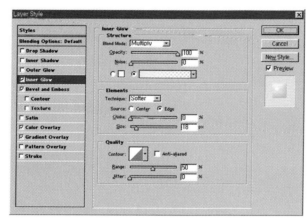

5.

Apply styles

After applying all the effects, drag the mouse to the bottom of the Styles Palette and click on an empty space.

When the New Style dialog box opens, enter the name **star1** to save the styles that were applied to the image.

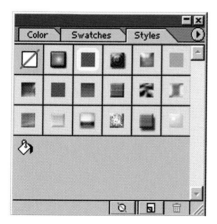

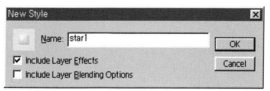

▲ *New Style dialog box.*

The offset filter

The Offset filter lets you symmetrically divide the image, from top to bottom and side to side, to create equal, repeating tiles. To create precisely partitioned tiles, you need to apply a pixel size half that of the image work window to the Offset. For example, if your work window is 200 x 200 pixels, you need to apply a size of 100 x 100 pixels to the Offset.

Applying Offset

You will now apply the Offset filter to convert your image into a repeating pattern. You first set the background color to yellow to match the color of the star and then flatten all the layers.

1.

Choose Filter⁀Other⁀Offset.

2.

Set both the Horizontal Offset and the Vertical Offset to 50 and then verify the result.

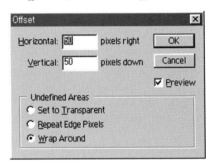

Rubber Band

When using the Path Tool to draw shapes, the Rubber Band function in the Options Bar creates denotation lines, making it easier to draw your shape.

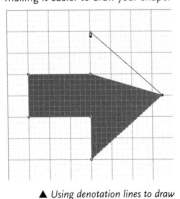

▲ *Using denotation lines to draw the shape.*

Making a Small Star

1.

Select the grid again and draw a small star in the center.

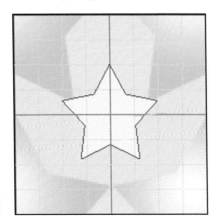

2.

From the list of styles in the Styles Palette, select star1, which was applied to the large star, and apply it to the small star.

using the patterned background image

Surfing through the Internet, I frequently come across pages that use patterned images for their backgrounds. Each of the image units in the pattern are of very low size and the arrangement of the units into a pattern makes it appear as one large image, thus making it a very attractive choice for homepages limited by file size.

3.

Adjust the Bevel and Emboss and Gradient Overlay effects of the small star so that it stands out from the image of the large star.

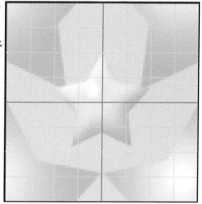

Saving as a Pattern and Applying It to the Image

1.

Choose Edit⬥ Define Pattern. After entering the name, star pattern, save the pattern.

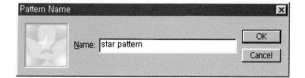

Load the **Samples⇨Chapter2⇨
Pattern.Psd** file from the supplementary CD-ROM into Photoshop.

2.

Open the main image file and select the background layer in the Layers Palette.

▲ *The main image file.*

3.

Select Edit⇨Fill. In the Fill dialog box, set Use to Pattern and Custom Pattern to Star Pattern and then verify the result.

You can verify the result by loading **Samples⇨Chapter2⇨Pattern-after.Psd** from the supplementary CD-ROM.

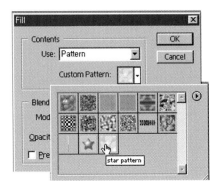

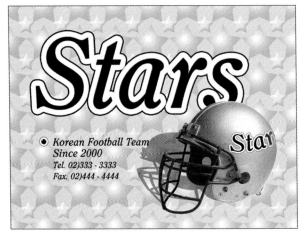

◀ *The result after applying the main image file to the background pattern image.*

::

chapter 3

Photoshop for Web Graphics

In this chapter, you will look at the overall graphic design process using Photoshop and how to use Photoshop to create Web graphics. Included are examples, collected from an analysis of the image trend in more than 300 actual venture enterprise Web sites, to provide more realistic and practical examples.

Distorted 3-D Text

In this lesson, you'll use Photoshop's Style Library to add embellished text. You'll also find out how to use and apply Text Styles and Warped Text Styles.

Photoshop offers a total of 32 text-style effects. In the example here, you'll learn how to apply one of these effects and then apply Warped Text to create distortion.

LESSON HIGHLIGHTS

Styles can be called the star of Photoshop 6. You can style Web graphic images to artistic craftsmanship using Styles and the Layer Style dialog box. The function sequence is Create Warped Text and Styles (Brushed Metal).

▲ *After the toggle button at the top is used to extract the menu list, the Text Effects.Asl file is loaded.*

getting ready

Copy the **Samples⇨Chapter3⇨Warpedtext.Psd** file from the supplementary CD-ROM onto the hard disk and remove the Read-Only property. Then, load it into Photoshop.

Applying Styles

1.
___

After loading the example image into Photoshop, click the toggle button at the top right-hand side of the Styles Palette and change the basic palette to Text Effects.Asl.

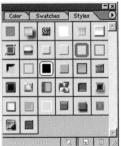

▲ *The Text Effects.Asl file applied to the Styles Palette.*

2.

Select the layer to which the style has been applied. Then, after selecting Brushed Metal from the Styles Palette, apply it to the selected layer.

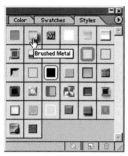

▲ *The result after applying the style to the text.*

3.

To add a slight yellowish tint to the word WEB, click Add A Layer Style in the Layers Palette and choose Color Overlay.

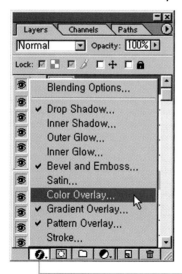

Add A Layer Style

91

color picker

The Color Picker dialog box, which you open by clicking the Color Selection box in the Style options, is largely divided into Select Color on the left, the Hue selection bar in the center, and the value window on the right.

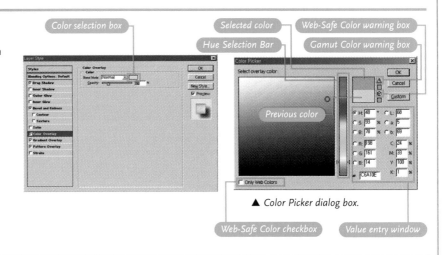

Color selection box
Selected color
Web-Safe Color warning box
Hue Selection Bar
Gamut Color warning box
Previous color

▲ *Color Picker dialog box.*

Web-Safe Color checkbox
Value entry window

The value entry window

1. Used to enter the percent values for Cyan, Magenta, Yellow, and Black in the CMYK color mode when using the PostScript printer.

2. Used to enter values from o to 255 for Red, Green, and Blue in the RGB color mode for viewing on the monitor.

3. Used to enter the HSB mode (Saturation, Brightness, and 0° to 360°) for the Hue that divides the Web-safe color at the bottom left.

4. Includes four methods of color entry using Lightness from o to 100, the A-axis (Green and Magenta) from −128 to +127, the B-axis (Blue and Yellow), and the # value at the bottom to verify the HTML color code of the selected color.

In addition, this dialog box uses the Gamut Color and the Web-Safe Color warning boxes to show you whether the selected color is appropriate for use on the Web and then allows you to modify it.

The Gamut refers to the spheres that can be seen on a color system or printed. The three color modes in Photoshop, in order of decreasing color domains, are the Lab mode, the RGB mode, and the CMYK mode.

The RGB color mode includes the color domain that can be seen on television or on a monitor, and the CMYK color mode includes the printable color domain. If the color does not appear correctly in the printout, users should

verify that the color has not extended beyond the CMYK color domain.

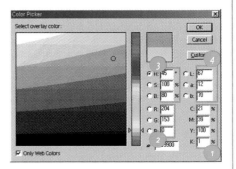

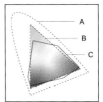

▲ *A: Lab color gamut;*
B: RGB color gamut;
C: CMYK color gamut.

4.

After specifying the desired color in the Color Overlay pane, lower the opacity so that only a slight hint of color is applied to the text.

> ### color overlay
>
> **Blend Mode:** Normal
> **Opacity:** 21%
> **Color Picker settings:** R: 255, G: 204, B: 0

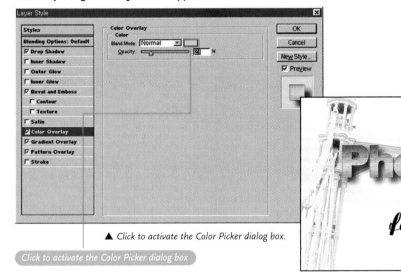

▲ *Click to activate the Color Picker dialog box.*

Click to activate the Color Picker dialog box

▲ *Color Overlay applied to WEB.*

Applying Warped Text

In order to specify the font type, color, and size, double-click Layer Thumbnails in the Layers Palette and then on the respective text in the image window to convert the text to the editable, inverted shaded state.

1.

First edit the word Photoshop.

▶ *Double-clicking Layer Thumbnail in the text layer.*

> ### changing image color
>
> You can change the color of an image in Photoshop in many ways. You can choose Adjust⇨Hue/Saturation from the Image menu or create an Adjustment Layer and make the color change in that layer or add color using Color Overlay in Layer Style. The first option, Adjust⇨Hue/Saturation, is the most frequently used method. However, because this option damages the original image, many people are now chosing to use the Color Overlay option.

93

convert to paragraph text

In order to convert a regular layer to a Paragraph Text, use Layer⇨Type⇨ Convert To Paragraph Text. In the converse operation, the Convert To Point Text menu will appear.

2.

After you've converted the text into editable form, click Create Warped Text from the Options Bar.

When the Warped Text dialog box opens, select Arc from the Style list. Then, at the bottom, set the Bend to 40% and the Horizontal Distortion to −42%.

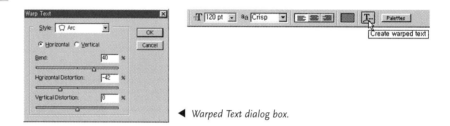

◀ *Warped Text dialog box.*

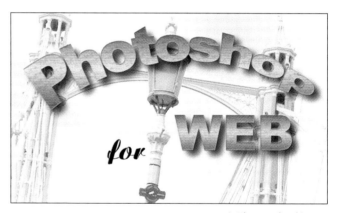

▲ *The completed image.*

3.

After bending the text, convert the word WEB to the editable state.

When one word is in the editable state, you can double-click another word to convert it into an editable state as well. In this case, you can click Commit Any Current Edits in the text Option Palette to exit the changes and then select another word of the text.

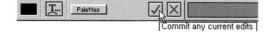

94

4.

Apply Arc to the word WEB as well, but to add a bigger arch, set the Bend to 50% and the Horizontal Distortion to –35%.

▲ *The completed image (Warpedtext-after.Psd).*

option configuration

Warp Text
Style: Arc
Horizontal: (selected)
Bend: 50%
Horizontal Distortion: –35%
Vertical Distortion: 0%

Warped Text Style in Photoshop 6

The Warped Text function is used to transform text, entered using the Text Tool, in various ways after converting the text in the layer to an editable format. In other words, you cannot apply Warped Text to a Rasterized Layer. In addition, because the Warped Text changes are saved in the text layer, future changes to and deletions of the style are possible.

The following figure displays a list of styles in the Warp Text dialog box that you can apply. You'll now look at what happens when you apply the text to Style in the Warp Text dialog box and adjust the Bend, Horizontal Distortion, and Vertical Distortion.

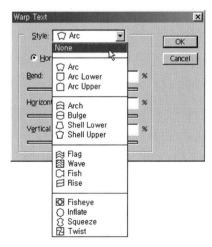

▲ *The Styles of Warped Text.*

95

getting ready

Copy the **Samples⇨Chapter3⇨ Wind.Psd** file from the supplementary CD-ROM onto the hard disk and remove the Read-Only property. Then, load it into Photoshop.

⬠ arc

⬡ arc Lower

⬡ arc upper

⬔ arch

⬓ Bulge

Distorted 3-D Text

shell lower

shell upper

flag

wave

fish

Rise

Fisheye

Inflate

Squeeze

Twist

Text Effects in the Styles Palette

The default styles offered by Photoshop 6 in the Styles Palette include Buttons, Glass Button Rollovers, Glass Buttons, Image Effects, Text Effects, and Textures Styles.

Next, you'll look at the various Text Effects in the Styles Palette.

getting ready

Load the **Samples⟡Chapter3⟡ Image.Psd** file from the supplementary CD-ROM to get ready.

blue gradient with stroke

brushed metal

candy

chalk

chisled sky

chrome—polished

99

chrome—fat

chromed satin

clear emboss—inner bevel

clear emboss—outer bevel

clear die cut

clear double black stroke

clear with heavy stroke

clear with medium stroke

fat black and white

frosted glass

Green Gradient with stroke

Liquid Rainbow

Rainbow

Router

Shade Red Bevel

Hot Burst

Over Spray

Red, white, Blue contrast

Satin

South Beach

sprayed stencil

stamped sunset

sunset sky

swimming pool

toy

wood

Jagged and Transparent Bubble Letters

After using a pattern to create a background and applying the Warped Text command to add distortion, the Displace function, located in the Filter menu, is used to create a sunken-in effect. Then, Layer Style is applied to create bubble letters and trim the overall text.

To have the letters stand out from the black and white background, the Bevel and Emboss effect is used. The yellow color of the text further aids in catching the attention of the viewer.

Preparing the Background

You can use the File⇨New command to create a new, 30 x 30 image window. After drawing a circle on a black background and saving it as a pattern, choose Edit⇨Fill to fill in the entire window with this pattern, which will then be used as the background.

LESSON HIGHLIGHTS

You can use the Displace filter in the Filter menu to add jagged effects image patterns. The function sequence is Edit⇨Define Pattern, then Edit⇨Fill, Text, Warped Text, Transform⇨Rotate, Channel, Filter⇨Distort⇨Displace, and Layer⇨Layer Style.

▲ *Transparent bubble letters.*

1.

Draw the circle of the pattern.

In the Toolbox, set the Foreground
Color to white and the Background
Color to black. Then prepare the
new image by setting the Width to
30 pixels, the Height to 30 pixels,
and the Contents to Background
Color.

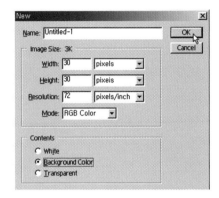

2.

***Choose Ellipse Tool from the Toolbox and click Create Filled Region from the Option
Palette.***

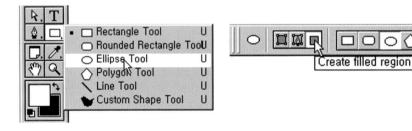

3.

***Draw an appropriately sized circle in the center to complete the pattern that will be
used as the background.***

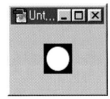

4.

Select the entire image by selecting Select⇨All or by pressing Ctrl+A. Save the selection frame as a pattern by applying Edit⇨Define Pattern.

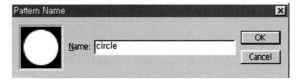

▲ *The Pattern Name dialog box.*

5.

Draw the main image.

In order to draw the main image, set the Width to 500 pixels, the Height to 600 pixels, and the Contents to White.

6.

Open the Fill dialog box by choosing Edit⇨Fill. Under Contents, set Use to Pattern and select and apply the newly created circle from Custom Pattern.

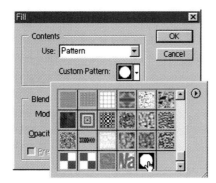

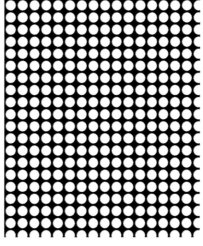

▲ *The resulting image.*

Entering Text

After you use the Text Tool to enter text and the Warped Text command to twist it, you can rotate the text and arrange it in the desired location. (In this example, you'll use Arial Rounded MT Bold, 350 pt, anti–alias:bold, and the text color yellow.)

1.

After typing the word verb, select Warped Text in the Text Options Bar.

2.

In the Warp Text dialog box, select and apply Arc from the Style list and set the Bend to 50%.

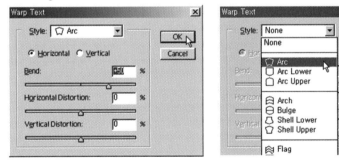

3.

Click Palettes in the Text Options Bar to activate the Character Palette. This palette will allow you to add more detailed configurations to the text.

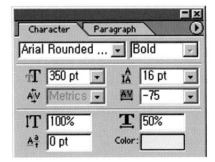

Within this palette, set the Horizontally Scale option to 50% to create a more distorted text.

Choose Edit⇨Transform⇨Rotate to rotate and arrange the text in the desired location.

Choose Edit⇨Transform⇨Rotate to rotate and arrange the text in the desired location.

A Sunken-In Effect

Choose Stroke from within Layer Style and specify this as the Alpha Channel. Apply Gaussian Blur to the new channel. Then, in order to save this channel as a new file, right-click the mouse (Control–click on a Mac) on the channel and select Duplicate Channel.

Choose Filter⇨Distort⇨Displace to give the pattern a sunken-in effect; choose Layer⇨Layer Style to add depth.

1.

From the Blending Options list in the Layers Palette, select Stroke. In the Stroke dialog box, set the Size to 16 px and the Color to red.

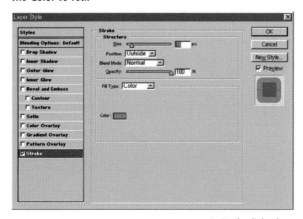

▲ *Stroke dialog box.*

▲ *The Add A Layer Style list menu.*

2.

Choose Select⇨Color Range. After selecting the red portion of the main image using the Eyedropper Tool, click OK. This region will be shown in white.

With the Color Range dialog box activated, dragging the mouse cursor to the image will convert the cursor to an Eyedropper Tool, which allows you to select the color.

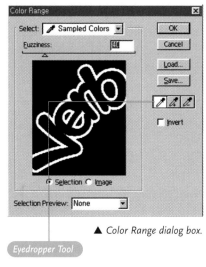

▲ *Color Range dialog box.*

Eyedropper Tool

3.

With the frame selected, open the Channels Palette and choose Save Selection As Channel to create a new channel for the frame.

◀ *The copied layer with the applied pattern.*

4.

To soften the Displace Filter, apply Filter⇨Blur⇨Gaussian Blur to the channel frame. Then, save this channel as a new image file by right-clicking the mouse on the channel and selecting Duplicate Channel.

▲ *Applying Duplicate Channel.*

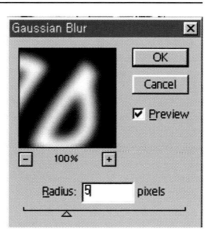

▲ *Gaussian Blur dialog box.*

5.

In the Duplicate Channel dialog box, set the Document text box to New to create and save a new channel. (Here, I named the new file Blurredtext.Psd.)

Blurredtext.Psd is used in the existing image frame to create a sunken-in effect.

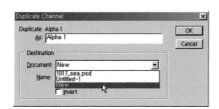

▲ *Setting the Document to New in the Duplicate Channel dialog box.*

6.

To create the sunken-in portion in the Layers Palette, the layer in which the pattern has been applied is copied.

▶ *The copied layer with the applied pattern.*

7.

With the duplicated layer activated, choose
Filter⇨Distort⇨Displace. In the Displace
dialog box, set both the Horizontal Scale and
the Vertical Scale to 5% and click OK. In the
resulting window, select Blurredtext.Psd to
apply the filter to the outer edges of the text.

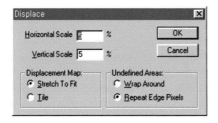

▲ *Displace dialog box.*

▲ *Filter applied to the outer edges
of the text.*

8.

Control + click (Command-click on a Mac) on
the channel of the Blurredtext to specify it as
a selection frame in the Alpha Channel.

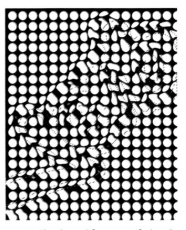

▲ *The channel frame specified as the
selection frame.*

9.

After activating the distorted layer in the Layers Palette, choose Select⇨Inverse to invert the selection frame and then delete it.

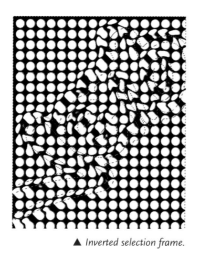

▲ *Inverted selection frame.*

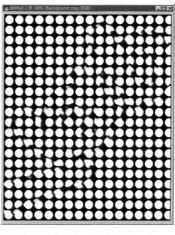

▲ *Deletion of the inverted selection frame.*

```
option configuration

Inner Shadow
Structure
Blend Mode: Multiply
Opacity: 75%
Angle: 120°
Use Global Light: Selected
Distance: 5 px
Choke: 0%
Size: 5 px
Quality
Contour: Linear
Noise: 0%
```

10.

Cancel the selection and select Inner Shadow from Layer Style to create the sunken-in effect.
In the dialog box, set the Blend Mode to Multiply, the Opacity to 75%, the Distance to 5 px, and the Size to 5 px.

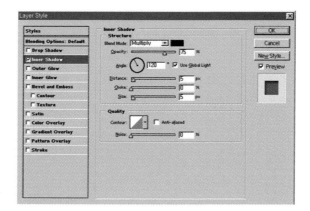

▲ *Configuring the Inner Shadow.*

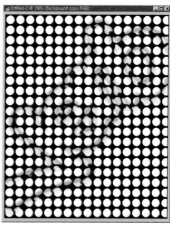

▲ *Application of the Inner Shadow to create the sunken-in effect.*

Creating Transparent Bubble Letters

You can make transparent, bubble letters by using Inner Shadow, Inner Glow, and Bevel and Emboss in Layer Style. You can manipulate the Style values to create the ultimate design.

```
option configuration
```

Inner Shadow
Structure
Opacity: 31%
Distance: 18 px
Size: 9 px

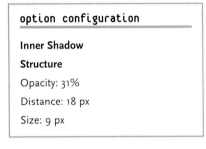
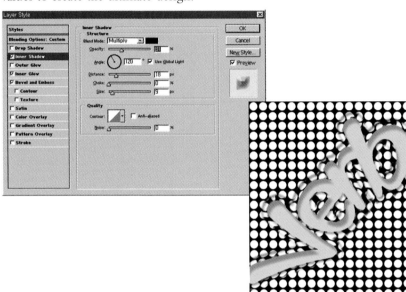

```
option configuration
```

Inner Glow
Structure
Blend Mode: Normal
Opacity: 100%
Elements
Size: 29 px
Quality
Range: 50%

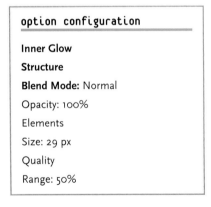
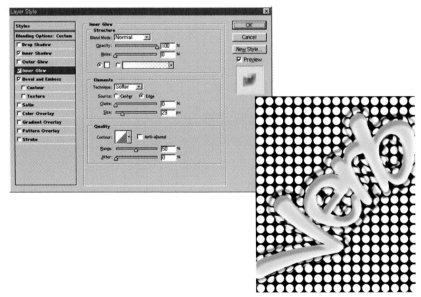

You can load **Samples⊃Chapter3⊃Plastic-after.Psd** from the supplementary CD-ROM to verify the result.

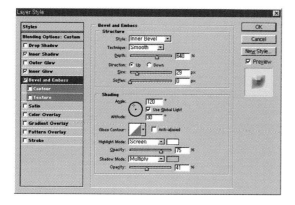

option configuration

Bevel and Emboss

Structure

Depth: 640%

Size: 29 px

Shading

Shadow Mode: Multiply

Color: Yellow (R: 255, G: 174, B: 0)

Opacity: 41%

▲ *The completed image (Plastic-after.Psd).*

Bevel and Emboss

Bevel and Emboss is usually used to
add a jagged appearance to images,
and Lighting Effects are applied to the
background or to the entire image.
The Distort Filter creates a more
realistic image, which is why mastering
this filter will be helpful in improving
your skill.

Quartz Effect

You can create many different styles in Photoshop by combining the Layer Style effects. In this lesson, you'll create a quartz effect by combining the marbling and transparent effects. Continuing to practice with combining these different styles is a great asset in creating new and unique effects.

Applying an Embossed Effect

You can add embossing by using Bevel and Emboss.

▲ *The original Amethyst.Psd image.*

LESSON HIGHLIGHTS

You can create marbling effects by repeatedly applying Satin (in Layer Style) to give a shiny, irregular appearance. The function sequence is Bevel and Emboss, Inner Glow, Satin, Inner Shadow, and Drop Shadow.

getting ready

Copy the **Samples↪ Chapter3↪Amethyst.Psd** file from the supplementary CD-ROM onto the hard disk and load the image into Photoshop.

1.

Select the Amethyst layer in the Layers Palette and choose Bevel and Emboss from the Add A Layer Style pop-up menu.

Add A Layer Style

2.

In the Structure menu in the Style dialog box, set the Style to Bevel and the Technique to Chisel Hard. Raise the values for Depth and Size and lower the value for Soften to create the Embossed Effect.
The values for this example are as follows: Depth: 231%, Size: 106 px, Soften: 0 px.

In the Shading menu, set the Highlight Mode to Screen, white, and Opacity 75%, and the Shadow Mode to Normal, pink, and Opacity 60%.

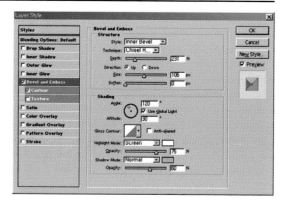

option configuration

Structure
Style: Inner Bevel
Technique: Chisel Hard
Depth: 231%
Direction: Up
Size: 106 px
Soften: 0 px
Shading
Angle: 120°
Use Global Light: Yes
Altitude: 30°
Gloss Contour: Linear
Anti-aliased: Off
Highlight Mode: Screen, Color: White
Opacity: 75%
Shadow Mode: Normal, Color: Pink
   (R: 240, G: 142, B: 246)
Opacity: 60%

3.

To have the embossing appear to flow smoothly outwards, select Cone-Inverted from Contour.

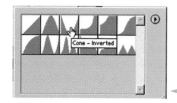

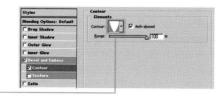

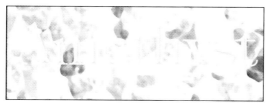

▶ *After applying the results.*

option configuration

Contour Elements
Contour: Cone-Inverted, Anti-aliased:
On, Range: 100%

Adding a Smooth Outline

You can use the Inner Glow effect to create color that softly flows in toward the interior from the borders.

1.

Select Inner Glow from the Styles List/menu (Mac) in the Layer Style dialog box. In the Structure menu, set the color style to Gradient and create a gradient that flows from pink to transparent.

Then, in the Elements menu, set the Source to Edge and the Size to 10.

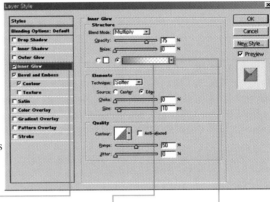

Inner Glow   Click to execute the Gradient Editor   Click to execute the gradient list

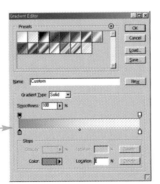

▲ *The addition of a smooth outline due to Inner Glow.*

Adding an Inner Shine

1.

Select Satin in the Layer Style dialog box. In the menu on the right, select the color pink using Multiply mode and Opacity 50%. Choose Gaussian from Contour to add a random shine.

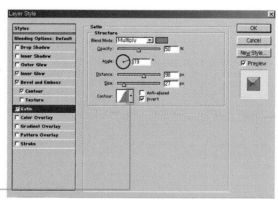

`Contour picker`

The Inner Shadow adds an internal shadow to emphasize the transparency of the image. In this example, this effect was used to emphasize one particular color.

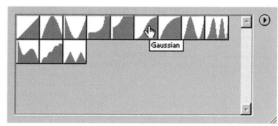

▲ *The screen that appears from clicking on Contour Picker.*

▲ *The random shine that appears due to the Satin effect.*

---

satin

This effect adds a shiny luster to the images to create a bumpy and luminous diffused reflection.

---

option configuration

Satin

Structure

Blend Mode: Multiply

Color: Pink (R: 239, G: 63, B: 224)

Opacity: 50%

Distance: 98 px

Size: 27 px

Contour: Gaussian

Anti-aliased: Deselect

Invert: Select

---

contour editor

The Drop Shadow, Inner Shadow, Inner Glow, Outer Glow, Bevel and Emboss, and Satin effects are all adjusted using the curved graph of the Contour Editor. By directly adjusting this graph, you can have direct control over the finished results.

The Contour Editor is executed by right-clicking the mouse on the

▲ *Contour Editor dialog box.*

Contour thumbnail. Then, after making the adjustments using the curved mapping, the results are saved.

117

option configuration

Inner Shadow

Structure

Blend Mode: Hard Light

Color: Pink (R: 233, G: 83, B: 196)

Opacity: 73%

Angle: 120°

Use Global Light: Select

Distance: 29 px

Choke: 0%

Size: 0 px

Quality

Contour: Linear

Anti-aliased: Deselected

Noise: 0 px

2.

Set the Blend Mode of the Inner Shadow to Hard Light at pink and the Distance to 29.

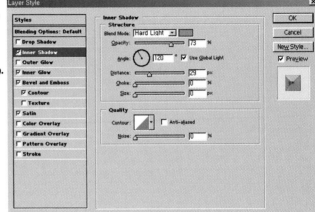

FYI

In the Gradient Editor dialog box, you can adjust the color and transparency using a slide bar that has two pencil-shaped icons, one at the top and one at the bottom, on either side. The icons at the bottom of this bar indicate the color, and the ones at the top represent the transparency. You can change this configuration by first clicking one of these icons with the mouse and then making the appropriate changes to the Stops menu at the bottom.

To add a new color or to change the transparency in the color bar, the mouse is clicked on the top or the bottom of the bar at the location of the desired transparency/color.

▲ *Entering values in the Color and Location boxes to change the color.*

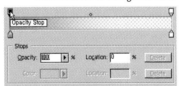

▲ *The Opacity and Location values for adjusting the transparency.*

▲ *Adding a new color and transparency at the center of the gradient.*

Option Configuration

Stops

Opacity: Can be adjusted from 0 to 100%.

Color: Color is selected using the Color Picker.

Location: The position of the gradient is adjusted from 0% on the left to 100% on the right.

Applying Noise to the Gradient Type makes for a more colorful effect.

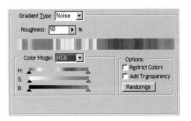

▲ *Emphasizing portions of the color using
Inner Shadow.*

Adding a Shadow

1.

*The tone and contrast of the overall image is very high and bright. Therefore, by
adding the Drop Shadow effect, you can have the main image stand out more from
the background.*

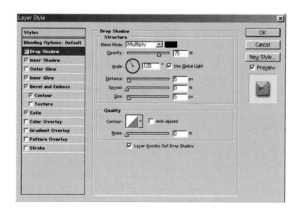

▲ *Configuring Drop Shadow.*

119

option configuration

Outer Glow

Structure

Blend Mode: Screen

Opacity: 75%

Noise: 0%

Elements

Technique: Softer

Spread: 0%

Size: 5 px

Quality

Contour: Linear

Anti-aliased: Deselect

Range: 50 px

Jitter: 0%

2.

You'll also add the Outer Glow effect to brighten up the outline of the text.

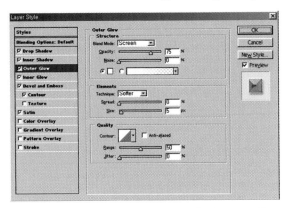

▲ *Configuring Outer Glow.*

3.

Add the newly created effect to the Styles Palette.

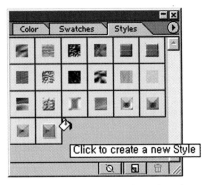

▲ *Adding the new style to the Styles Palette.*

4.

Click an empty space in the palette and
enter the name of the new style in the
New Style dialog box that appears.

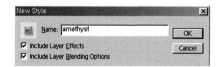

▲ *New Style dialog box.*

5.

*The quartz effect that you made here needs to be adjusted slightly according to
where and how it will be used. Making small changes to the highlight, the reflection,
and the internal refraction will produce drastically different results. You should practice making changes to the configuration to obtain the desired results.*

▲ *Completed image (Amethyst-after.Psd).*

Transforming the Quartz Effect

In this lesson, you'll apply the quartz effect to a text design and adjust the configurations to create the desired effect.

LESSON HIGHLIGHTS

You can use Layer Style to transform the quartz effect. The function sequence is Bevel and Emboss, Inner Glow, Inner Shadow, and Color Overlay.

▲ Original image.

▲ The final image with the application of the quartz effect.

Applying an Embossed Effect

You'll apply Bevel and Emboss to create an image with a carved appearance. By selecting Use Global Angle, the same light angle will be applied to all the effects.

getting ready

Copy the **Samples⟲Chapter3⟲ Jade.Psd** file onto the hard disk and then load it into Photoshop.

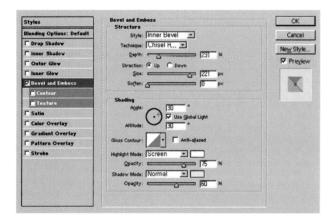

▲ *Configuring Bevel and Emboss.*

option configuration

Bevel and Emboss

Structure

Style: Inner Bevel

Technique: Chisel Hard

Depth: 231%

Size: 221 px

Soften: 0 px

Shading

Angle: 30°

Use Global Angle: Select

Highlight Mode: Screen, white

Shadow Mode: Normal

Color: Light Pink (R: 255, G: 206, B: 206)

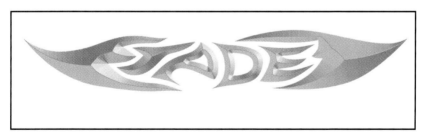

▲ *After applying the embossing.*

123

option configuration

Inner Glow

Structure

Blend Mode: Multiply

Opacity: 75%

Noise: 0%

Color: Gradient, Pink (R: 192, G: 0, B: 220)

Elements

Technique: Softer

Source: Edge

Choke: 0%

Size: 44 px

Quality

Contour: Cone-inverted

Anti-aliased: Off

Range: 50%

Jitter: 0%

Bevel and Emboss

This option is used to create protruding and sunken-in effects. Used mostly to create buttons or slightly protruding shapes, this function was originally included in the Lighting Effects filter. However, in the latest version of Photoshop, this feature has been improved and is now included in Layer Style. With five different styles to choose from, including Outer Bevel, Inner Bevel, Emboss, Pillow Emboss, and Stroke Emboss, you can vary the configuration to create diverse and unique results.

Adding a Smooth Outline

To add a smooth outline, apply Inner Glow.

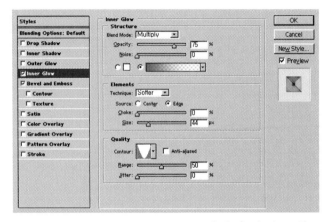

▲ *Configuring Inner Glow.*

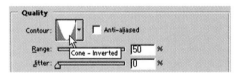

▲ *Setting the Contour in Quality to Cone-Inverted.*

▲ *After applying a smooth outline.*

Adding Transparency

After applying Inner Shadow, you'll add a shadow to the rear.

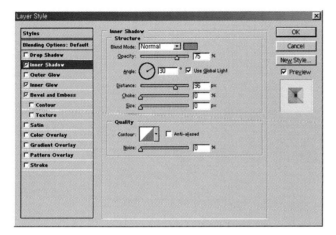

▲ *Configuring Inner Shadow.*

▲ *After applying the Inner Shadow.*

125

```
About Layer Style
```

The Layer Style Palette is made more powerful because the individual effects of Drop Shadow, Inner Shadow, Outer Glow, Inner Glow, Bevel and Emboss, Satin, Color Overlay, Gradient Overlay, and Pattern Overlay can be combined and applied to one object.

It's a good idea to learn how to combine these effects, rather than stick to just one particular style. Looking through the examples, you can see that Gradient Overlay is not merely used for gradations but also to create highlights and default colors, that Satin can also be used as a source of light to emphasize the other effects, and that Inner Shadow is not only used to add internal shadow but to add contrast to circular shapes. The possibilities are endless. It is up to you to practice with combining the different effects of the Layer Style to create new and unique results.

Adjusting the Overall Color

You can use Color Overlay to create a unified color throughout the image.

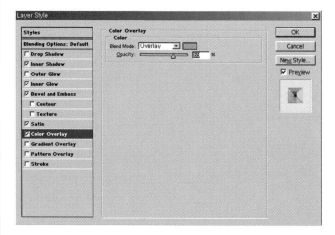

▲ *Configuring Color Overlay.*

▲ *The completed image (Jade-after.Psd).*

You can verify the result by loading **Samples⇨Chapter3⇨Jade-after.Psd** from the supplementary CD-ROM.

126

Gold and Enamel Effects

In this lesson, you'll create gold letters to be placed on a shiny, enamel texture. You'll apply Satin and Inner Glow to a protruding background, made using Layer Style's Bevel and Emboss option, to create a shiny effect.

▲ A gold and enamel effect.

A Softly Protruding Effect

You'll use the Bevel and Emboss effect in Layer Style to create a protruding background. In order to soften the protrusion, the Soften value is adjusted.

▲ The original image, Gold_enamel.Psd.

LESSON HIGHLIGHTS

You can use dark colors and strong, partial highlights to create a shiny texture. Here, you'll use Inner Glow and Satin to create a shiny, enamel effect. The function sequence is Bevel and Emboss, Satin, Inner Glow, Gradient Overlay, and Color Overlay.

getting ready

Copy **Samples⇨Chapter3⇨ Gold_enamel.Psd** from the supplementary CD-ROM onto the hard disk and then load the image into Photoshop.

option configuration

Bevel and Emboss

Structure

Style: Pillow Emboss

Technique: Smooth

Depth: 100%

Direction: Up

Size: 5 px

Soften: 5 px

Shading

Angle: 120°

Use Global Light: Select

Altitude: 28°

Gloss Contour: Linear

Anti-aliased: Off

Highlight Mode: Screen, white

Opacity: 75%

Shadow Mode: Multiply, black

Opacity: 75%

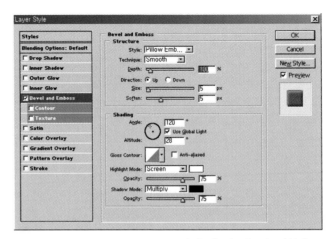

▲ *Configuring Bevel and Emboss.*

▲ *After applying the protruding effect.*

bevel and emboss style

You can use Stroke Emboss only when Stroke Effect is used. Here, you see the different Bevel effects depending on the Stroke.

outer bevel

inner bevel

emboss

pillow emboss

stroke emboss

Adding More Shine

After using Satin, in Layer Style, to create a shiny effect, Inner Glow is added to further emphasize the lighter areas.

Set Opacity to 91%, Distance to 8 px, and Size to 13 px. Then, after setting the Contour to Cove–Deep, select Invert.

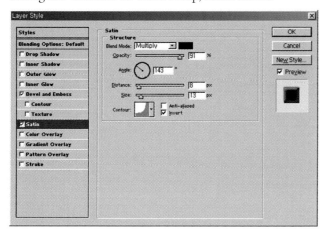

▲ *Configuring Satin.*

▲ *Setting Contour to Invert and Cove-Deep.*

option configuration
Satin
Structure
Blend Mode: Multiply, white
Opacity: 91%
Angle: 143°
Distance: 8 px
Size: 13 px
Contour: Cove-Deep
Anti-aliased: Off
Invert: On

▲ *After applying Satin to the image.*

After selecting Inner Glow from the Styles dialog box, under the heading Structure, set the Blend Mode to Overlay, and under the heading Elements, set the Size to 15 px.

option configuration

Inner Glow

Structure

Blend Mode: Overlay

Opacity: 60%

Noise: 0%

Elements

Technique: Softer

Source: Edge

Choke: 0%

Size: 15 px

Quality

Contour: Linear

Anti-aliased: Off

Range: 50%

Jitter: 0%

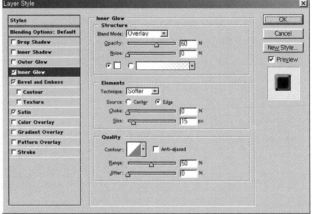

▲ *Configuring Inner Glow.*

▲ *The shiny effect created using Inner Glow.*

Applying a Gold Texture to the Text

You can use Gradient Overlay in Normal mode to create a background color where the light flows from top to bottom and then use the Color Overlay in Multiply Mode to designate the color. You can then apply Inner Bevel and Inner Glow to the gold texture created in this way so that the shape of the texture is more prominent.

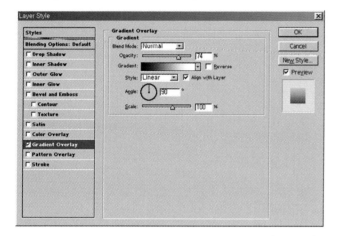

▲ *Gradient Overlay.*

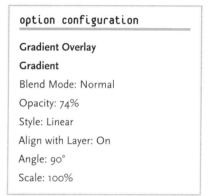

option configuration

Gradient Overlay

Gradient

Blend Mode: Normal

Opacity: 74%

Style: Linear

Align with Layer: On

Angle: 90°

Scale: 100%

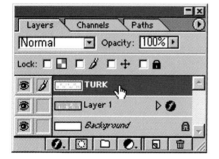

▲ *Selecting the text layer in the Layers Palette.*

▲ *After applying the Gradient Overlay.*

131

option configuration

Color Overlay

Color

Blend Mode: Multiply

Color: Yellow (R: 255, G: 222, B: 0)

Opacity: 41%

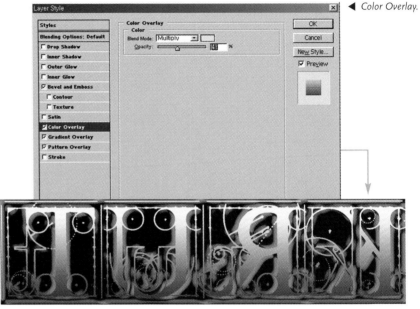

◀ *Color Overlay.*

You can verify the result by loading **Samples⤳ Chapter3⤳ Gold_enamel-after.Psd** from the supplementary CD-ROM.

option configuration

Inner Glow

Structure

Color: Light Yellow (R: 255, G: 255, B: 190)

Elements

Size: 5 px

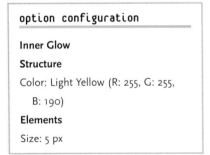

▶*Inner Glow.*

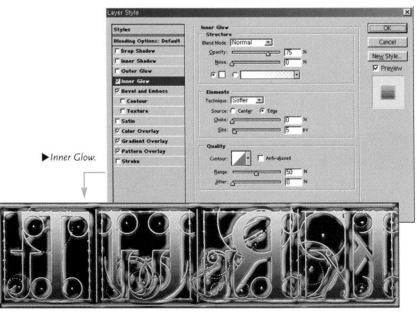

▲ *The completed image with the gold texture.*

Metallic Textures

In this lesson, you'll look at how to create metallic textures by applying Curves and various styles as well as how to create matching fluorescent, bubble letters, encircled by a metallic band.

▲ *Completed image.*

Highlights, in Image⇨Adjust⇨Curves, contains a feature that uses curves to create detailed modifications in brightness and color, much like that seen in Shadows. You'll use this feature in this example to create a metallic feel by strongly emphasizing the contrast. You'll combine a metallic band and fluorescent letters with this image to create a background using several Layer Styles.

A Metallic Effect

1.

Load the image file and then copy it in the Layers Palette to make a new layer.

In the Paths Palette, switch the selection frame by setting the OUTLINE path to Loads Path As A Selection and then choose Select⇨Inverse to invert the frame.

Delete the inverted selection frame from the duplicated layer so that the areas outside the image appear transparent.

LESSON HIGHLIGHTS

You can apply metallic textures to images by choosing Image⇨Adjust⇨Curves to create strong contrast. In addition, you can use Inner Glow to create a glow-in-the-dark effect. The function sequence is Image⇨Adjust⇨Curves, Image⇨Adjust⇨Desaturate, Edit⇨Transform⇨Skew, and Layer⇨Layer Style.

---

getting ready

Load the **Samples⇨Chapter 3⇨Basketball.Jpg** image file from the supplementary CD-ROM and copy it onto the hard disk.

curves

The Curves function allows you to use curves to naturally modify the color frame, including Highlights, Midtones, and Shadows. The point on the left is used to modify Shadows. The middle point is for Midtones, and the point on the right is used for Highlights. These points are used, or a new point is added to the center, to adjust the color tones and contrast and modify the color of the overall image.

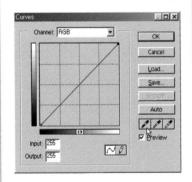

▲ *The Eyedropper Tool indicating Black, White, and Gray.*

option configuration

Gradient Overlay

Gradient

Blend Mode: Overlay

Opacity: 100%

Style: Linear, Align with Layer

Angle: 90°

Scale: 100%

2.

Choose Image⟳Adjust⟳Desaturate to convert the color image to monotone.

To add a strong contrast, choose Image⟳ Curves. In the dialog box, brighten the Highlights and Shadows and darken the Midtones.

▲ *Curves dialog box.*

▲ *Metallic effect added to the image.*

3.

Choose Layer Style to add shadows and a blue color to the top of the image. Apply Layer⟳Layer Style⟳Gradient Overlay. Create a white to blue gradient (R: 0; G: 40, B: 116) by setting the Blend Mode to Overlay and the Angle to 90°.

In the Layers Palette, use the Add A Layer Style function or double-click on the empty space next to Layer thumbnail.

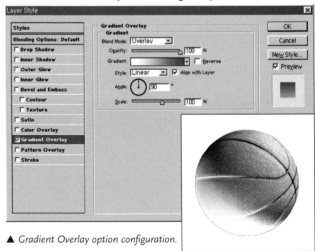

▲ *Gradient Overlay option configuration.*

▲ *Gradient Overlay applied to the image.*

4.

To add shadows to the bottom of the image, select Inner Shadow and set the Distance to 37 px, the Size to 40 px, the Opacity to 75%, and the Blend Mode to Multiply.

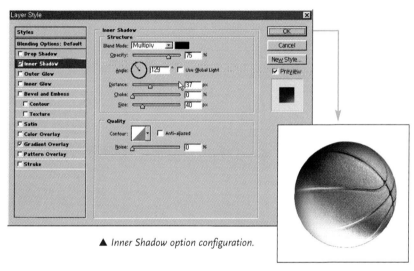

▲ *Inner Shadow option configuration.*

▲ *Inner Shadow applied to the image.*

```
option configuration

Inner Shadow
Structure
Blend Mode: Multiply
Opacity: 75%
Angle: 129°
Use Global Light: Off
Distance: 37 px
Choke: 0%
Size: 40 px
```

Completing the Background Image

1.

Make a new window with the dimensions Width: 770 px and Height: 250 px to create the main image.

After loading and positioning the image of the basketball, apply a slight gradient effect to the Background Layer to complete the background.

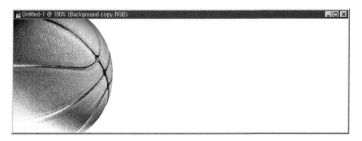

The Path Tool Team

In the Toolbox, the Text Tool is in the same category as the Path and Shape Tools. Text Layers converted to Paths or Shapes through Create Work Path or Convert to Shape can use the Path function.

When modifying or creating new text, the work will proceed much easier if it's first converted into a Path.

▲ *The Path Tool team in the Toolbox.*

2.

Choose Gradient Tool from the Toolbox and change the color in the Options Bar.

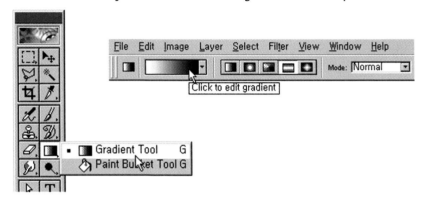

Apply a white to blue-gray gradient (R: 134, G: 150, B: 179) to the Background Layer.

Entering Text and Applying Skew

Select Type Tool from the Toolbox and enter the text. (In the example here, you'll use Zrnic, 168 pt.)

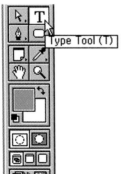

Creating the Metal Band Using Stroke and Bevel and Emboss

1.

Select Stroke from the Layer Styles dialog box and set the Size to 5 px, the Blend Mode to Luminosity, and the Position to Outside.

▲ *Stroke option configuration.*

▲ *Stroke applied to the image.*

option configuration

Stroke

Structure

Size: 5 px

Position: Outside

Blend Mode: Luminosity

Opacity: 100%

2.

Select Bevel and Emboss from the Layer Styles dialog box and set the Style to Stroke Emboss, the Size to 5 px, and the Gloss Contour to Ring. These settings add a metallic band to the Stroke frame.

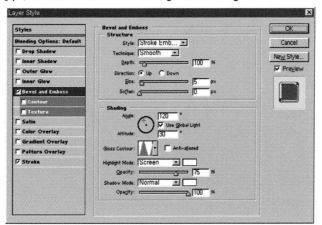

option configuration

Bevel and Emboss

Structure

Style: Stroke Emboss

Technique: Smooth

Depth: 100%

Direction: Up

Size: 5 px

Soften: 0 px

Shading

Angle: 120°

Use Global Light: On

Altitude: 30°

Gloss Contour: Ring, Anti-aliased: Off

Highlight Mode: Screen, White

Opacity: 75%

Shadow Mode: Normal, White

Opacity: 100%

137

◀ *Stroke and Bevel and Emboss used to add a metallic band to the image.*

Applying Pattern Overlay

The created pattern is saved and used as a Pattern Overlay.

1.

An image that will be used as the stripe pattern is made and applied to the Pattern Overlay. Open a new work window with the dimensions Width: 1 px and Height: 2 px and fill in the frame of 1 pixel in black. Choose Edit⇨Pattern and save this pattern as bnw.

2.

Choose Layer⇨Layer Style⇨Pattern Overlay and select bnw from the Pattern list. Then set the Blend Mode to Multiply and the Scale to 150%.

---

option configuration

Pattern Overlay

Pattern

Blend Mode: Multiply

Opacity: 100%

Pattern: bnw

Scale: 150%, Link with Layer: On

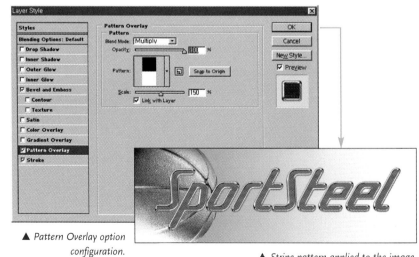

▲ *Pattern Overlay option configuration.*

▲ *Stripe pattern applied to the image.*

138

Applying Gradient Overlay, Color Overlay, and Inner Glow

1.

Set the Gradient Overlay to a blue gradation (R: 2, G: 11, B: 126) with a 30% transparency applied to the center. Then set the Blend Mode to Hard Light and the Angle to 90°.

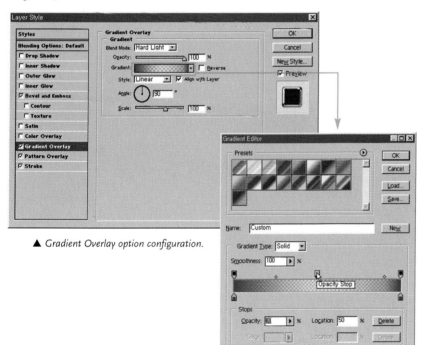

▲ *Gradient Overlay option configuration.*

▲ *Gradient Editor dialog box.*

option configuration

Gradient Overlay

Gradient

Blend Mode: Hard Light

Opacity: 100%

Style: Linear, Align with Layer: On

Angle: 90°

Scale: 100%

▲ *Gradient Overlay applied to the image.*

2.

To brighten up the color overall, set the Overlay Mode of the Color Overlay to a jade green (R: 0, G: 255, B: 234).

option configuration

Color Overlay

Color

Blend Mode: Overlay

Color: Bright Jade Green

(R: 0, G: 255, B: 234)

Opacity: 100%

▲ Color Overlay option configuration.

▲ Color Overlay applied to the image.

3.

option configuration

Inner Glow

Structure

Blend Mode: Color Dodge

Opacity: 75%

Noise: 0%

Elements

Technique: Softer

Source: Center

Choke: 75%

Size: 5 px

To emphasize a fluorescent effect, open the Inner Glow dialog box and set the Blend Mode to Color Dodge, the Source to Center, the Choke to 75%, and the Size to 5 px.

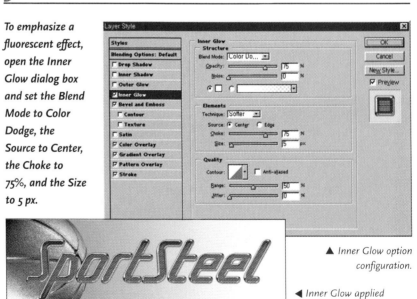

▲ Inner Glow option configuration.

◀ Inner Glow applied to the image.

Applying Drop Shadow

To create text that appears to protrude from the background, apply Drop Shadow and set the Distance to 12 px and the Size to 7 px.

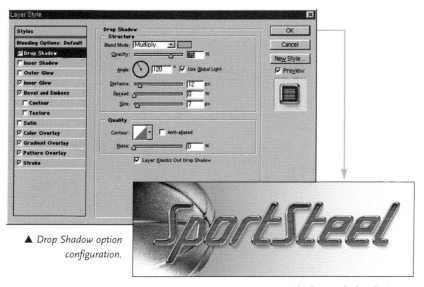

▲ Drop Shadow option configuration.

▲ Drop Shadow applied to the image.

Saving Styles

You can save the various styles applied to the layer as one style in the Styles Palette. With the text layer activated, click an empty space in the Styles Palette to save the style.

You'll save this style as steel and rubber.

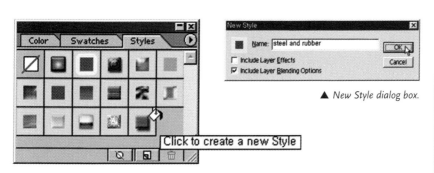

▲ Saving a new style in the Styles Palette.

▲ New Style dialog box.

option configuration

Drop Shadow

Structure

Blend Mode: Multiply

Opacity: 75%

Angle: 120°

Use Global Light: On

Distance: 12 px

Spread: 0%

Size: 7 px

141

Making the Text Background

1.

Select the Rectangle Tool from the Toolbox.

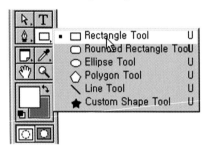

2.

Make sure that the Create New Shape Layer is checked in the Options Bar. Draw in a rectangle that will serve as the background for the text and insert this new layer in between the text and basketball layers.

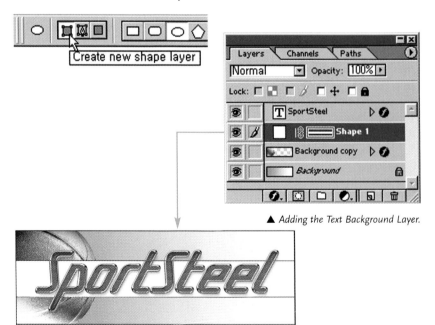

▲ *Adding the Text Background Layer.*

3.

Apply the new steel and rubber style to the Text Background Layer. Adjust the tone and contrast so that the text can be differentiated from its background.

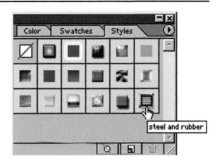

▲ *Selecting the steel and rubber style from the Styles Palette.*

4.

When the Shape Tool is used to create the Layer Clipping Path, you can modify the color of the Shape frame through the Color Picker, which is executed by double-clicking the Layer thumbnail.

A low-tone blue (R: 86, G: 91, B: 158) is selected for the Shape Layer.

▲ *Layer thumbnail.*

▲ *Color Picker is displayed by double-clicking the Layer thumbnail.*

▲ *A low-tone blue color is applied to the bar in the background.*

Gamut

When printing the completed image, remember that certain colors will look good in the printout, while others won't. Gamut is the function that gives you this information. Choose View⇨Gamut Warning to verify the nonprintable colors; change these colors by choosing Edit⇨Preferences⇨Transparency & Gamut.

▲ *Original image.*

▲ *The nonprintable colors are shown in white when the Gamut Warning is applied.*

143

5.

You can remedy an overly bright background by making adjustments to the Inner Glow that was applied to the background image.

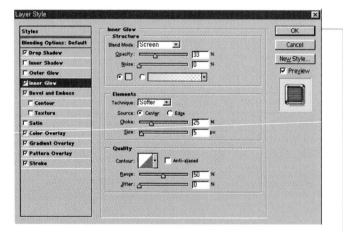

▲ *Inner Glow option configuration.*

▲ *Completed image (Sportsteel-after.Psd).*

You can verify the completed image by loading **Samples⇨Chapter3⇨ Sportsteel-after.Psd** from the supplementary CD-ROM.

Plastic Buttons

Connections to other Web pages are made through hyperlinks. You're probably familiar with clicking an underlined piece of text on a Web site to move to another page. Just as these text links transport you to other pages, a more graphical representation of a hyperlink comes in the form of buttons.

Button graphics are simpler than text links and convey the information in a more direct fashion. On a more aesthetic level, buttons play a huge role in adding decorative detail to a page, and they're the first things to catch your eye.

In this lesson, you'll learn how to draw and create buttons in Photoshop. You'll create transparent, plastic buttons. Transparent textures usually utilize bright colors, and Inner Bevel is used to emphasize the inner shadow created by the embossed effect.

LESSON HIGHLIGHTS

You can use Layer Style's Gradient Overlay to add highlights. You'll also find out what kinds of effects can be created by the transparent Inner Shadow. The function sequence is Gradient Overlay, Color Overlay, Inner Bevel, Inner Shadow, and Drop Shadow.

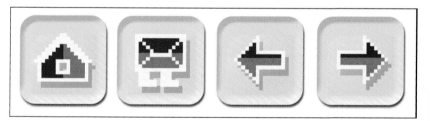

▲ *The completed transparent, plastic buttons.*

getting ready

Copy the **Samples⇨ Chapter3⇨Button_ plastic.Psd** file onto the hard disk and then load the image into Photoshop.

Creating Highlights

Load the example image and use Layer Style's Gradient Overlay to create a protruding form on the rounded rectangular layer. You can add highlights to a portion of the image that is portrayed in this way.

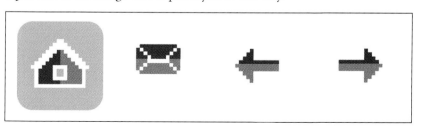

▲ *Original image (Button_plastic.Psd).*

FYI

You can use the Normal mode of
Color Overlay to apply Styles.

1.

*After selecting the Square layer, click Add A Layer Style in the Layers Palette and
select Gradient Overlay.*

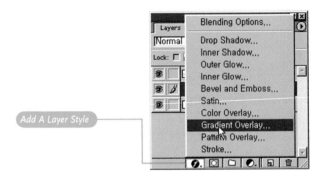

▲ *Selecting Gradient Overlay from
the Add A Layer Style list.*

option configuration

Gradient Overlay

Gradient

Blend Mode: Normal

Opacity: 100%, Reverse: On

Style: Radial

Angle: 90°

Scale: 100%

2.

*Set the Blend Mode to Normal and the Opacity to 100% so that the style will be
applied to the existing rounded rectangle, without regard to the color.*

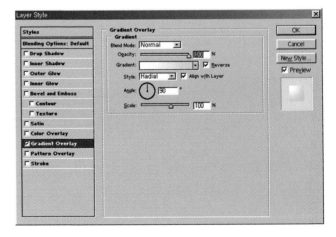

▲ *The Gradient Overlay Options configuration.*

Adding Color

Use the Multiply mode of Color Overlay so that a new color, along with the gradient, is applied to the style.

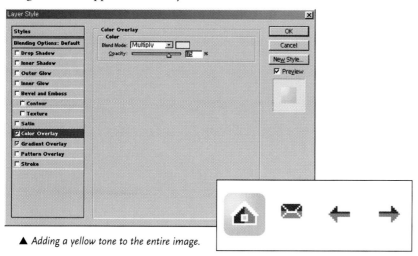

▲ Adding a yellow tone to the entire image.

▲ The highlight effect added to the image.

option configuration
Color Overlay
Color
Blend Mode: Multiply
Color: Yellow (R: 255, G: 222, B: 0)
Opacity: 75%

Applying Inner Bevel

The Depth and Size are appropriately applied, and the Direction is made to go down.

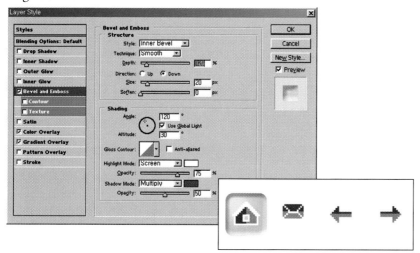

▲ Applying the Inner Bevel for dimensionality.

option configuration
Bevel and Emboss
Structure
Depth: 120%
Direction: Down
Size: 20 px
Soften: 0 px

147

Adding a Transparent Shadow

An Inner Shadow at Normal mode is added to emphasize the transparency.

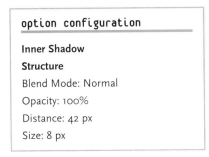

option configuration

Inner Shadow

Structure

Blend Mode: Normal

Opacity: 100%

Distance: 42 px

Size: 8 px

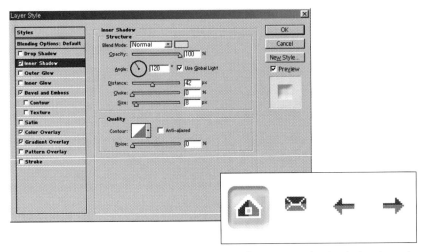

▲ *The transparent interior shadow due to the application of Inner Shadow.*

Adding Shadow Effects

You can use Drop Shadow to add shadow.

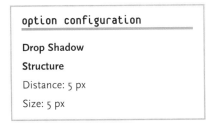

option configuration

Drop Shadow

Structure

Distance: 5 px

Size: 5 px

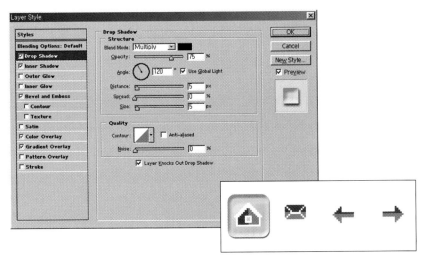

▲ *Using Drop Shadow to create protrusion.*

Saving New Styles

1.

After activating the layer in which the Style has been applied, click an empty space in the Styles Palette to save the new style.

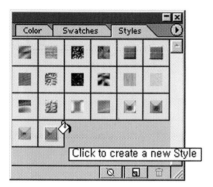

▲ *Adding a new style to the Styles Palette.*

2.

In the New Style dialog box, save the style under the name yellow plastic.

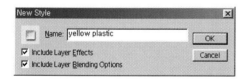

▲ *New Style dialog box.*

149

тhe Lock Function in the Layers palette

1. **Lock transparent pixels:** This option preserves the transparent frame in the selected layer. This prevents a selection frame from being selected in the layer (Ctrl+clicking on the layer) and prevents it from being effected by external frames.

2. **Lock image pixels:** When the transparent section is automatically checked, it prevents editing of the respective layer.

3. **Lock position:** This prevents the layer image from being moved.

4. **Lock all:** This applies all three previous Lock commands.

3.

This completed button layer is then double-clicked and applied to another symbol.
Copying the layer itself is done using the Move Tool. With the layer that you want to copy activated, use the tool to move it to the desired location while pressing the Alt (Option on Mac) key. This copies the original layer and creates a new duplicate image layer.

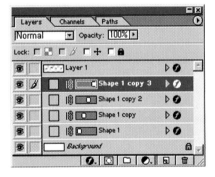

▲ *The three copied layers duplicated using the Move Tool.*

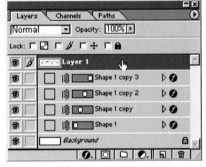

▲ *Selecting the Symbol layer.*

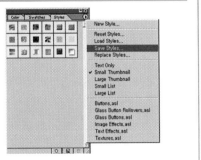

Adding Shadow to the Symbols

1.

To make it appear as if the symbol has been placed on top of the yellow plastic, you apply Drop Shadow.

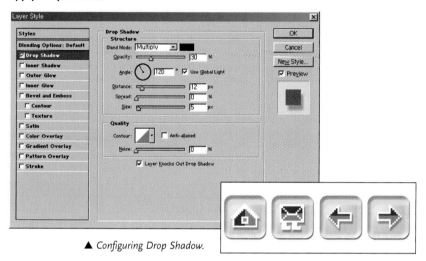

▲ *Configuring Drop Shadow.*

▲ *Shadow has been added to the symbol to create depth.*

2.

In order to change the color of the symbol to a light yellow, a yellow Color Overlay Effect, at a low Normal mode Opacity, is applied.

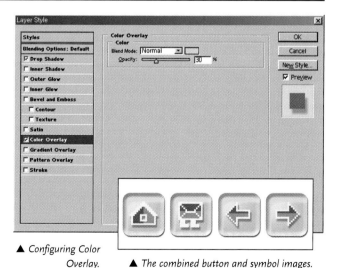

▲ *Configuring Color Overlay.*

▲ *The combined button and symbol images.*

151

Preserving the Overall Color

You can use the Adjustment Layer to change the color of the completed plastic button without affecting the entire layer.

With the Symbol layer activated, select Hue/Saturation from Create New Fill Or Adjustment Layer at the bottom of the Layers Palette.

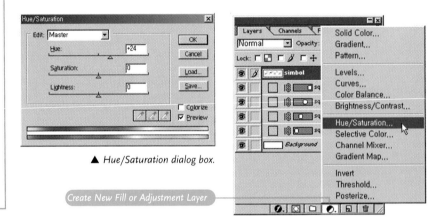

▲ Hue/Saturation dialog box.

Create New Fill or Adjustment Layer

Adjust the Hue value to the desired color and then check the result. (In this example, I used a Hue value of +24.)

▲ The color has been changed for all the layers within the Adjustment Layer.

▲ The completed button image (Button_plastic-after.Psd).

You can verify the result by loading **Samples⇨Chapter3⇨ Button_plastic-after.Psd** from the supplementary CD-ROM.

Up until now, you've looked at using Style Effects to create buttons. Style Effects is a very diverse toolset that can be combined in many ways to create a wide array of different styles, just as you saw earlier with the text design, and is one of the biggest advantages of using Photoshop. It is now up to you to make this tool your own and master it to create your own new styles and techniques.

Making Illustrations
Using the Path Tool

The function sequence is Ellipse Tool, Pen Tool, Path Component Selection Tool, Direct Selection Tool, Combine, and Layer Style.

One of the biggest reasons that many people were awaiting the release of Photoshop 6 was the inclusion of Illustrator functionality. People familiar with Adobe's Illustrator will not find Photoshop 6's Illustrator function to be very exciting. This is because the only thing that you can do with Photoshop 6's Illustrator is to use Paths to draw a basic shape and use Combine to trim/combine shapes. You will soon find that you are restricted in terms of how much you can do with this functionality, especially when drawing very complex images. However, looking just in terms of Web design, Photoshop's vector-graphic functionality can be a very useful tool.

In this lesson, you'll use the Path Tool and the Shape Tool to create a simple illustration.

▲ *Illustration created using the Path Tool and the Shape Tool.*

LESSON HIGHLIGHTS

This chapter deals with how to use Selection Tools, Pen Tools, and Shape Tools to create or edit paths and shapes. In addition, by following along with illustrated images in Photoshop, you'll enhance your image creation techniques and broaden your efficiency of using clipping paths for mask effects.

Preparing the Work Environment

1.

Create a new 600 x 500 pixel work window.

2.

Choose Edit⇨Preferences⇨Guides & Grid to create a more precise and exact image.

▲ *Choosing Guides & Grid from the Edit⇨Preferences menu.*

3.

In the Preferences dialog box, set the Guideline Every to 50 pixels and the Subdivision to 4.
Choose View⇨Show⇨Grid to activate the grid and then select View⇨Snap to convert to Snap form.

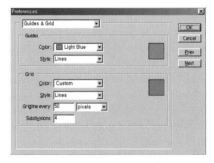

▲ *Guides & Grid dialog box.*

Making the Bowl

1.

Select the Ellipse Tool from the Toolbox.

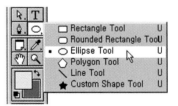

2.

In order for the ellipse to be created in a new layer, make sure that Create New Shape Layer is selected in the Options Bar.

Drawing a fixed shape

In the Option Palette of the Shape Tool is the Geometry option, hidden in the toggle menu that is used to specify the size and proportions of the shape to be drawn. You can use this option to create a more precise and exact shape.

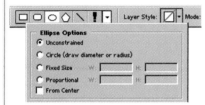

▲ *The Geometry option toggle button in the Shape Tool.*

Rectangle Options

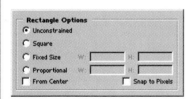

▲ *The Geometry of the Rectangle Tool.*

Unconstrained: Nonstipulated shape

Square: Square shape

Fixed Size: A shape with a fixed width and height

Proportional: A shape with a proportional width and height

From Center: The center of the square is designated as the starting point

Rounded Rectangle Options

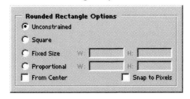

▲ *The Geometry option of the Rounded Rectangle Tool.*

Ellipse Options

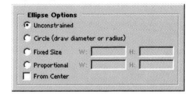

▲ *The Geometry option of the Circle Tool.*

Circle (draw diameter or radius):
Circular shape

Polygon Options

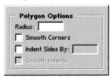

▲ *The Geometry option of the Polygon Tool.*

Radius: A specified radius

Smooth Corners: A shape with rounded corners

Indent Sides By: The space between the corners is rounded inwards

Smooth Indents: Softens the Indent effect

Arrowheads (Line Options)

▲ *The Geometry option of the Line Tool.*

Start, End: Creates arrowheads at the start or end points of a line

Width, Length: The width and length of the arrowheads relative to the line thickness

Concavity: The degree to which the ends of the arrow appear sunken in

Custom Shape Options

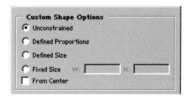

▲ *The Geometry option of the Custom Shape Tool.*

FYI

You can tell whether a path in the Layers Palette is activated by clicking on the Clipping Path. This allows you to turn the path on and off.

3.

Draw the ellipse that will serve as the foundation for the bowl. In the example, I drew a 350 px x 200 px ellipse.

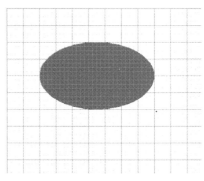

▲ *The ellipse with a clipping path.*

4.

Next, you'll draw in the remaining parts of the bowl.

Select the Pen Tool from the Toolbox. In order to add a shape or remove portions from the existing ellipse layer, the path must be activated. Make sure that the path of the ellipse layer is selected. The path is selected when the outline of the ellipse appears.

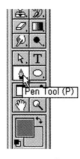

▲ *Selecting the Path Tool in the Toolbox.*

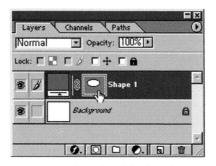

▲ *The outline of the shape becomes activated when the path is selected.*

▲ *The inactivated path.*

156

5.

The Path Tool is used to complete the lower half of the bowl. The rounded bottom of the bowl is drawn using the Ellipse Tool.

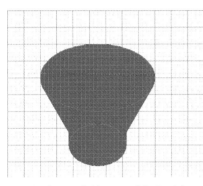

▲ *The rounded bottom of the bowl drawn using the Ellipse Tool.*

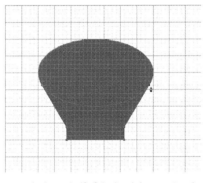

▲ *The lower half of the bowl drawn using the Path Tool.*

6.

In order to be able to use a portion of the path later, make sure that the three shapes overlap in the Layers Palette.

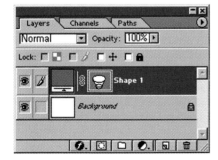

▲ *The overlapping shapes in one layer.*

Aligning two or more paths

▲ *The Align (left) and Distribute (right) options of the Path Component Selection Tool.*

Align

Top edges: Aligns the paths to the top edges of the upper path.

Vertical centers: Aligns the paths to the vertical centers of each path.

Bottom edges: Aligns the paths to the bottom edges of the lower path.

Left edges: Aligns the paths to the left edge of the path on the left.

Horizontal centers: Aligns the paths to the horizontal centers of each path.

Right edges: Aligns the paths to the right edge of the path on the right.

Distribute

Top edges: Three or more paths are each lined up proportionately along the top edge.

Vertical centers: Three or more paths are each lined up proportionately along the vertical center.

Bottom edges: Three or more paths are each lined up proportionately along the bottom edge.

Left edges: Three or more paths are each lined up proportionately along the left edge.

Horizontal centers: Three or more paths are each lined up proportionately along the horizontal center.

Right edges: Three or more paths are each lined up proportionately along the right edge.

157

Drawing the Bottom of the Bowl

After combining the two paths below, copy and trim them to create the bottom of the bowl and then apply a different color to this portion.

1.

Select the Path Component Selection Tool from the Toolbox.

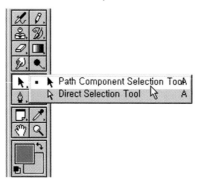

2.

Using the mouse, drag the cursor over the two paths to select them.

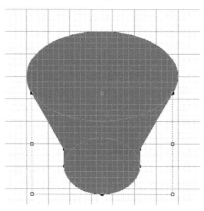

▲ *Using the Path Component Selection Tool to select the two shapes.*

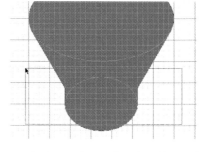

▲ *The two shapes selected simultaneously.*

Making Illustrations Using the Path Tool

3.

With the Add To Shape area (+) selected in the Option Palette, click the Combine button.

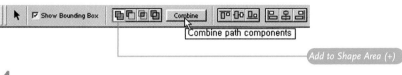

4.

To make the bottom support, copy the Shape 1 layer to make a new layer. Hide the Shape 1 layer.

After removing the upper ellipse, select the entire path. Then move this path while pressing the Alt key to create a copy of this path on the same layer.

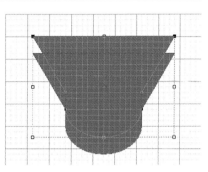

5.

After selecting the entire path, click Exclude Overlapping Shape Areas from the Options Bar.

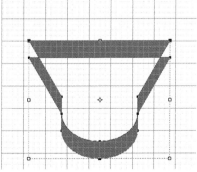

▲ *After selecting Exclude Overlapping Shape Areas.*

6.

Next, delete all the sections, excluding the area at the bottom. Use the Direct Selection Tool to transform or remove a portion of the path.

Select the Direct Selection Tool from the Toolbox. After selecting the frame to remove, press the Del key to delete this area.

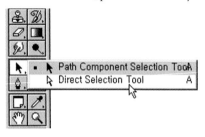

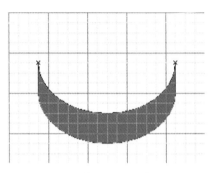

▲ *After removing the unnecessary portions of the shape.*

7.

You'll now change the color of the layer to which the Layer Clipping Path has been applied. Double-click the Layer thumbnail and then select the color from the Color Picker that appears.

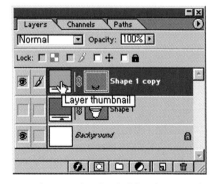

▲ *The Layer thumbnail of the Clipping Path.*

8.

Select and apply an appropriate color from the Color Picker Palette and verify the result. Here, I used sky blue (R: 62, G: 160, B: 225).

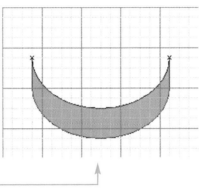

9.

Right-click the mouse on the layer and select Layer Properties from the pop-up menu. Enter the name Support.

▲ Layer Properties dialog box.

Making the Shadow Field

In order to portray the darkened areas of the image, you need to create a shadow field.

1.

Make a copy of the Shape 1 layer in the Layers Palette to create a new layer. Hide the Shape 1 layer.

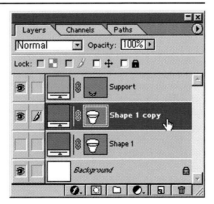

2.

Select the Path Component Selection Tool from the Toolbox.

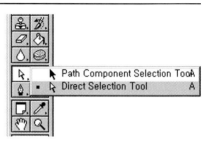

3.

Select the entire path and then, after selecting Exclude Overlapping Shape Area from the Options Bar, click Combine.

4.

Use the Direct Selection Tool to select the top portion of the merged shape and remove it.

In the remaining shape, use the Path Tool to create the area that will be used as the shadow field.

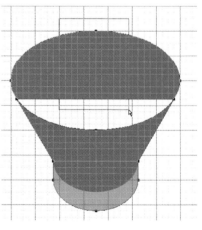

▲ *Selecting the area to be deleted using the Direct Selection Tool.*

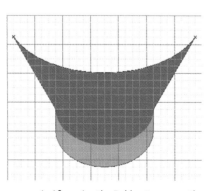

▲ *After using the Del key to remove the selected portion.*

5.

Use the Path Tool to draw in the remaining shadow field.

▲ Working in the same layer in order to combine the two paths.

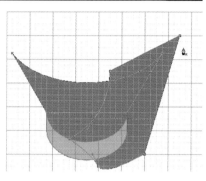

▲ The shadow field drawn in using the Path Tool.

FYI

The same color was used in this example, and both the shadow and support layers were set to the Multiply mode at Opacity 50% to portray the color.

6.

Use the Direct Selection Tool to select the entire path and then, after selecting Intersect Shape Areas from the Options Bar, click Combine.

Name the layer, shadow, and the Shape 1 layer bowl. Then apply color to each layer to portray the shadow.

Intersect shape areas

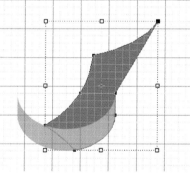

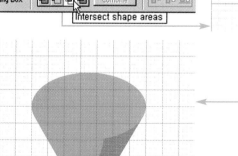

▲ After applying the color.

▲ Applying the Multiply mode at Opacity 50% to the shadow and support layers.

163

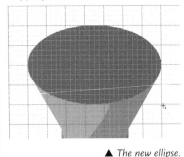

▲ *The new ellipse.*

Drawing the Top of the Bowl

Draw another ellipse, with the same dimensions as the previous one, in a new layer.

1.

Copy the new ellipse layer to create a second ellipse layer.

2.

In the second ellipse layer, choose Edit⇨Transform Path⇨Scale. This will display the Options Bar, which allows you to edit the shape using precise numerical values. In order to create an ellipse slightly smaller than the existing one, you enter the values W: 95% and H: 93% in the Transform option.

3.

Click the Commit Transform button to complete the execution of the Transform option.

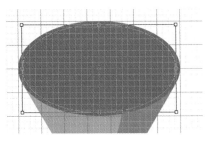

▲ *Transform applied to the second ellipse.*

4.

Name the existing ellipse layer Edge and the scale-adjusted layer Bowl_In.

Brighten the color of the Edge layer to complete the formation of the bowl.

In the example here, I applied a bright blue to the Edge layer (R: 128, G: 200, B: 240).

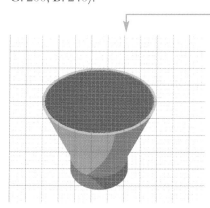

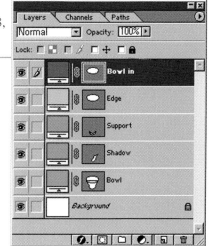

▲ *The completed bowl image.*

Drawing a Linear Shape

A linear shape, as opposed to a planar one, is created by first drawing the basic shape using Path and then applying Stroke Effect in Layer Style.

1.

The food inside the bowl will be drawn in a new layer using the Path Tool.

In order to cut out the areas that extend beyond the Bowl_In layer, select the path for this layer and press Ctrl (Cmd)+C to copy. After activating the new layer, press Ctrl (Cmd)+V to load the elliptical path.

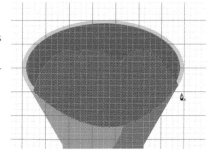

2.

After selecting the entire path using the Path Component Selection Tool and clicking Intersect Shape Areas in the Options Bar, click Combine.

3.

To create noodles, use the Path Tool to draw in many linear strands and then apply Stroke Effect to adjust the thickness of the lines. To cut out the areas that extend out of the bowl, this time you'll apply the Layer↪Group With Previous command.

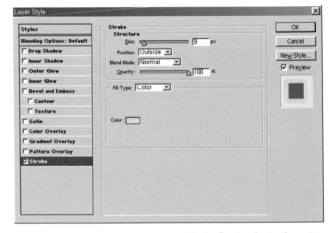

▲ *Configuring the Stroke option.*

---

option configuration

Stroke

Size: 9 px

Position: Outside

Fill Type: Color

Color: Mustard Yellow (R: 226, G: 206, B: 81)

▲ *The Stroke Effects applied to the path.*

tip

You can group two layers together by placing the cursor between them and clicking while holding down the Alt key or by using the shortcut keys Ctrl+G.

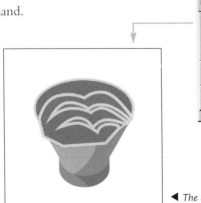

◀ *The completed noodles.*

4.

When the food/noodle layer is grouped with the Bowl_In layer, the bottom-most layer, Bowl-In, acts as a mask for the two upper layers to hide them.

▲ *After applying Group with Previous.*

▲ *The grouping of the Shape 1 and Shape 2 layers due to the Bowl_In layer.*

5.

The remaining elements are drawn in using Path and trimmed to complete the illustration.

The images created using vector graphics in Photoshop, despite differences in size and shape distortion, are similar in quality to those created using Illustrator.

You can verify the result by loading **Samples⇨Chapter3⇨Illust_cup.Psd** from the supplementary CD-ROM.

◀ *Completed illustration.*

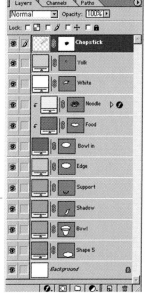

▲ *All the layers used to create the illustration.*

Using Satin to Create Irregular Light Sources

You can use Lighting Effects to have the main image appear to pop out from the background. In this chapter, you find out about Alpha Channels and Paths and learn how to use Layer Styles Satin effect to create irregular light rays. The Layer Style methods used to create buttons in the previous lesson will be adapted to create unique symbols.

▲ *Complete image.*

To create a protruding main image, you first establish a domain using the Path Tool, apply Blur, and then save to a new channel.

Choose Filter⇨Render⇨Lighting Effects to create a Texture Channel. For the first channel, create a large enough domain to accommodate the protruding edges. For the second channel, create a frame slightly larger than the main image to accommodate the sunken in areas around the main image. The standard ellipse used to set up the domains is saved in the Paths Palette and used as needed.

The remaining, jagged frames (created using Lighting Effects) are deleted as selection frames with configured Feather values so that the jagged effect and the background image blend together more naturally.

After using Style Effects to create the rounded ellipse of the main image, you can add highlights manually.

A Protruding Effect

FYI

Before creating the ellipse, make sure that Create New Shape Layer is checked in the Options Bar.

1.

Create a new 850 x 300 pixel image window.
Use View⟹Show⟹Grid to activate the Grid and Snap.

2.

Use the Ellipse Tool in the Toolbox to draw the ellipse for the main image.
The ellipse created here is quite wide. Take the Direct

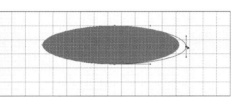

Selection Tool and select the points for the width on either side of the ellipse and increase the size to create an ellipse with sharper edges. Because you're using the Shape Tool to draw the main image, you can adjust the precise shape and position of the image after applying the effects.

3.

Draw two ellipses that will be saved as Alpha Channels.
Open the Paths Palette and make a copy of the Shape 1 Clipping Path.

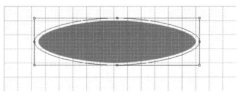

4.

Use Edit⟹Free Transform Path to adjust the frame of the new path so that it's slightly larger than the existing ellipse. When applying Transform, numerical values are entered in the Options Bar to adjust the size. You use the numerical values in order to create a new shape that is proportional to the existing shape.

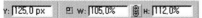

By clicking Maintain Aspect Ratio, you can adjust the width/height ratio at the same time. This option, along with Grid and Clipping Path, makes it easier to create a precise and proportional image.

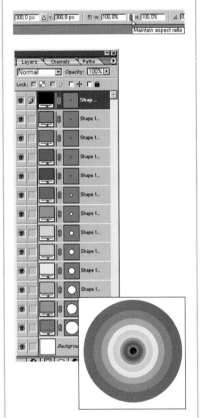

▲ *The color combination image showing repeated 80 percent reductions in the size of the circle and the Layers Palette created using the Margin aspect ratio option.*

5.

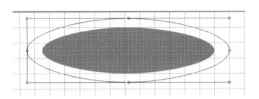

Because this is an ellipse, the percentage of the height is magnified slightly more than the percentage of the width. After adjusting the size of the first path, use the same method to create a slightly larger second path.

6.

Specify the second ellipse as a selection frame by clicking the layer while pressing the Ctrl key or by clicking Loads Path As A Selection in the Paths Palette.

7.

Save this selection frame as a new channel by selecting Save Selection As Channel in the Channels Palette. In the same way, save the small ellipse as a new channel and name the channels Big and Small, respectively.

8.

Now, apply Filter⇒Blur⇒Gaussian Blur to both channels. To add more of a protrusion to the Big Channel, set the Radius to 15 px; to add a slight concavity to the Small Channel, set the Radius to 2 px.

9.

Create a new layer to which the Lighting Effects will be applied and add color.

10.

Choose Filter⟿Render⟿Lighting Effects and select Big from the Texture Channel. Check White Is High and set the Height to 35.

To offset a too bright effect, set the Intensity to 21.

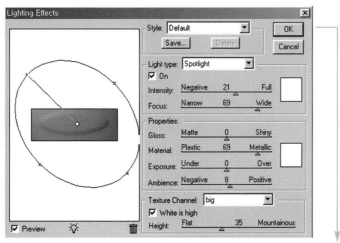

▲ *A protruding Lighting Effect applied to the image.*

11.

Again, create a new layer and apply Lighting Effects to the Small Channel to create a concave shape. In the configuration window, select Small for the Texture Channel and deselect the White Is High option.

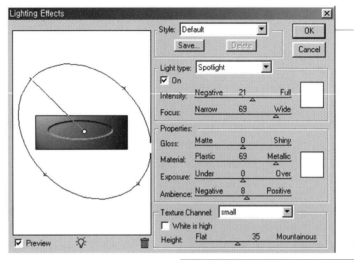

▲ *Lighting Effects dialog box.*

▲ *A concave Lighting Effect applied to the image.*

12.

In the Layers Palette, name each layer Big and Small, respectively, as you did for the channels.

▲ *Layer Properties dialog box chosen by right-clicking (Control-clicking on a Mac) the mouse.*

13.

Use Paths to remove the unnecessary areas around the outside of the two layers.
After activating the Small layer, load the small ellipse in the Paths Palette into the
selection frame.

Apply Select↦Inverse to invert the selection
frame and set Select↦Feather to 3 px in order to
soften the cut edges.

▲ *The selection frame with the Small layer.*

14.

Remove the selection frame by
pressing the Del key.

Using the same method,
remove the area outside the
Big layer. To extend the
smooth frame, set the Feather
value to 5 px.

▲ *The outer area removed from the selection frame*
and softened using the Feather value.

15.

Fill in the Background layer with color so that it blends in well with the protruding
image.

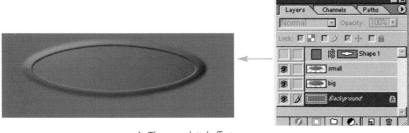

▲ *The completed effect.*

Applying Layer Style to the Main Image

Apply the Gradient Overlay Effect to the Shape 1 layer.

In this example, you'll use Gradient to give the symbol a protruding effect.

1.

Apply a vertical Linear Gradient (Normal Mode, Opacity 100%) to create the convex effect.

option configuration

Gradient Overlay

Gradient

Blend Mode: Normal

Opacity: 100%

Gradient: Blue (R: 8, G: 57, B: 195)

Sky Blue (R: 138, G: 228, B: 251)

Angle: 90°

▶ *Configuring Gradient Overlay.*

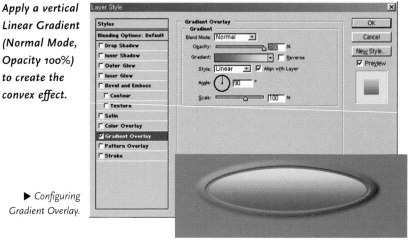

▲ *Application of the Gradient.*

2.

To give a blue tone to the overall image, apply Color Overlay Effect in Multiply mode.

option configuration

Color Overlay

Color

Blend Mode: Multiply

Color: Sky Blue (R: 0, G: 198, B: 255)

Opacity: 100%

▶ *Configuring Color Overlay.*

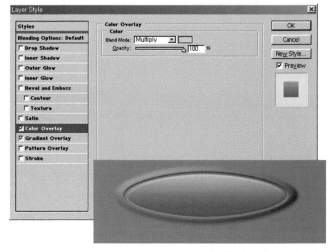

▲ *Application of Color Overlay.*

3.

You create the irregular light rays in the background of the main image by using the Satin effect.

Adjust Contour to create an irregular form and then brighten it by applying color in the Color Dodge mode. Adjust Distance and Size until the desired shape is achieved.

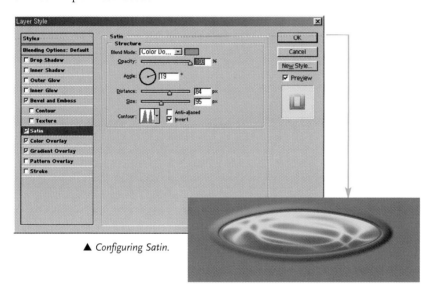

▲ *Configuring Satin.*

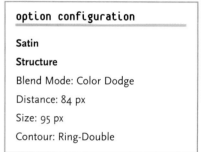

▲ *Application of the Satin effect.*

option configuration

Satin

Structure

Blend Mode: Color Dodge

Distance: 84 px

Size: 95 px

Contour: Ring-Double

4.

option configuration

Inner Shadow

Structure

Blend Mode: Multiply

Distance: 42 px

Size: 46 px

Apply Inner Shadow to create the dark background for the highlight.

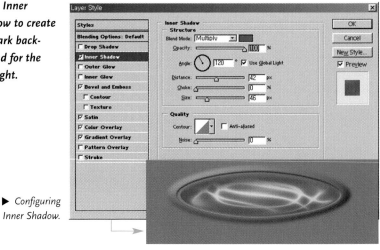

▶ *Configuring Inner Shadow.*

▲ *Application of Inner Shadow.*

5.

option configuration

Inner Glow

Structure

Blend Mode: Overlay

Opacity: 75%

Elements

Size: 92 px

To soften and slightly smear the effects of the Satin option, apply Inner Glow in Overlay mode. Save the current layer style in the Styles Palette.

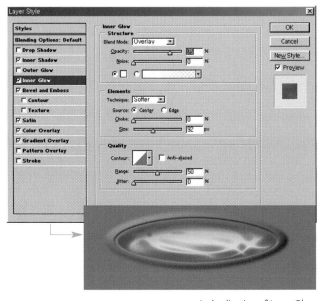

▶ *Configuring Inner Glow.*

▲ *Application of Inner Glow.*

Applying Highlights

1.

Use the Pen Tool in the Toolbox to draw in the frame that will make up the highlight region.

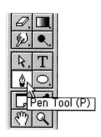

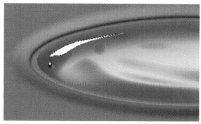

2.

Apply Filter⇨Blur⇨Gaussian Blur to soften the outline of the shape.

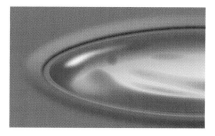

3.

Use the Text Tool to enter the text and then apply Drop Shadow Effect so that the letters stand out from the background.

▲ *The completed image (Chaosskyline.Psd).*

You can verify the result by loading **Samples⇨Chapter3⇨ Chaosskyline.Psd** from the supplementary CD-ROM.

Arranging Text and Images

In this lesson, you'll apply an embossing effect to the image to create the effect of protruding tiles and design text that blends in with the background.

To apply an embossing effect, you first need to create the pattern of the transparent background, which will be used as a mask, in a new layer.

You then copy the background image and create a new copy of the image that shows only the pat-tern frame. Then, you apply Layer Style to cre-ate an embossed effect.

If you want the background reflected in the text, use the text, created using Style Effects, as a mask in the copied image.

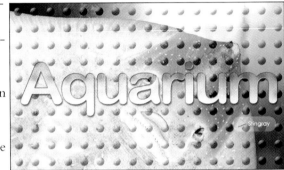

▲ Completed image.

Making a Patterned Image

1.

Create a new 50 x 50 pixel image
window with a transparent
background.

▲ The transparent background created for the pattern.

2.

With the grid activated, draw a circle with a diameter of 25 pixels in the center. You
cannot save an image drawn using the Ellipse Tool and the Clipping Path as a pattern.

In the Options Bar, click Create Filled Region
so that you can save the layer as a pattern.

▲ Creation of the image using
Create Filled Region.

3.

Choose Edit⇨Define Pattern and save the pattern as TransparentBCK_Circle.

getting ready

Copy **Samples⇨Chapter 3⇨ Aquarium.Psd** onto the hard disk and then load the image into Photoshop.

4.

Open the example image file and create a new layer in the Layers Palette that will be used for the pattern.

Choose Edit⇨Fill. Set Use to Pattern and then select TransparentBCK_Circle from the Custom Pattern list.

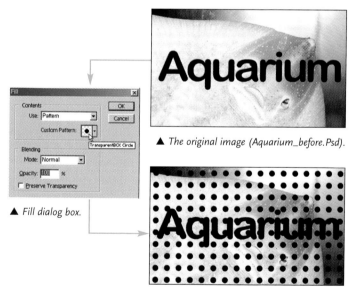

▲ *Fill dialog box.*

▲ *The original image (Aquarium_before.Psd).*

▲ *Application of the pattern to the transparent background.*

Application of the Mask and the Embossing Effect

1.

Copy the background image in a new layer.

Move this copied layer to right above the pattern layer and change the layer mode to Hard Light.

Choose Layer⇨Group With Previous so that the pattern layer is applied as a mask to the image layer.

▲ *The copied background image that has been grouped with the pattern layer.*

▲ *After applying Group With Previous.*

2.

In the Layer Style of the pattern layer, select Bevel and Emboss and set the Size to 5 px and Soften to 10 px to apply a smooth embossing.

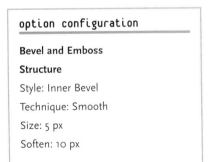

option configuration

Bevel and Emboss

Structure

Style: Inner Bevel

Technique: Smooth

Size: 5 px

Soften: 10 px

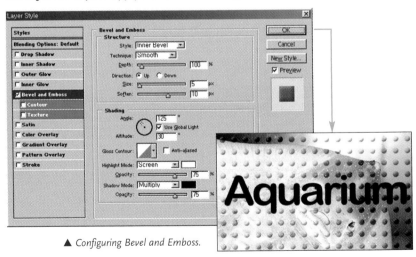

▲ *Configuring Bevel and Emboss.*

▲ *The application of Bevel and Emboss to the pattern layer.*

Reflecting the Background in the Text

1.

After copying the background image in a new layer, move it to right above the text layer and slightly darken the image by choosing Image⊃Adjust⊃ Hue/Saturation. By doing this, the area that shows through the text is more strongly emphasized.

▲ *Hue/Saturation dialog box.*

2.

Choose Layer⊃Group With Previous so that the only the image that shows through the text is visible.

▲ *The copied background image grouped with the text layer.*

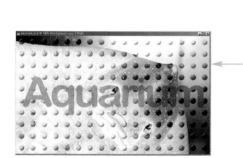

▲ *The image applied to the text.*

selectively modifying the color in hue/saturation

To apply another color (besides Master from the Edit menu), the Eyedropper Tool at the bottom of the dialog box must be activated. In this state, drag the mouse to the image and click the desired color to adjust the Hue/Saturation/Lightness. In addition, if the color has already been changed, you can click the Eyedropper Tool on a particular color to apply the effects immediately. You can then use the Add To Sample and Delete From Sample tools to add/subtract this change in another color.

▲ *The Eyedropper Tool used to select color.*

Group with previous

The Layer ⟲ Group With Previous command applies the image or text frame in the lower of the two layers as a mask in the upper layer. A mask is applied and only the portions that will be edited remain visible so that a uniform effect can be applied without affecting the entire image. In addition, because you can group many layers together, you're able to apply a single mask to several layers at a time.

▲ *Identical styles applied using the mask.*

The mask that you apply through the Group With Previous command can be applied to layers with clipping paths, layers with masks, or layers with applied layer styles. However, grouping masks cannot be applied to fill or adjustment layers.

By applying a style to the layer that acts as the mask (the bottom-most layer), this same style can be applied simultaneously to all the grouped layers. The use of this mask is shown here in creating the Contact Sheet, Image thumbnail list.

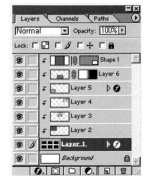

▲ *Several layers grouped into one layer.*

Applying Layer Style

You can apply Layer Style to the text to enhance its overall appearance.

option configuration

Gradient Overlay
Gradient
Blend Mode: Overlay
Angle: 90°

1.

A blue, Gradient Overlay effect (in Overlay mode) is applied to the text to create a bright and refreshing appearance.

▶ *Configuring Gradient Overlay.*

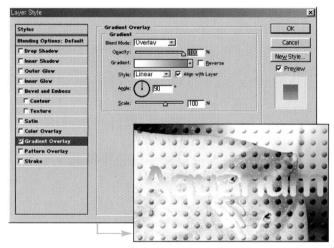

▲ *Application of Gradient Overlay.*

2.

You now use the Bevel and Emboss and Drop Shadow effects so that the text stands out more from the background image.

option configuration

Bevel and Emboss
Structure
Style: Inner Bevel
Direction: Down
Size: 2 px

▲ *Configuring Bevel and Emboss.*

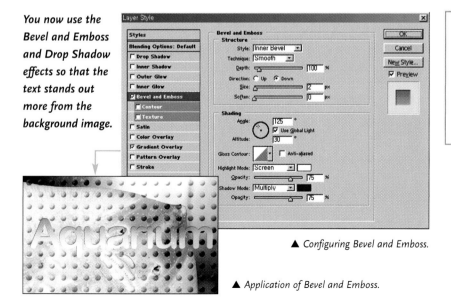

▲ *Application of Bevel and Emboss.*

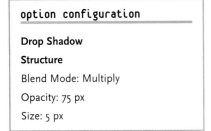

option configuration

Drop Shadow

Structure

Blend Mode: Multiply

Opacity: 75 px

Size: 5 px

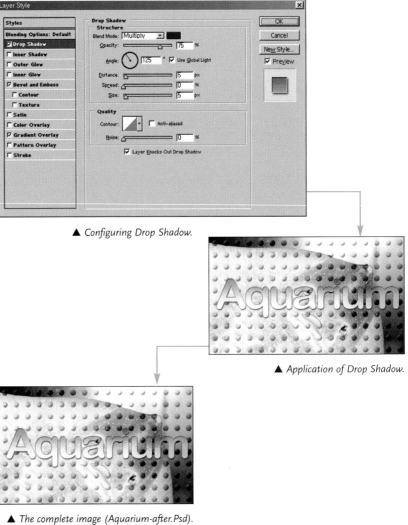

▲ *Configuring Drop Shadow.*

▲ *Application of Drop Shadow.*

▲ *The complete image (Aquarium-after.Psd).*

You can verify the result by loading **Samples⇨Chapter3⇨Aquarium-after.Psd** from the supplementary CD-ROM.

Adding Dimensionality to Text

You enter text onto a picture image and adjust it to create harmony between the two. To have the image and the text blend well together, you need to apply the perspective of the picture image and the rough-ened texture of the image to the text. You also use the Group With Previous command to apply the color and light of the image to the text, without affecting the entire layer.

▲ The completed image.

LESSON HIGHLIGHTS

A grid is placed on a picture image and adopted as the perspective that will be applied to the text. Also, free-flowing text is created using Edit⇒Transform⇒Distort.

The function sequence is Lasterize Layer, Edit⇒ Transform⇒Distort, Duplicate Layer, Filter⇒Distort⇒ Displace, Layer⇒Group With Previous, and Image⇒Adjust⇒ Hue/Saturation.

In dealing with images that have severe depth, like the outside of the building in the example image, you must use your sense of space to tackle the difficult task of matching the perspective of the text to that of the building. If the building had been made up of lines instead of planes, it would be pretty easy to line up the text with the building. All you'd have to do is distort the text along the grid lines of the building. Using this concept, you'll create a grid on the building.

▲ Original image.

▲ The organization of the layers of the example image.

getting ready

Copy the **Samples⇒ Chapter3⇒Join.Psd** file from the supplementary CD-ROM onto the hard disk and remove the Read-Only property. Then load the image into Photoshop.

Creating the Grid

1.

First, hide all layers except Background.

▶ *Hiding all layers except Background.*

2.

Looking at a close-up of the surface of the wall, you can see that you can position the grid over the vertical slats and the nails that were used to hold the slats in place.

▶ *The nails and the slats that will form the foundation of the grid.*

3.

Create a new layer for the grid and place it right above the Background layer. Then select the Line Tool from the Toolbox and set the foreground color to white so that the grid lines will stand out from the background.

▲ *Selecting the Line Tool from the Toolbox.*

4.

In the Line Options Bar, click Create Filled Region and check the Anti-alias option.

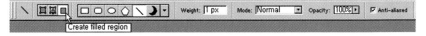

▲ *Creating the horizontal grid line based on the nails in the building.*

5.

Draw in the grid on the new layer using the nails and the slats as a guide.

▲ *Horizontal grid lines drawn in along the position of the nails.*

▲ *One vertical grid line drawn in along the slats.*

Arranging the Text on the Grid Lines

1.

Convert the text layer into an image layer so that you can apply the Distort command. Right-click the mouse on the text layer and select Rasterize Layer from the pop-up menu.

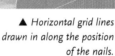

◄ *Application of Rasterize Layer.*

2.

Choose Edit⇨Transform⇨Distort.

Adjust the four corner vertices so that the text is placed on top of the grid.

The Distort function places eight vertices around the image, which you can use to adjust the shape and position of the image.

▶ *Using Distort to align the image on the grid.*

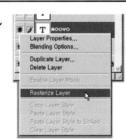

3.

When the image is in place, exit this command by
double-clicking the mouse, pressing Enter on the
keyboard, or by clicking the Commit Transform
button in the Options Bar.

▲ *The Commit Transform button
in the Options Bar.*

4.

Convert the remaining text layers into a Rasterize Layer and choose
Edit➪Transform➪Distort to align them on the grid.

▲ *Arranging the
WEBDESIGN layer.* ▲ *Arranging the WITH
PHOTO layer.* ▲ *Arranging the 6 layer.*

Applying the Roughened Texture of the Building to the Text

You've now finished arranging the text on the grid.
Now, in order to make the text look as if it has been
painted onto the building, you need to apply the
roughened texture of the building to the text.

1.

First, erase the grid layer by dragging and dropping the layer
that you want to erase onto the Delete Layer button at the
bottom of the Layers Palette or by selecting the layer in question
and then clicking this button..

Delete Layer button

▲ *Removing the
grid layer.*

2.

Next, merge all the text layers into one layer. Select one of the text layers and then link the others.

▶ *The Indicates If Layer Is Linked button.*

3.

Open the list menu by clicking the toggle button at the top right-hand side of the Layers Palette and choosing Merge Linked to combine the layers.

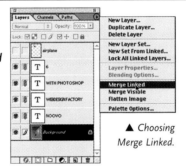

▲ *Choosing Merge Linked.*

4.

Copy the Background layer into a new layer. Right-click the Background layer to open the list menu and choose Duplicate.

In the Duplicate dialog box, select New under Document to create a copy of the layer in a new image window.

Save the copy as Pattern.Psd.

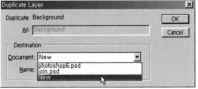

▲ *Duplicate dialog box.*

5.

Select the text layer and choose Filter⇨Distort⇨Displace.

▶ *Selecting the text layer.*

6.

In the Displace dialog box, select Stretch
To Fit and Repeat Edge Pixels and set
Horizontal Scale to 0% and Vertical Scale
to 3%.

▲ *Configuring the Displace dialog box.*

7.

Select the Pattern.Psd file in the Choose A Displacement
Map dialog box. This will create the roughened texture on
the text.

▲ *Selecting Pattern.Psd.*

▶ *The roughened texture applied to the image.*

Applying Color to the Text

Next, you'll apply color to the text. To apply the reflection of light on the
outer wall of the building to the text, you use the Grouped Layer function.

1.

Copy the Background layer into a new layer. Move this layer right
above the image layer and apply Layer↷Group With Previous.

▶ *Copying the Background layer.*

2.

Due to the application of the command in Step 1, the copy of the Background layer is set up to show only the text image frame. However, because this is the same image as the original Background layer, it is difficult to verify the result of the application.

Change the color of the duplicate Background layer using Image⟶Adjust⟶Hue/Saturation and apply Group With Previous to verify the result. (In changing the color, you applied a Hue and a Lightness of +30.)

▲ *Group with Previous.*

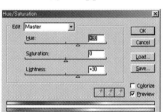

▲ *Hue/Saturation dialog box.*

You can verify the result by loading **Samples⟶Chapter3⟶ Join-after.Psd** from the supplementary CD-ROM.

▲ *After changing the color of the text image (Join-after.Psd).*

The Various Effects of the Group Layer

LESSON HIGHLIGHTS

You can apply the Layer❖ Group With Previous command to use the sublayers as a mask that will hide or display portions of the image without disrupting the original image itself. The function sequence is Ellipse Tool, Path Component Selection Tool, Combine Path Components, Edit❖ Define Pattern, Edit❖ Fill, Adjustment Layer, and Group With Previous.

In this lesson, you'll create an image without disrupting the entire image by displaying only a portion of the image and by using the Group function, which applies one mask to several layers. In addition, you'll use the Shape Tool and Grid to create a figure that will be used as an image pattern.

▲ *Completed image.*

▲ *Original image (Group.Psd).*

Making a Pattern Image

First, you need to make a work environment for a transparent image.

1.

Create a new transparent 100 x 100 pixel background image window.

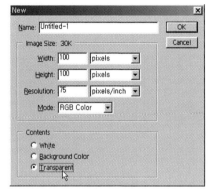

▲ *Selecting the Transparent option to create an image window with a transparent background.*

2.

Choose View⊃Show⊃Grid. In Edit⊃ Preferences⊃Guides & Grid, set Gridline to 50 pixels and Subdivisions to 4.

Now you're ready to design using the Shape Tool

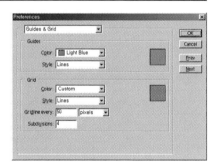

▲ *Adjusting the width and spacing of the gridline.*

Using the Shape Tool

1.

Select the Ellipse Tool from the Toolbox.
In this lesson, you'll create a design by creating a work path and then converting it into a Clipping Path. (Using the Shape Layer to create designs is detailed in Lesson 23 where the Path Tool was used to draw an illustration.)

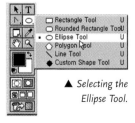

▲ *Selecting the Ellipse Tool.*

getting ready

Copy **Samples⊃Chapter3⊃ Group.Psd** from the supplementary CD-ROM onto the hard disk and then load the image into Photoshop.

setting up the color of the Gridline or Guideline.

The color of the gridline or guideline will depend on the image color. Complementary or contrasting colors are used so that the color of the image lines is not buried in the grid, which would prevent you from verifying the result. Use the color list in Edit⊃Preferences⊃Guides & Grid or click the color box to use the custom color of the Color Picker.

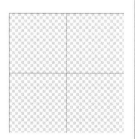

▲ *The activated gridline on the transparent background.*

193

2.

Select Create New Work Path in the Options Bar.

3.

The work window is divided into four even boxes.
Draw a circle in the top-right box. (Hold down
the Shift key to generate the path and then draw
the circle.)

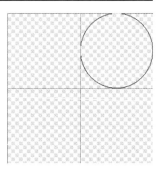

4.

Make sure that Subtract From Shape Area (-)
is checked in the Options Bar.

▲ Selecting Subtract from
shape area(-).

5.

Draw in a frame that includes the lower part of the
circle using the Rectangle Tool in the Toolbox.

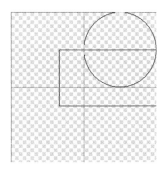

▲ Generation of the shape
that includes the frame that will
be cut out.

6.

To combine the two shapes, select the
Path Component Selection Tool in the
Toolbox.

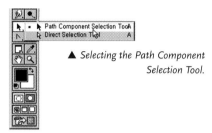

▲ *Selecting the Path Component
Selection Tool.*

7.

Select the two shapes as you would a selection frame.

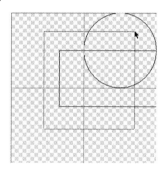

▲ *Selecting the two shapes.*

8.

Select Combine Path Components from the Options Bar to remove the frame at the
bottom of the circle.

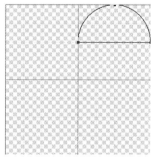

▲ *After removing the lower part
of the circle.*

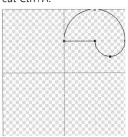
9.

Select the Ellipse Tool from the Toolbox to draw in a small circle and then click the Add To Shape Area (+) button in the Options Bar so that the newly drawn shape is added to the existing shape.

▲ *Selecting Add To Shape Area (+).*

10.

Draw a circle 1/4 the size of the original circle and place it on the right edge as shown here.

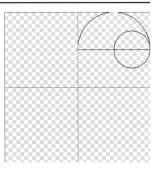

11.

Use the Path Component Selection Tool in the Toolbox to select the two shapes and then combine them using the Combine Path Components command in the Options Bar.

▲ *Selecting Combine Path Components.*

You're now ready to complete the design and copy and move the shape.

Completing the Shape

1.

Use the Path Component Selection Tool in the Toolbox to select the two shapes and press the Alt key to select only the paths of the two shapes. Then drag it to the lower left box to copy the shape.

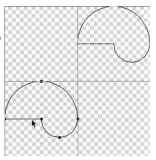

▶ *Generating the copy of the shape.*

2.

Choose *Edit⇨Transform Path⇨Rotate 180° to rotate
the duplicated shape and then select the two shapes
using the Path Component Tool and combine them
into one shape.*

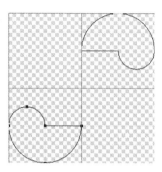

3.

*To link the separated shapes and to draw in the
curved line, enlarge the outer domain of the image
window.*

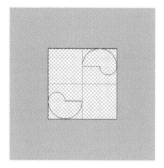

4.

*Draw in a large ellipse that connects the center
point of the top shape and the bottom point of the
lower shape.*

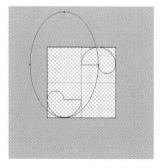

▲ *The outer domain of the
image window.*

5.

Select the ellipse using the Path Component Selection Tool and press the Alt (Option) key to make a copy. Then move the duplicate so that it's symmetrical to the original to create the curved lines.

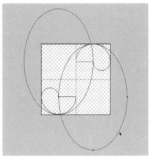

▲ *Formation of the curved lines.*

6.

Select the two ellipses while pressing the Shift key and, after clicking Intersect Shape Areas from the Options Bar, combine the two circles.

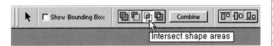

▲ *Intersect Shape Areas button.*

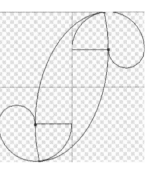

▲ *After combining the two circles using Intersect Shape Areas.*

7.

Select the two shapes using the Path Component Selection Tool and after selecting Add To Shape Area (+) from the Options Bar, combine the shapes to complete the curved figure.

▲ *Add to Shape Area (+).*

▶ *The external shape is complete.*

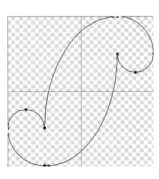

8.

Add two small circles to the inside of the shape for embellishment and then select the entire shape using the Path Component Selection Tool. With Exclude Overlapping Shape Areas selected in the Options Bar, click Combine to create the empty spaces inside the small circles.

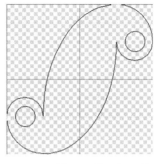

▲ *Adding small circles inside the shape.*

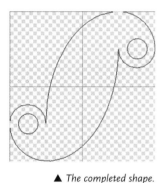

▲ *Exclude overlapping shape areas.*

▲ *The completed shape.*

Applying Color

Up until now, you've looked at using the Path Tool to create designs. Now, you'll convert the design into a Clipping Path layer, add color, and apply the Offset filter to use it as a pattern.

1.

Click the Default Foreground And Background Colors box located at the lower left of the color box in the Toolbox to convert the foreground color to black.

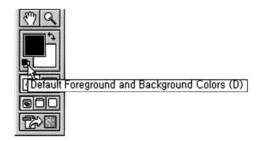

2.

Press Alt (Option) + Delete to apply the foreground color to the current layer. (Ctrl [Cmd]+Delete is used to apply the background color.)

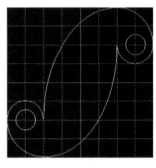

▲ *Color applied to the layer.*

3.

Choose Layer⇨Add Layer Clipping Path⇨Current Path so that the layer color is only applied to the inside of the shape.

▲ *Converting the layer frame to a Clipping Path.*

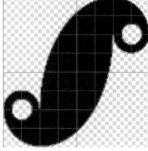

▲ *Color applied to the shape.*

value-adjusted transform

Value-adjusted Transform is used to draw precise images in design, logo type, and character development.

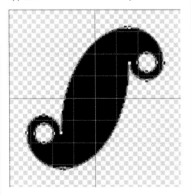

▲ *Eighty percent scale.*

Adjusting the Scale by Entering Values

1.

Choose Edit⇨Free Transform Path.
With Maintain Aspect Ratio checked in the Options Bar, enter 80% for the Height. (Due to the Maintain Aspect Ratio, the Width will be set automatically to 80% as well.)

▲ *Checking Maintain aspect ratio.*

▲ *Value-adjusted scale.*

2.

Select Commit Transform to apply the scale changes.

▲ Selecting Commit transform.

Applying the Offset Filter

You cannot apply a filter to the Clipping Path, so the layer is converted into a general image layer.

1.

In the Layers Palette, create a copy of the layer.

▲ Generation of the layer copy.

2.

Right-click the mouse on the layer name to reveal the pop-up menu and choose Rasterize Layer to convert the Clipping Path to a Layer Mask.

▲ The Clipping Path converted to a Layer Mask.

3.

Drag Layer mask thumbnail to the trash can (Delete layer) at the bottom of the Layers Palette. In the dialog box that asks Apply Mask To Layer Before Removing?, click Apply.

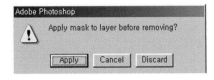

▲ Conversion into an image layer.

4.

Choose Filter⇨Other⇨Offset.

In the Offset dialog box, set Horizontal to 50 pixels right and Vertical to 0 pixels. Click Wrap Around and then apply it to the layer.

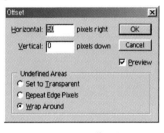

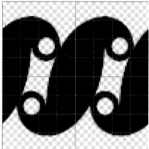

▲ *Offset dialog box.*　　　　　▲ *After applying the Offset.*

Completing the Pattern

1.

Link the two layers in the Layers Palette. Then use the Move Tool in the Toolbox to move the linked layers to make a space at the top where the small circle can be drawn.

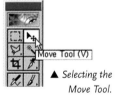

▲ *Selecting the Move Tool.*

▲ *The two linked layers.*

▲ *Moving the layers to the bottom of the screen.*

2.

Select the Ellipse Tool from the Toolbox and click Create New Shape Layer in the Options Bar. Then, draw a small circle in one small box of the grid.

▲ *Checking Create New Shape Layer.*

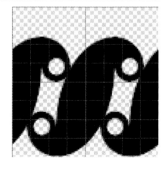

3.

After drawing in the small circle, press the Alt key while moving it to create three additional copies.

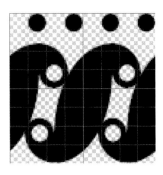

▲ *The completed pattern shape.*

Saving the Pattern in the Preset

1.

Of the three layers, select the image layer and choose Edit⇨Define Pattern.

▲ *Selecting the image layer.*

2.

In the Pattern Name dialog box, enter Shape as the Name and save.

Next, you'll look at how to use the Group function to apply the completed pattern to the image.

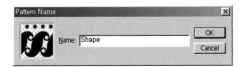

▲ *Pattern Name dialog box.*

Applying the Pattern to the Image

Here's how you make a pattern layer.

1.
___

Prepare the Group.Psd file.

▲ *Group.Psd.*

2.
___

In the Layers Palette, make a new layer in which to apply the pattern.

3.

Apply the pattern using the Edit⇨Fill command.

In the Fill dialog box, set Use to Pattern. Then, after clicking the Pattern Picker button to the right of Custom Pattern to reveal the list, select the Shape pattern and apply it to the layer.

▲ *After applying the pattern.*

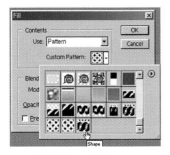

▲ *Selecting the Shape pattern.*

▲ *The Pattern Picker button.*

Trimming the Applied Pattern

1.

Select the Rectangular Marquee Tool from the Toolbox.

▲ *Selecting the Rectangular Marquee Tool.*

2.

Select the two upper lines of the pattern as you would a selection frame and press the Delete key to remove.

▲ *Selecting the frame.*

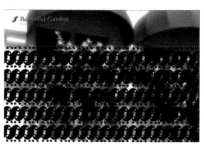

▲ *After removing the two upper lines of the pattern.*

3.

Choose Select⇨Deselect to undo the selection of the frame.
With the Marquee Tool selected, press the Alt (Option) key to switch to the Move Tool and move the remaining pattern to the center of the screen.

4.

Use the Marquee Tool to select the center frame of the pattern (excluding the top and bottom portions) and press Alt + Delete to apply the black foreground color to the selected frame.
Choose Select⇨Deselect to undo the selection of the frame.

▲ *The selection frame filled in with the foreground color.*

Applying a Threshold Layer

1.

Make a copy of the original image layer in the Layers Palette and place it above the Pattern layer. Deselect Indicates Layer Visibility to hide the duplicate layer.

2.

Select the original image layer again and click the Create New Fill Or Adjustment Layer at the bottom of the Layers Palette.

▲ *Create new fill or adjustment layer.*

3.

Choose Threshold from the pop-up menu.
In the Threshold dialog box, set Level to 112 and apply it to the layer.

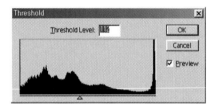

▲ *Threshold dialog box.*

▲ *The Threshold layer added to the Layers Palette.*

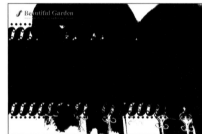

▲ *Application of the threshold to the original image layer.*

Applying a Gradient Layer

1.

From the Create New Fill Or Adjustment Layer pop-up menu at the bottom of the Layers Palette, select Gradient.
In the dialog box, click the Gradient bar to launch the Gradient Editor.

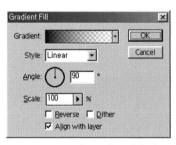

▲ *Gradient Editor dialog box.*

2.

In the Gradient configuration bar, move the lower pencil icons on both sides to the color white. After applying this configuration, set the direction of the gradient to -90° to complete the effect.

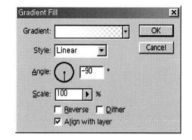

▲ Angle configuration.

▲ The added Gradient Fill layer.

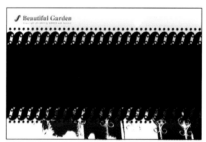

▲ Application of the Gradient.

Applying Group With Previous

1.

Select the original image_copy layer and choose Layer⇨Group With Previous.

▲ Application of Group With Previous to convert the Pattern layer to the mask of the original image_copy layer.

209

2.

Select Hue/Saturation from the Create New Fill Or Adjustment Layer list menu at the bottom of the Layers Palette.

In the dialog box, set the Hue to +42 and the Lightness to +17.

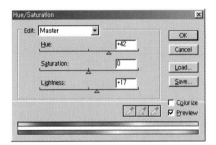

▲ *Hue/Saturation dialog box.*

3.

To the Hue/Saturation layer created in this way, choose Layer⇨Group With Previous to configure the group on the Pattern layer.

▲ *After applying Hue/Saturation.*

▲ *The Hue/Saturation layer configured as the group of the Pattern layer.*

Adjusting the Opacity of the Group Layer

After selecting the Pattern layer, go to the top of the Layers Palette and set the Opacity to 34%.

After entering the value, the same transparency that was applied to the Pattern layer is applied to the Group layer.

▲ *After applying the opacity.*

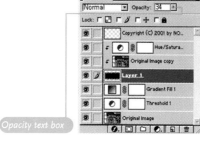

▲ *Modifying the layer opacity.*

Saving the Group Layer and Creating an Application Field

1.

To preserve the image of the flowers in the original image, a new Group is created, and only the layer with the flowers is allowed to show. Make a layer for the new group.

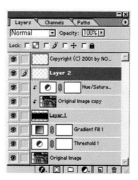

▲ *Creating a new layer.*

211

2.

Copy the original image layer to create the original image_copy2 layer and place it above the layer created in Step 1.

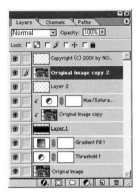

▲ The original
image_copy2 layer.

3.

Choose Layer⇨Group With Previous so that the original image_copy2 layer is applied as the group of the new layer.

As a result, due to the layer with the empty frame, a mask is applied to the original image_copy2 layer.

▲ Applying Group With
Previous.

4.

Select the Paintbrush Tool from the Toolbox and set the Brush size to 45 in the Options Bar.

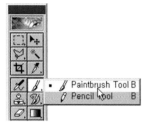

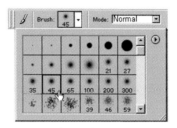

▲ *Selecting the Paintbrush Tool.*   ▲ *The Brush Preset in the Options Bar.*

5.

With the Layer2 layer activated, selectively color the frame within the frame with the flowers to reveal the respective layer in the original image_copy2 layer.

▲ *The mask frame drawn in the Layer2 layer.*

213

▲ *Completed image (Group-after.Psd).*

You can verify the result by loading **Samples⇨Chapter3⇨Group–after.Psd** from the supplementary CD-ROM.

Up until now, you've looked at the various uses for the Group layer. You can extract a portion of the image without affecting the original image. Applying color information using values, such as Hue/Saturation or Gradient, allows this to have a wide variety of uses. First and foremost, you can now verify the applied color information continuously throughout the working process.

Through the verification of the values applied to the Adjustment Layer, you can easily search for previously entered color information to aid in the construction of a uniform color template. In addition, the ability to apply the same color information to another image is another helpful tool. Finally, it is now much easier to edit the work. Because the previously applied color and image information is included in the Group Layer, you can reconfigure the image simply by making changes to this layer. I urge you to make these new changes your own as you use them to create unique styles.

Using Layer Style to Create a Soft Embossing

Instead of applying the effects of the Layer Style to one layer, you'll combine the effects applied to separate layers and make them look like one effect. As an example, you'll slice the Bevel and Emboss effect and apply the slices separately as an Outer Bevel and Inner Bevel to create an embossed effect and look at the solid image that results from this application.

Lesson 28

LESSON HIGHLIGHTS

To add an embossed effect, apply Layer Styles Bevel and Emboss to the layer separately as an Out Bevel and an Inner Bevel. The function sequence is View⇨Show⇨Grid, Ellipse Tool, Path Component Selection Tool, and Bevel and Emboss.

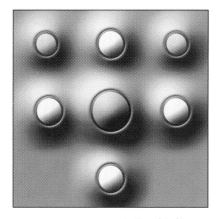

▲ Completed image.

Preparing the Image Window

Prepare a new 750 x 750 pixel image window by choosing File⇨New.

When generating the image to be viewed on a monitor, like in a Web browser, set the image resolution to 72 pixels/inch and the monitor color to RGB color mode. When the image is set up to be printed, switch the units to centimeters with the image resolution set to 300 pixels/cm and the color mode set to the CMYK color mode.

▲ New dialog box.

Configuring and Activating the Grid

For a project that relies on numerical values or images that require precisely arranged slices, the Grid is a helpful tool.

Choose Edit⇨Preferences⇨Guides and Grid to open the dialog box and set the Gridline Every to 50 pixels and the Subdivisions to 4.

Choose View⇨Show⇨Grid to display the grid on the screen.

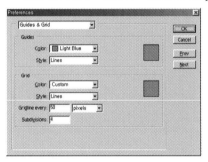

▲ *Guides & Grid dialog box.*　　▲ *The activated grid.*

Drawing a Circle Using the Ellipse Tool

1.

Select the Ellipse Tool from the Toolbox.

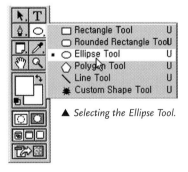

▲ *Selecting the Ellipse Tool.*

2.

About 50 x 50 pixels from the top left of the screen, draw a 150 x 150 pixel circle.

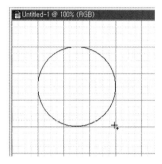

▲ *The first circle.*

3.

Select the Path Component Selection Tool from the Toolbox and move the circle while pressing the Alt key to copy it. Place the copied circle at a distance of 100 pixels from the first circle. Continue until a total of seven circles are made.

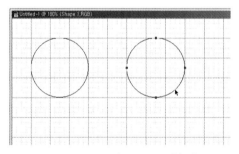

▲ *The creation of the first copy.*

▲ *Path Component Selection Tool.*

▲ *After creating seven identical copies.*

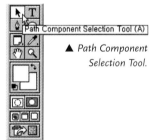

▲ *The layer clipping path for the seven circles are created in the layer.*

Layer clipping path

Shapes drawn using the Create New Work Path option of the Shape Tool or the Path Tool all possess a path line that makes up the external form. This supports the vector graphic postscript method and allows for free transformations. (In other words, instead of storing the information of bitmap images in the smallest unit of pixels, postscript images store information on the external form making it easy to alter the size and raising the quality of the result.)

The Path in the previous version of Photoshop did not support Transform or Clipping Path and cannot compare to the Path seen in Photoshop 6.

One of the noteworthy changes in the new Path is the use of the Layer Clipping Path. In contrast to the previous version where the image information on the entire layer had to be saved, in Version 6, the image information is composed of the Layer Contents, which contains the color information, and the Clipping Path, which contains the frame information.

▶ *Comparing the image layer concept in the previous (top) and current (bottom) versions of Photoshop.*

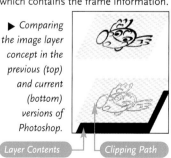

217

Applying the Bevel and Emboss Effect

1.

From the Add A Layer Style pop-up list at the bottom of the Layers Palette, choose Bevel and Emboss.

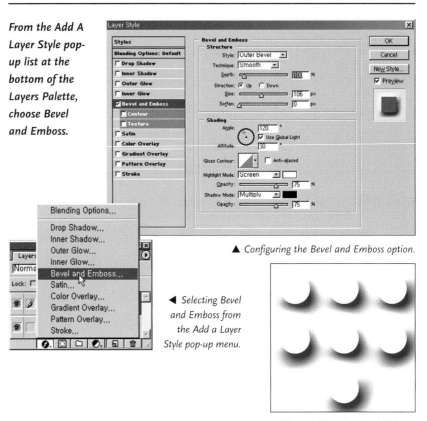

▲ *Configuring the Bevel and Emboss option.*

option configuration

Bevel and Emboss

Style: Outer Bevel

Direction: Up

Size: 106 px

Use the default configuration for the other values.

◀ *Selecting Bevel and Emboss from the Add a Layer Style pop-up menu.*

▲ *After applying Bevel and Emboss.*

2.

Change the color of the Background layer to a midtone gray (R: 147, G: 147, b: 147) so that the embossing effect is better portrayed.

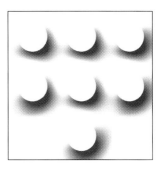

▶ *After applying a gray color to the Background layer.*

3.

Select the foreground color in the Color Palette. After entering each value, press Alt (Option) + Delete to apply the effect.

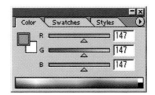

▲ *Entering the values in the Color Palette.*

4.

Copy the upper portion of the embossing as a layer and change the applied Bevel and Emboss to Inner Bevel.

You can make the copy of the layer either by right-clicking the layer name and choosing Duplicate Layer from the pop-up list or by dragging and dropping the original layer onto the Create New Layer button.

Double-click Bevel and Emboss at the bottom of the duplicate layer to open the Layer Style Palette and convert the Style to Inner Bevel.

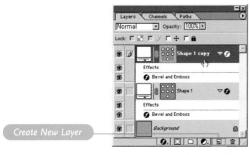

Create New Layer

▲ *Creating the copied layer.*

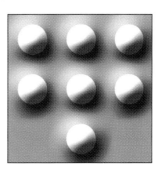

▲ *Inner Bevel applied to the copied layer.*

5.

Change the color of the layer to gray (R: 147, G: 147, B: 147) to create a natural blend between the top and the bottom of the embossing.
(Select the color as you did for the back-ground color in the Color Palette and press Alt [Option] + Delete to apply.)

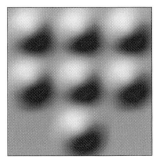

▲ The naturally blended embossing.

6.

Looking closely at this embossing, you can see that although it was created using shapes of the same size, the link between the shapes is too prominent. You can fix this problem by increasing the size of the shape in the upper layer just to the point where the link between the shapes is no longer visible.
In order to increase the size of the shape while maintaining the current center point, you use the Scale Value window in the Options Bar of the Path Component Selection Tool.

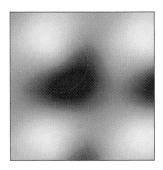

▲ The visible link between the two shapes.

7.

Use the Path Component Selection Tool in the Toolbox to select the shape that will be altered.

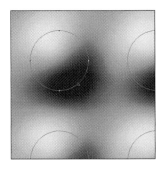

▶ Selecting the shape that will be altered.

8.

Choose Edit⇨Free Transform Path to activate the Scale Value window in the Options Bar and, after checking on the Maintain Aspect Ratio, raise the Height or Width to 101%.

▲ *Checking Maintain aspect ratio.*

9.

Select the remaining shapes and adjust their size so that the link between them is no longer visible. (A convenient way to apply Free Transform Path to the selected shape is to use Ctrl (Cmd) + T.)

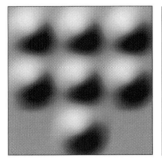

▲ *The image after dealing with the visible link between the shapes.*

▲ *After removing the link between the shapes.*

Applying Bevel and Emboss for a Concave Shape

1.

To create a concave shape, make a copy of the copied layer.

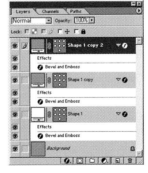

▲ *Creating a new layer copy.*

2.

Select the shape at the top left using the Path Component Selection Tool and choose Edit⟿Free Transform Path to scale the shape down to 62%. Scale down the remaining shapes in the same way.

(When you apply Free Transform Path with the Layer Clipping Path activated, you can uniformly modify the size of the entire shape. When this method is used, you need to move the shapes to the precise location. This can be a difficult task, so it's advised that the shapes be modified individually.)

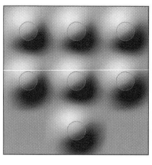
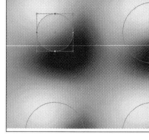

▲ *Scaling the shape down to 62%.*　　▲ *After adjusting the size.*

3.

option configuration

Bevel and Emboss

Style: Outer Bevel

Direction: Down

Size: 20: px

Highlight:

Highlight Mode: Opacity 100%. To create a bright highlight, set the Opacity of the Highlight Mode to 100%.

Double-click Bevel and Emboss at the bottom of the layer to open the dialog box and configure the options.

Finally, change the color of the layer to white. (You can change the color of the Layer Content by using Alt (Option) + Delete as shown earlier or by double-clicking Layer Thumbnail and selecting the color from the Color Picker that appears.)

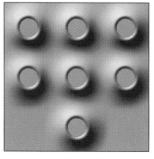
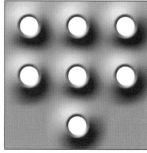

▲ *After applying a concave shape.*　　▲ *Completing the application of the embossing and concave effects.*

Adding an Adjustment Layer to Adjust the Overall Brightness

adjustment Layer

The Adjustment Layer applies the result to all the sublayers and also applies the result to only specified areas when a mask or Clipping Path is present. In addition, you can apply the Adjustment option to an average layer with a Clipping Path by choosing Layer⟹Change Layer Content.

Taking advantage of this property, you can create the image using the method of adding an Adjustment Layer for each color to a grayscale template image.

1.

Select Brightness/Contrast from the Create New Fill Or Adjustment Layer pop-up list at the bottom of the Layers Palette.

▲ *Adding the Brightness/Contrast layer.*

2.

In the dialog box, adjust the Brightness to 18 to brighten the overall image.

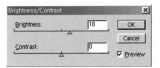

▲ *Configuring Brightness/Contrast.*

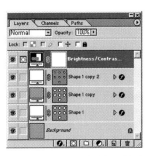

▲ *The added Brightness/Contrast layer.*

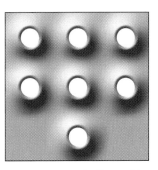

▲ *After applying Brightness/Contrast.*

223

option configuration

Bevel and Emboss

Style: Inner Bevel

Direction: Up

Size: 100 px

Adding a Color Layer

1.

Make a copy of the layer that you used to apply concavity.
Move this copied layer above the Brightness/Contrast layer and make sure that the applied color shows up properly.

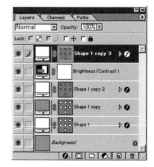

▲ *Addition of the copied layer.*

2.

Change the configuration of the Bevel and Emboss.

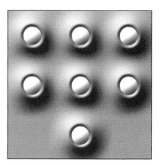

▶ *Addition of the protruding embossed effect.*

3.

Change the blending mode of the layer to Multiply by selecting it from the Blending Mode menu at the top left of the Layers Palette so that the images of the lower layers show through.

▶ *Selecting the layer blending mode.*

4.

Use the Path Component Selection Tool to select the shape at the top left and choose Edit⇨Free Transform Path to scale the shape up to 120%.

(The application of the Multiply mode will create a band around the shape.)

Scale up the remaining shapes to 120%.

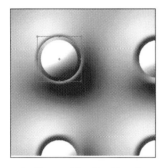 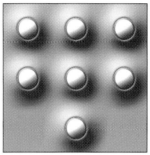

▲ After applying Free Transform.   ▲ After scaling the shapes to 120%.

5.

Change the color of the layer to yellow (R: 251, G: 244, B: 156).

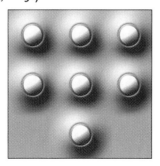

▲ After applying the color to the
Multiply layer.

6.

You use the copy of the current layer to make color changes to the other layers. First of all, make two copies of the layer and deactivate them. Use the Path Component Selection Tool, used in the yellow layer, to select the shape that you'll apply a different color to and press Delete.

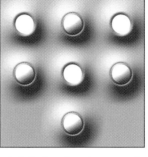

▲ *Only the yellow shapes remain.*

▲ *Addition of the copy of the color layer.*

7.

Turn on the second color layer and change the color of this layer to purple (R: 198, G: 159, B: 202). As in the previous step, erase all the shapes excluding the ones to which you'll apply the color.

▶ *Creation of the purple layer.*

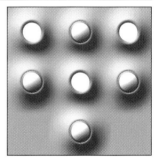

8.

Change the color of the final color layer to a light green (R: 172, G: 215, B: 157) and remove the unnecessary shapes.

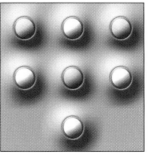

◀ *The Clipping Path of the color layer added to the Layers Palette.*

▲ *After applying all the colors.*

Completing the Image

The seven differently colored images of the same size are arranged on the window. You've already seen that, because these shapes were created using Path, the application of the Transform command is quite easy. You'll now complete the image by applying Scale to some of the shapes to create a final image with differently sized shapes.

1.

Scale down the four embossed shapes on the top left to 85%.
First, adjust the size of the color layer.

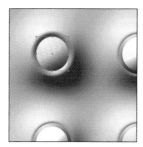

▲ *The shapes reduced by 85%.*

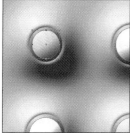

▲ *Adjusting the scale of the concave shapes.*

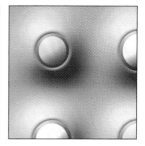

▲ *After adjusting the top and bottom of the embossing to 85%.*

There are two ways to select the path using the Path Component Selection Tool. First, the path is selected while the Layer Clipping Path is activated. This method is used when the shape of a particular layer on a Layer Clipping Path page with many layers needs to be selected or when the shape needs to be selected while the path is visible.

The other method is to select the path while the Layer Clipping Path is deactivated. In this method, you can select the clipping path despite the status of the upper and lower layers.

When several paths overlap, the path of the topmost layer gets selected. In order to select the path of another layer, you need to use the first method mentioned.

2.

Apply the same scale to the remaining light green shapes. Scale the shape in the middle to 150% and then check the final result.

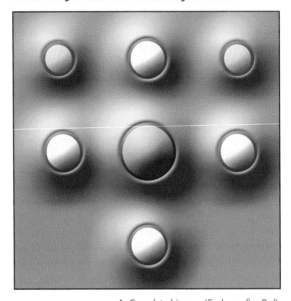

▲ *Completed image (Emboss-after.Psd).*

Verify the completed image by loading **Samples⇨Chapter3⇨Emboss-after.Psd** from the supplementary CD-ROM.

::

chapter 4

Web Graphic Design Using ImageReady

ImageReady is a software program specifically for Web design. Although the basic Web design methods are the same as in Photoshop, ImageReady's own image optimization and Web application techniques are used. In this chapter, you'll look at the Web graphic design methods of ImageReady.

ImageReady's Workflow

LESSON HIGHLIGHTS

Understanding the general workflow of Web graphics will help you grasp a clearer understanding of the tools of ImageReady.

In this lesson, you'll look at the overall Web graphics workflow in ImageReady and at how and when the various ImageReady tools are used.

Step 1: Editing Picture Images, Creating Button Images, and Organizing Web Layouts

ImageReady, like Photoshop, contains many functions for graphic design but is limited to only simple work environments. For this reason, both ImageReady and Photoshop have a Jump To feature in the Toolbox that allows a work in process to be moved back and forth between the two programs. It's recommended that you conduct the graphics work in Photoshop and image optimization in ImageReady.

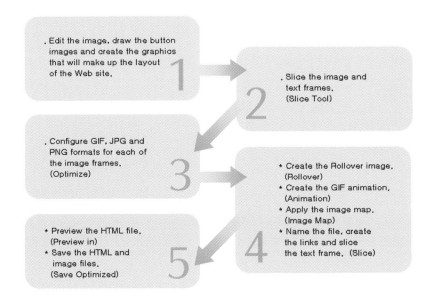

▲ Web graphic workflow in ImageReady.

Step 2: Slicing Text and Image Frames

After organizing the Web site layout and design, you can use the Slice Tool to slice up the image frames. It can be said that characteristic ImageReady functions are put into use from this step on. In order to understand how the Slice function works, you'll look at an example of slicing and arranging an image on the Web.

Several pages of images and text are combined together on a Web page that appears in the browser in order to minimize the loading time while displaying as much information as possible.

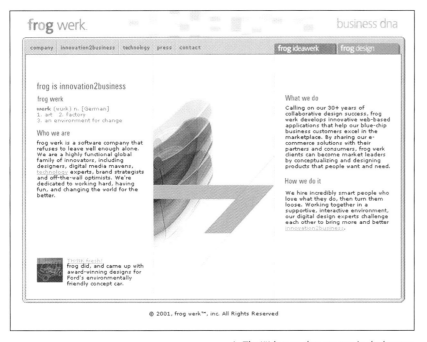

▲ *The Web page that appears in the browser.*

Photoshop's Save For Web and ImageReady's Optimize save the images that will appear on the Web page, such as GIF, PNG, and JPEG files, in optimized format so that they maintain their original graphic state while taking up as little file size as possible.

Users can convert the window to 2-UP or 4-UP status, which allows them to open up several sample pages at a time. As a result, they can compare the optimized image and the image size and choose the one that they want.

This type of image comparison is a necessity for Web environments of lower capacity and should be a standard tool in all Web-related software.

Observing this page closely, you can see that the images that appear to be composed on one page are actually fragmented into many pieces. This fragmentation is used to combine the graphical embodiment of the JPG format and the low-file capacity of the GIF format. In addition, patterns or blank spaces can be used for the areas outside the image.

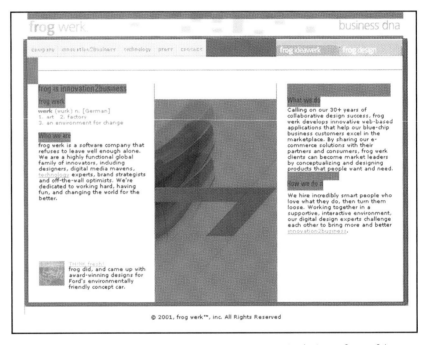

▲ *The image frame of the page.*

Also, you need to slice frames because GIF animations and Rollover buttons frequently have their own independent images.

For these purposes, the Web site, literally, gets hacked to bits, and the tool that does that is the Slice Tool.

The Slice command divides and saves the window in different frames comprising the JPG/GIF format image frame, the Rollover/button frame, the GIF animation frame, the text frame, and the blank spaces.

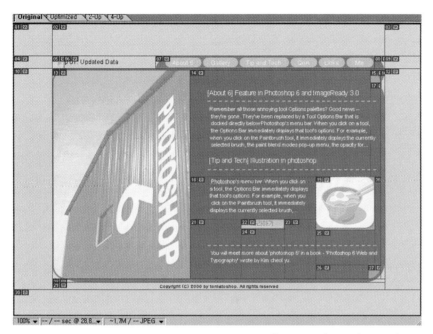

▲ Yellow: Image frame; Blue: Text frame;
Gray: Blank space.

Step 3: Optimizing Each Image Frame to GIF, JPG, and PNG

After slicing the window into three frames, you now optimize the image contained in the image frame. To do this, you use the Optimize function.

▲ JPEG Medium format
configuration (above) for
the image frame (right).

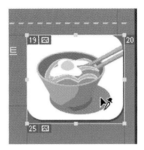 

▲ *Configuring the GIF 32 No Dither format (right) for the illustration (left).*

The Optimize function optimizes each slice frame and saves each slice in the optimized format. The Optimize Palette offers the JPEG, GIF, and PNG image formats, and you can use the Settings list to apply an average image format.

Step 4: Using Rollover, Animation, Image Map, and Slice

In this step, you'll give the optimized image a file name and an image map and specify the text frame. In addition, you'll create a Rollover image and a GIF animation on the sliced frame.

Rollover

The palette is used to distinguish the buttons drawn in two layers as Normal or Rollover and save them. The Rollover image, along with the Image Swap script, gets divided into two image files and saved on the HTML file through the Save Optimized command.

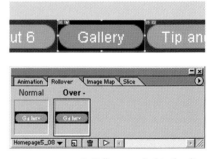

▲ *Rollover applied to the slice.*

Animation

GIF animation comes about by changing the layer position or color of the selected slice frame or by turning on/off the layer.

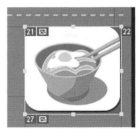

▲ *The GIF animation slice frame.*

One disadvantage of the Animation Palette is that, because it shows the image in its entirety, the animation specified by Slice cannot be seen in detail.

▲ *Creating the animation in the Animation Palette (left) and the Layers Palette (right).*

Image Map

The Image Map Tool is a new addition to ImageReady 3.0. It's used to add hyperlinks to images that do not or cannot be sliced and to images that will increase in file size due to more slicing.

▲ *Image Map Tool.*

▲ *The image configured with the image map and the Image Map Palette.*

▲ *Configuring the Image Map Palette.*

HTML support in ImageReady

ImageReady is not an HTML editor. It does not support any function for editing automatically created HTML files or for adding other tags. However, it has a Jump To function that allows you to move the image to an HTML editor. It's enough for you to know that ImageReady's HTML function automatically creates a partial tag for your convenience. When a rollover image is created and saved, an <IMG> tag and a JavaScript for the Image Swap are added automatically. In addition, ImageReady can also add the <TABLE> and <MAP> tags.

spacer.gif

Homepages created using HTML make use of many <TABLE> tags for splitting up the screen. In creating tables, the <TABLE> tag itself does not support frames that are 1 or 2 pixels long and wide. However, for precise frame splicing, these types of frames are used often. The image used for this is the transparent, 1 x 1 pixel Spacer.Gif. When Spacer.Gif is inserted into the tag <td>, within the <TABLE> tag, the <TABLE> can give rise to a 1 or 2 pixel frame. This is why Spacer.Gif files are created automatically in image folders created using ImageReady. Also, through the width and height properties in the <IMG> tag, the Spacer.Gif file can be changed into a variety of different sizes, or it can appoint the complex table as the topmost frame.

Step 5: HTML Preview (Preview in)

This step converts and saves the optimized image into a Web page. After configuring the HTML file name, the rule for the automatic naming of the image file, the location where the image will be saved, and the background image, ImageReady will then automatically create an HTML table, Spacer file, and an image folder based on the slice frame. It will also arrange the image in a perfect HTML page.

Image Frame Slicing

The Slice command in ImageReady is like the Guide option that you used in Photoshop, with the addition of an image-saving Properties option. More specifically, the sliced frame in ImageReady can contain within itself information on how the image was saved, the file name, the file format, and other diverse information on Rollover, Animation, and Image Map. It also includes the convenient feature of allowing you to edit and modify several pages of images within one file. In this lesson, you'll learn how to slice frames and how to apply image optimization properties to detailed frames.

You'll use Guides to create the basic slice frame. After using Slices⇨Create Slices from Guides to convert it into a slice frame, you'll fragment or combine the frame to complete the detailed slice frame. The configurations of the Optimize Palette and the Slice Palette will then be applied to the slice, and you'll obtain the result in an HTML page.

LESSON HIGHLIGHTS

In this lesson, you'll learn how to use Guides to create a slice frame, how to use the Slice Tools, and how to configure Optimize and Slice options for each slice frame. The function sequence is Guides, Slices⇨ Create Slices from Guides, Optimize Palette, Slice Palette, and File⇨ Save Optimized.

▲ Original image.

getting ready

Copy **Samples⇨Chapter4⇨ Slice_sample.Psd** from the supplementary CD-ROM onto the hard disk and then load it into ImageReady.

Slicing Frames Using Guides

The original image is like a cross between a picture and an illustration with a body of text on the right side. You can divide this image into an image frame and a text frame. More specifically, you can divide it into an image frame for JPEG and an image frame for GIF.

Referring to the image, Frame Sliced Using Guides, you can see how the image and text frames were divided for HTML coding. The picture portion of the image was configured in JPEG format, the illustration in GIF, and the story line as TEXT.

Display the ruler by choosing View⇨Show Rulers and then drag on Guide in the divisions of the ruler to create each frame.

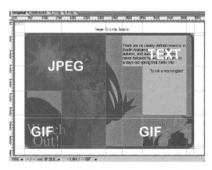

▲ *The sliced frame created using Guides.*

Creating Slice Frames

1.

Use the Slices⇨Create Slices From Guides command to convert the Guides frame into slices.

▲ *The Guides frame converted into slices.*

2.

Select the Slice Select Tool from the Toolbox.

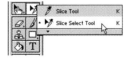

▶ *The Slice Select Tool.*

3.

Select all the slices of the owl image while pressing the Shift key and choose Slices⊃Combine Slices to convert the individual slices into one big slice.

In the same way, combine all the other slices that will be converted to JPEG format.

▲ *Selecting the slices to combine (left) and after the slices are combined (right).*

▲ *Selecting the two slices that will be saved in JPEG format.*

4.

Edit the slice for the remaining GIF and TEXT frames.

▲ *The organized slice frame.*

---

dither

There are two kinds of dithering, which combines two scattered colors and makes them look like one. When an image is saved in GIF format and there are colors that are not included in the 8-bit (256 color) palette, Application Dither is provided so that all the colors will appear to be present.

You can select No Dither, Diffusion, and Pattern in Photoshop's Save For Web and ImageReady's Optimize Palette so that when dithering has not been applied, the gradation image will appear in step-like fashion.

Browser Dither is a pixel pattern that is used to display colors used by the browser that are not included in the 8-bit system. You can apply this dither by selecting Browser Dither from the pop-up menu, indicated by the arrow button at the top right of the image window in the Save For Web dialog box in Photoshop or by choosing View⊃Preview⊃Browser Dither in ImageReady.

Optimizing Images

1.

You'll now look at how to save JPEG, GIF, and TEXT frames and how to apply the optimal file size. Convert the image window to Optimized and verify the optimal color.

▲ *The Optimized image window.*

2.

Prepare the Optimize Palette and Slice Palette and select the slice of the owl.
In the Optimize Palette, set the settings to the low capacity JPEG Low and then see how blurry the image has become.

▶ *The Optimize Palette set to JPEG Low.*

▲ *Selecting the slice of the owl.*

3.

In the Slice Palette, enter owl as the file name. In the same way, optimize the slice of the light bulb.

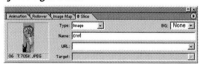

▲ *The slice of the owl entered into the Slice Palette.*

▲ *Configuring the name of the light bulb image in the Slice Palette.*

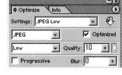

▲ *Optimizing the image of the light bulb.*

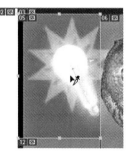

▲ *Selecting the slice of the light bulb.*

240

4.

You optimize the GIF frame by using the Colors box in the Optimize Palette. Select each slice and then specify GIF in the Optimize Palette.

In the Colors box, select an optimal color that will not alter the image. (The slices selected as GIF frames and the Optimize Palette properties are contained in Optimal file size of the GIF-formatted slices.)

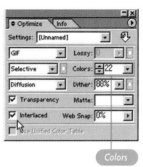

Click the Interlaced option to create a GIF image that progressively gets clearer upon loading. You can apply this same effect to JPEG-formatted images by clicking the Progressive option.

5.

The Transparency, Matte, Interlaced, and Web Snap that has been applied to the GIF image were selected from the menu that appears and disappears upon clicking the triangular buttons at the top of the Optimize Palette.

▲ *This window displays the slice number and the optimal file size that has been applied.*

▲ *The button to reveal the submenu of the Optimize Palette.*

6.

You specify the TEXT frame by selecting No Image From Type in the Slice Palette. After converting the background color of the text to the foreground color in the Toolbox, you select Foreground Color and match the two colors.

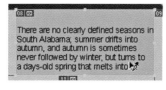

▲ *Text frame slices.*

interlacing

When some images are first loaded onto a Web page, they start out very blurry and progressively get clearer. This effect is referred to as Interlacing. With the appearance of the GIF89a file format, GIF files now support background transparency, animation, and interlacing. Also, JPEG has recently added Progressive JPEG, which adds Interlacing functions to JPEG files.

optimal file size of the GIF-formatted slices

▲ *03: 8 Colors, Interlaced (202 Bytes).*

▲ *07: 8 Colors, Interlaced (204 Bytes).*

▲ *09: 8 Colors, Interlaced (586 Bytes).*

▲ *10: 8 Colors, Interlaced (1.38 KBytes).*

▲ *12: 8 Colors, Interlaced (2.11 KBytes).*

▲ *13: 8 Colors, Interlaced (2.50 KBytes).*

configuring Transparency, Matte, interlaced (progressive), and web snap

Transparency is applied when an image slice is optimized into GIF format. This option makes transparent the spaces around the image and therefore makes this a popular option for homepages that use a tile image as their background. However, you must keep in mind that the result of this method of GIF optimization depends largely on the application of Matte.

Matte applies a color to the outline of the image when Transparency is applied. Due to the transparent background, there can be discrepancies between the background color and the image or within the image itself. This option, therefore, is used to remove these differences and create a homogenous blend between the background and the image. In addition, when the Transparency option is not selected, Matte uses the background color in its application.

Interlaced creates an effect of an image that grows steadily into focus as the Web page loads. This is useful in downloading large images and allows you to predict what the image will be. The corresponding option for JPEG-formatted images is Progressive.

Web Snap converts the image to 100% Web-safe colors and 0% of the colors that are currently in use. This is done to prevent the colors of the image from breaking up when loaded.

◀ *Transparency applied to the image (left) and the Optimize Palette (right).*

◀ *Transparency and Matte applied to the image (left) and the Optimize Palette (right).*

◀ *Application of a background color through Matte (left) and the Optimize Palette (right).*

◀ *Web Snap at 100% (left) and the Optimize Palette (right).*

◀ *Web Snap at 60% (left) and the Optimize Palette (right).*

7.

The text entry line in HTML does not recognize text with more than two spaces between characters and text written on more than one line. Therefore, you first enter the text and edit it using the HTML editor.

▲ *Configuring the Slice Palette to No Image for the text frame.*

Saving HTML Files and Images

When all the configurations are complete, you can choose File⥱Preview In to preview the image in the basic browser. After checking for any errors, choose File⥱Save Optimized to save the entire file.

Using Preview In to extract the HTML allows you to verify the source code. You can see here the addition of the spacer.Gif file that has been modified to fit the empty space of the image.

▲ *The HTML file extracted in the browser (Slice_sample.Html).*

HOW to express blank spaces in HTML

You apply a 1 pixel spacer.Gif file to the empty spaces of the HTML file created in ImageReady. For example, if you have a 200 x 200 pixel empty space in the HTML file, you insert a spacer.Gif file that has been expanded to 200 x 200 pixcls. Because you can adjust the size of the image in the HTML tag, you can enlarge the 1 pixel file for your use.

▲ *The slice of the empty space.*

DitherBox filter

Filter⥱Other DitherBox in Photoshop and ImageReady allows you to apply user-defined dithers to the images. When non-Web safe RGB colors have been used in the Color Picker, you can load it into the DitherBox and convert it into a dither.

▲ *DitherBox dialog box.*

Creating GIF Animation

LESSON HIGHLIGHTS

One of the biggest advantages of creating animation in ImageReady is that it can be created using layers. In this lesson, you'll use the Layers Palette and the Animation Palette to create a simple GIF animation. The function sequence is Layers Palette and Animation Palette.

GIF animation in ImageReady requires turning the several pages of frames that were prepared beforehand into layers and using the frame creation/link feature of the Animation Palette to create a continuously moving GIF89a format file.

The Animation Palette contains several simple functions that you can use to create and move frames, adjust the time interval between frames, preview the animation, create repeated loops, and apply Tween.

The Illustrator functionality in Photoshop is useful for drawing simple graphics. Because this function allows for easy drawing and modification of the graphic, it's extremely useful for creating the graphical symbols and icons seen on the Web.

In this lesson, you'll draw the source image of the animation using Photoshop's Illustrator functionality and then complete the GIF animation in ImageReady.

Setting Up the GIF Animation Frame

getting ready

Copy **Samples**⸱ **Chapter4**⸱ **Gifanimation.Psd** from the supplementary CD-ROM onto the hard disk and then load it into ImageReady.

1.

Look closely at the arranged layers. Looking at the thumbnails, you can see that the layers are included in each frame of one animation. You'll create an animation of a full cup of water that empties progressively.

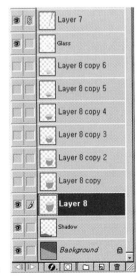

▶ *The layers prepared for creating the animation.*

2.

The first frame, which shows a full cup of water, will be displayed for 0.2 seconds.
In the Layers Palette, activate the thumbnail of the full cup and the respective straw layer and deactivate all the other layers.

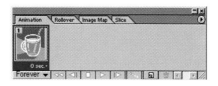

▲ *Animation Palette.*

3.

You can adjust the frame time by clicking the right toggle button at the bottom of each frame.

▶ *The time configuration toggle button and the pop-up menu.*

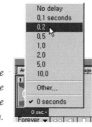

▲ *Animation Palette Option.*

4.

Create a new frame by clicking the Duplicates Current Frame button in the Animation Palette.
This causes new frames to be created as duplicates of the first frame. Using this method, the time interval that was applied to the first

▲ *Choosing Duplicates Current Frame.*

frame will be applied to the duplicate. Therefore, you can create several frames all with the same time interval in this way without having to individually configure the time for each frame.

For the second frame, activate only the respective layer.

245

The Create Droplet icon at the top right of the Optimize Palette has two functions. First, after configuring the settings of a slice, you can apply the same settings to another slice by simply dragging it onto this icon with the mouse. Second, you can save the settings as a Droplet file by clicking this icon. When this icon is clicked, the Save Optimized As Droplet dialog box will appear, and the settings are saved (with the extension .exe if you're working in Microsoft Windows). Then this file is loaded into the image file, and the settings will automatically apply themselves to the image.

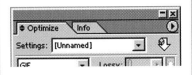

5.

Create all the other frames in the same way in the Animation Palette.

In most GIF anima-tions, in order to distin-guish the beginning and the end, the last

▲ *The seven frames configured for the animation.*

frame is set up to run slightly longer than the other frames. In this example, you configured the final frame to be on display for 1 second.

6.

Preview the animation by clicking the Plays Animation button at the bottom of the Animation Palette.

Adjusting Loops

After the animation is complete, you'll adjust how often the animation will loop. In Selects Looping Options at the bottom, you can make selections from 1 to infinity.

Optimizing Images

Apply the image optimization settings in the Optimize Palette to the entire animation.

▲ *Selecting Forever to infinitely loop the animation.*

1.

Convert the image window to Optimized and specify the GIF colors and Dither in the Optimize Palette.

▲ *Converting to Optimized.*

◄ *Configuring the Optimize Palette for the animation.*

2.

Save the complete animation by choosing File⇨Save Optimized and then verify the final animation in the browser.

Tween Animation

The Tween function, which was hidden in the toggle menu at the top right-hand side of the Animation Palette in ImageReady 2.0, has been moved to the menu at the bottom of the palette in Version 3.0. Tween converts the frame into an animation midway through the creation process to match the changes in the placement of the two frames, the opacity, and effects.

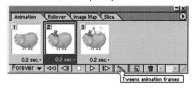

▲ *New elements added using Tween are displayed immediately in the animation.*

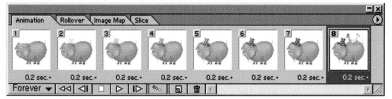

explanation of the Tween options

Layers: This option allows you to select unnecessary layers and prevent them from being used in the animation.

Parameters: You can use this option to adjust the position, opacity, and the effects.

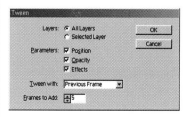

Tween with: The tween of the current active frame is applied to the previous or next frame. You can also use Select Frame to create an animation that moves in reverse.

Frames to Add: This allows you to specify the number of frames that you'll use in Tween. The more frames there are, the smoother the animation.

247

Using GIF Animation

LESSON HIGHLIGHTS

There is a type of GIF animation technique that cuts out all still cuts and uses only animation frames. In this lesson, you'll learn how file size is reduced and optimized in ImageReady.

The function sequence is Animation Palette, Actions Palette, Optimize Palette, and File⟶Save Optimized.

---

getting ready

Copy **Samples⟶Chapter4⟶Submarine.Psd** from the supplementary CD-ROM onto the hard disk and then load it into ImageReady.

In this lesson, you'll see what happens when the difference in time of an animation is based on one image and applied in parts. You'll also utilize the tools in the Actions Palette.

First, load **Samples⟶Chapter4⟶Submarine.Psd** from the supplementary CD-ROM into ImageReady and preview the final animation. You can see that only a part of the image is animated and that the animation frames appear one after another at fixed time intervals. This is done to show how much the file size can be reduced by using only a part of the image.

First, you'll discover how partial animation works by creating the animation, and then you'll apply the Spin effect from the Actions Palette and see how that affects the animation.

▲ *Original image.*

Moving Clipping Paths to Create Animation

1.

The submarine will have on its side flickering yellow lights. This effect is contained in the Light layer made using the Clipping Path in the Layers Palette.

2.

Make a duplicate frame by clicking Duplicates Current Frame in the Animation Palette.

I mentioned earlier that this is an easier way to create an evenly spaced animation rather than making each frame individually and configuring the speed.

Set the first frame to 0.2 seconds and apply this same time to all the frames from the second frame on.

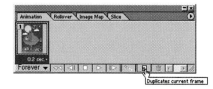

▲ *Adding a new frame in the Animation Palette.*

saving your work frequently

It is a good idea to get in the habit of saving your work frequently. If you've ever taken a computer lesson, you probably remember all your instructors telling you to frequently save your work. For any of you who have ever lost entire files, this is probably a deeply ingrained habit. Along with saving your work, it's a good idea to verify the end results. This is useful for preventing mistakes along the way.

In addition, if you verify the result after the application of each function, the source of the error is easier to find than it would be if you were to check the result at the end.

3.

In order to have the first light on the submarine be turned off in the duplicate frame, move the Clipping Path frame to the right.

You want to create an animation where the lights get turned off one at a time. In order to do this, repeat this step and move the Clipping Path to make frames 3, 4, and 5.

▲ *Using the Move Tool to move the Clipping Path.*

4.

Before moving onto the next step, press the Plays Animation button in the Animation Palette to make sure that the animation works properly.

▲ *Five frames made in the Animation Palette.*

Moving Layer Masks to Create Animation

1.

Next, you'll make the animated bubbles coming out of the fish's mouth. The water bubble layer is configured using the layer mask. To do this in ImageReady, a separate layer at the top is not necessary. What this means is that the frame itself contains the information on the moved layer. Then see what happens when you create an animation using a new, duplicate layer.

First of all, the shape modification, created using Transform, is not saved on the frame. You need to make a duplicate layer for each frame in order to adjust the size or to rotate the image. Then you change color by creating a new layer that contains the image with the changed color in order to apply it to the animation. Based on all the different effects that can be applied, you should be able to estimate how many layers you will need to create.

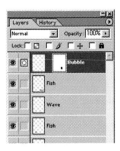

▲ The water bubble layer.

2.

The layer mask is applied in linked form when it's first created. Moving the layer mask frame to adjust the visible portion of the respective layer, you need to deselect Indicates Layer Mask Is Linked To Layer between the layer and the layer mask.

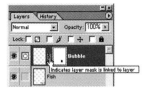

▲ The link between the layer and the layer mask.

3.

The water bubble animation is made in frames 6 to 10. In frame 6, the water bubbles are not visible. In other words, the layer mask completely hides the water bubble image. From the next frame on, the layer mask is moved slightly for each frame so that the water bubbles gradually appear.

Frame 6.   Frame 7.   Frame 8.   Frame 9.   Frame 10.

4.

To prevent the two animations that you created from running too quickly into each other, you set up frame 5 to be on display for 1 second. Test the animation by clicking the Plays Animation button.

▲ *Configuring the time for each frame.*

Applying Spin Action Animation

1.

You'll be applying a rotating effect on your final animation. In the Layers Palette, activate the Weather Vane layer.

▲ *The image that will be rotated (left) and the layer (right).*

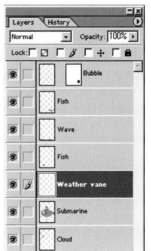

The animation actions in ImageReady.

There are a total of 12 frames of animation effects in the Actions Palette, and the time that you specified for the first frame will be applied to all the other frames.

Spinning Zoom In: The small image grows steadily to its original size as it rotates.

Spin: The image rotates half a revolution clockwise.

Zoom In: The small image grows to its original size.

Zoom Out: The image gets smaller and smaller until it becomes completely invisible. (The invisible frame is inserted for a total of 13 frames.)

Image quality and loading speed

In choosing between image quality and loading speed, you need to consider what kinds of users will be visiting your site.

You can divide the users into two categories: those that use a broadband connection (such as office workers and people with DSL or cable-modem) and those that use a modem (such as dial-in users).

If you know what kinds of users will be visiting your site, it will be very easy to choose between image quality and loading speed.

2.

In the Animation Palette, you make another duplicate frame for the new animation and then select Spin from the Actions Palette. Click Play Selection at the bottom of the palette so that the animation is created automatically.

The spin effect will be applied to a total of 12 frames, from frames 11 to 22. Because you applied the animation to the shape itself, you can see that a total of 11 layers, all at different angles of rotation, for each of the added frames have been created.

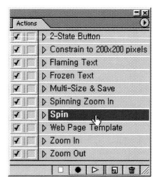

▲ *The Spin effect in the Actions Palette.*

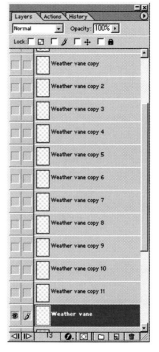

▲ *The layers created due to the Spin effect.*

Optimizing Images

You'll now convert the image window to 2-UP and apply color to the animation.

1.

You convert the image window to 2-UP so that you can compare the original and the modified images. This allows you to apply the optimal color with the least amount of damage to the original image.

In order to maintain the quality of the original image, you need more than 128 colors. If you apply fewer than 128 colors, you'll see that portions of the image will appear quite different from the original image.

▲ *The 2-UP image window.*

2.

In the example, in order to maintain a fair file size, you applied GIF 32 colors, No Dither, and Web Snap: 0%. If you use 128 colors at No Dither, the file size becomes 57.43KB, meaning that it will take 21 seconds for it to load using a 2.88 modem.

Using 32 colors and No Dither, the file size reduces to 33.37KB, and users are told that 13 seconds is required for loading at the bottom of the screen.

▲ *The Optimize properties for the animation.*

3.

Finally, choose File⇨Save Optimized to create the GIF animation file.

understanding GIF Animation

GIF Animation displays several pages of images in consecutive order.

Looking at Table 1, you see the running of a four-frame GIF animation. The next frame is on hold for the previous frame. This allows GIF animation to utilize a much smaller file size.

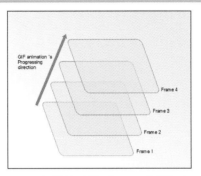

▲ *(Table 1) The frame on hold in the GIF animation.*

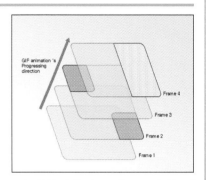

▲ *(Table 2) The image frame on hold and the newly appearing image frame.*

Table 2 shows the actual animation in frames 2, 3, and 4.

If frame 1 contains the background image and frames 2, 3, and 4 contain partial animations, the background shown in frame 1 does not need to be loaded again. In this case, in order to reduce the file size, the animation in frames 2, 3, and 4 are made without the background. (Table 3)

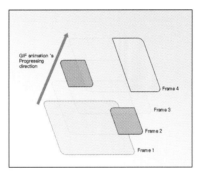

◀ *(Table 3) The actual image frame used to optimize the size of the animation.*

In ImageReady, when frames 2, 3, and 4 are separated by layers, the partial animation is created automatically. Using this method of partial animations makes for a smaller GIF animation.

The entire image is loaded in frame 1; therefore, only the actual image frame is saved in the next frame.

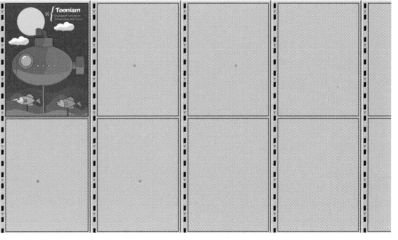

▲ *The GIF animation created using ImageReady is verified using GIF Movie Gear.*

Creating a Rollover Button

LESSON HIGHLIGHTS

The Rollover function is a tool that shows both the efficiency and the inefficiency of ImageReady. This function is effective in the sense that buttons that will be used in the HTML can be made while the layer is active and that the result can be previewed in ImageReady. However, this function is inefficient in that Rollover cannot be set up for each image that divides up one layer. For this reason, if you want to add a Rollover effect to a button and have it appear only in ImageReady, each button must have its own layer.

The function sequence is Layer⇨New Layer Based Slice, Slice Tool, Rollover Palette, Save Optimized, and Using Dreamweaver.

You'll apply Rollover to the image of a clock that has three buttons. Then, you'll add functions that you can use to control the image at the top of each button. In this lesson, you'll learn how to create a Rollover image and how to use Rollover buttons to stop/play animations.

Depending on the movement of the mouse, Rollover buttons can take on different forms. Users will feel as if they're operating 3-D buttons that appear and disappear based on some fixed conditions.

In this lesson, you'll save the images that result from three button operations as individual layers and learn how to use the Rollover Palette to use these layers as Rollover buttons.

---

controlling Rollover buttons

You can control Rollover buttons in six different ways:

Normal: The image as it was when it was first loaded.

Over: The image as it appears when the mouse is placed over the rollover image.

Down: The image as it appears when the (left) mouse button is clicked and held down.

Click: The image as it appears when the mouse is clicked.

Out: The image as it appears when the mouse moves away from the rollover image.

Up: The image as it appears when the right mouse button is clicked (or the mouse is Control-clicked on a Mac) or when the mouse is double-clicked.

---

getting ready

Copy **Samples⇨Chapter4⇨Rollover.Psd** onto the hard disk and then load it into ImageReady.

Slicing Frames

Each of the button layers will be sliced into a slice frame. If the frames are clearly divided into layers, you can do this by choosing Layer⇨New Layer Based Slice.

1.

In the Layers Palette, Button_left, Button_center and Button_right are the respective frames. First of all, activate the Button_left layer and choose Layer↪New Layer Based Slice.

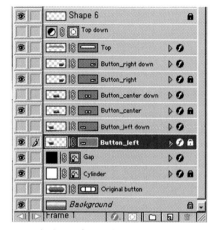

▲ *The layer after applying Layer↪New Layer Based Slice.*

2.

In the new slice frame that was just created, go to the Slices menu and choose Promote To User-Slice to convert the slice frame to an editable state. Now, you'll be able to adjust the size of the slice to fit the image frame.

In the same way, convert the Button_center and Button_right layers into slice frames and adjust their size.

There should now be exactly seven slice frames.

▲ *The slice applied to the Button_left layer.*

▲ *The slices applied to the three buttons and the remaining four slices.*

The New Layer Based Slice Function

The Layer↪New Layer Based Slice is a timesaving function that easily converts layer image frames into slice frames. However, you need to keep a few things in mind if you want to use this function.

Users cannot control slice frames created in this way, much like those created automatically using Auto-Slice. If you need to modify the frame, you need to change the property of the slice by using User-Slice. Also, the slice frames created using New Layer Based Slice are slightly wider than the layer image frames.

Although this is fine for sliced images that are spread far apart, slice frames that require precise slicing can overlap. In the example, there is no spacing between the images. Therefore, the slightly wider slice frames, created using the New Layer Based Slice function, need to be adjusted to fit the actual image frame.

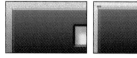

▲ *The actual layer image frame (left) and the slightly wider slice frame (right).*

Although the Slice Tool is extremely helpful and convenient for saving image slices, many first-time users will find themselves at a loss. Many will give up after trying to use the Slice Tool and finding that the wrong image has been saved or that hidden spacing will be inserted in between the slice frames to create uneven distributions.

This is because, compared to other tools, there are many more things that you must know before using the Slice Tool. Only after you understand numbered slices, information contained within slices, activated/deactivated slices, User-Slice, Auto-Slice, the Slice Palette, the Optimize Palette, and the Save Optimized function will you realize just how useful the Slice Tool is in creating Web graphics.

You must realize that although ImageReady takes on the external form of Photoshop, it is in itself an independent program and this is due to the Slice Tool. A lot of trial and error is required before you can master the Slice Tool. However, this is a necessary hurdle in the road to becoming an advanced user.

Naming the Sliced Frame

1.

Select Slice 03 using the Slice Select Tool from the Toolbox and enter button_left under Name in the Slice Palette. Name Slice 04 and Slice 05 button_center and button_right, respectively.

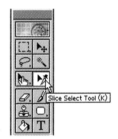

▶ *Selecting the Slice Select Tool.*

▲ *The Slice Palette configurations applied to the button_left slice.*

2.

Name slices 01-07 appropriately and, with all the slices activated, convert to User-Slice.

If a name is not entered, a name will be applied by default (the PSD file name plus a number). In order to specify a file name automatically beforehand, choose File⇨Output Settings⇨Saving Files.

Applying Rollover

The Rollover button is applied by first selecting each slice in the Rollover Palette and then specifying the symbol in the center to a color–changed Over state and a slightly lowered Down state.

1.

Select Slice 03 of the left button. Then execute Creates New Rollover State in the Rollover Palette and select Over.

▲ *Clicking Creates new Rollover State to select the Over state.*

▲ *Selecting Slice 03.*

> ### Auto-slice
>
> The slice created automatically by slicing the slice frame takes on the attributes of an Auto-Slice.
>
> The size and position of the Auto-Slice cannot be adjusted and only changes in response to changes in the slice frame that was made by the user. You can think of the Auto-Slice as having a Linked Slice functionality.
>
> This slice frame can be converted to the editable, User-Slice state by choosing Slice⮑Promote To User-Slice or by using the option configurations in the Slice Palette.

2.

Activate the symbol_left_over layer in the Layers Palette and apply an Over status to the color-changed symbol image.

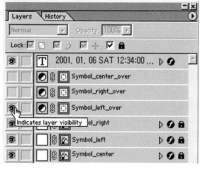

▲ *Activating the symbol_left_over layer.*

▲ *The Over button image.*

259

3.

Add the Down state to the Rollover Palette. This is done after activating the button_left_down layer in the Layers Palette.

▲ Adding the Down state to the Rollover Palette.

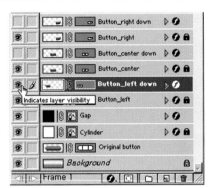

▲ Activation of the Button_left_down layer.

4.

Clicking Preview The Behavior Of Rollovers in the Rollover Palette allows you to preview the animation of the button images in the image window.

▲ The Preview button.

5.

Repeat the steps to convert the button_center and button_right slices to the Rollover state.

You can verify which slices have been converted to the Rollover state by looking at the list at the bottom left of the Rollover Palette.

In the menu at the bottom left, slices that have been converted to the Rollover state will be marked with an ★.

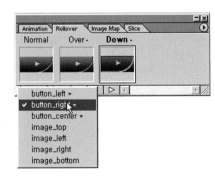

260

6.

The finished button can be previewed in the browser by selecting File⇨Preview In.

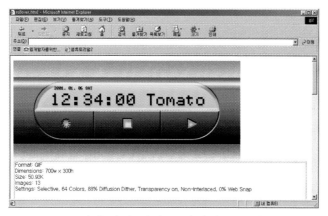

▲ *Previewing the button in the browser using Preview In.*

saving files

You can configure file-naming conditions beforehand by choosing File⇨ Output Settings⇨Saving Files so that files names will be applied automatically according to these conditions.

A total of eight conditions can be configured for the file name and are usually based on numbers, dates, or rollover status. You can also use this option to specify beforehand whether the file extensions will be in all uppercase or lowercase letters.

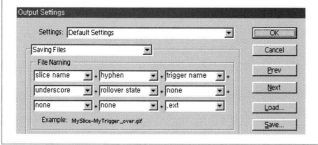

Adding a Light Switch Button

When the left button is clicked (the Down state of the button_left slice), you
want the background color of the screen to change. This effect is made by
adding the layer of the changing background to the button_left_down slice.

1.

First, use the Slice Tool to make a slice that contains the top of the screen. Then,
name this slice screen in the Slice Palette.

▲ *Entering the file name in the Slice Palette.*

▲ *The slice frame containing the screen.*

2.

Then open the Rollover Palette of the left button and add the active state of the top
down layer (the down state of the transformed screen).

▲ *Activating the Down state of the left button.*

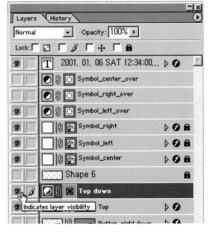

▲ *The top down layer added to the Down state.*

262

3.

Using Preview The Behavior Of Rollovers in the Rollover Palette, you can see the top screen changing with the click of the left button.

▲ *The screen effect of applying the mouse button down to the button_left slice.*

Save Optimized

After entering the names for the remaining slices, excluding the button and screen slices, in the Slice Palette, choose File⇨Save Optimized to save all the images and HTML files and then verify the result in the browser.

▲ *Entering the names for slices 01, 02, 04, and 08 in the Slice Palette.*

save slice selection

Slice⇨Save Slice Selection saves the information on the selected slice. You can save several groups of slices (useful when more than one slice is worked on at a time) at one time as well.

The configurations of the Optimize Palette are applied to all selected slices is a very useful option.

If Save information is created for slices that will be configured in the same way, slice selection can be more effectively managed. This information can then be loaded from Slice⇨Load Slice Selection.

1.

Choose File⇨Save Optimized. Entering the HTML file name rollover under File Name will automatically save the HTML file, images folder, and the images.

▲ *Entering the HTML file name in the Save Optimized dialog box.*

2.

Open the browser and extract the Rollover.Html file to see that the image and the HTML sources have been created properly.

▶ *Previewing the result in the browser.*

FYI

Choosing View⇨Snap to⇨Slices will
bestow the Snap function on the
slice frame so that you can easily
crop the slice frame.

▲ *The screen slice frame cut out
using the Crop Tool.*

Making a Screen GIF Animation

Next, you'll animate the screen and add an on/off control to the button
animation.

1.

Use the Crop Tool in the Toolbox to cut out the screen slice frame for the GIF animation.

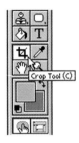

▲ *Selecting the Crop Tool.*

2.

Open the Animation Palette and make a new frame, making sure to hide the text layer.
Assign a time of 0.5 seconds to each frame so that the blinking lights look
natural. Name this screen_ani in the Slice Palette.

▲ *The text is now hidden in the second frame.*   ▲ *Hiding the text layer.*

3.

Choose File⇨Save Optimized As and then select Images Only for File Format so that the previously saved HTML file is not altered and remains coded as a cropped-only frame.

When Save Optimized or Save Optimized As is executed, the current PSD file name will be applied. In the example, the file name Rollover.Psd is applied.

▲ *Selecting Images Only under File Format.*

4.

Load the Screen_ani.Gif file from the Images folder in the browser and make sure that the animation runs properly.

Linking the GIF Animation to a Button

Macromedias Dreamweaver 4 is a popular HTML editor because it can be used to flexibly and easily create HTML files, add JavaScript, and create DHTML. You'll use Dreamweaver to link the buttons and the animation.

▲ *The GIF animation loaded in the browser.*

1.

Open Dreamweaver 4.0 and load the Rollover.Html file.

▲ *Loading Rollover.Html in Dreamweaver 4.0.*

> ## About file names
>
> The file name applied here corresponds to the standard name of the automatically applied slice. If a name is not entered and the name in the Save Optimized window is used, the name will take on the form of Entered File Name with a number attached to the end. In other words, if the name Rollover is applied automatically, the created file will be named Rollover_01.Ext.
>
> Whether the file format was set to Image Only or HTML And Images, the name that is applied when no name is entered in the Slice Palette is the same as the default name of the automatically occurring file.
>
> In the same way, when all file names are specified in the Slice Palette, the name entered in the Save Optimized window is not applied to the image file. The name of the saved GIF animation is given the name screen_ani. that was entered in the Slice palette.

265

2.

You can see that the name, screen, has been entered to the right of the image icon in the Properties Window by selecting the Screen image.

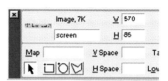

▲ *The name tag for the application of JavaScript.*

Trial version of Dreamweaver

You can download a 30-day trial version of the current version of Dreamweaver from the Macromedia homepage.

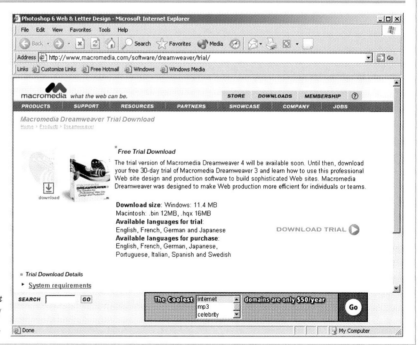

▶ *The Macromedia homepage at* www.macromedia.com/ software/dreamweaver/trial.

3.

After selecting the button on the right, open the Behavior Window and click the  toggle button. From the list that appears, select Swap Image.

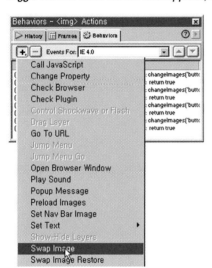

▲ *Applying Swap Image in the Behaviors Window.*

▲ *Selecting the button on the right.*

4.

In the Swap Image dialog box, select image screen* from the Images list and look for the screen_ani.gif file, located within the Images folder under Set Source to.

▲ *Swap Image dialog box.*

Deselect Restore Images onMouseOut at the bottom of the dialog box. This prevents the addition of the Swap Image Restore script. (When the mouse is placed on the button, the image changes shape. This script makes the transformed shape return to its original form when the mouse is removed from the button. Therefore, deselecting this option pre-vents the image from returning to its original form.)

Types of slices

Two types of slices are created by the Slice Tool: the User-Slice and the Auto-Slice.

A User-Slice contains the configuration frame and the optimization information. Therefore, it's not affected by overlapping slices. Auto-Slice is the complete opposite. All slices that are not User-Slices are Auto-Slices and change in size and position based on the changes in the User-Slices.

5.

After applying the script, convert Events from onMouseOver to onMouseDown using the toggle button in the Behaviors Window.

After using the File⇨Save command to enter the added condition to the HTML file, load it into the browser and see whether the animation runs when the button on the right is clicked.

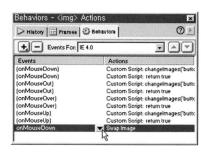

▲ *Modifying the mouse events.*

6.

A similar method that adds the script to swap the screen image for the original image entails selecting Screen from the Images list and selecting the screen.gif file from the Images folder under Set Source to.

As before, change the onMouseOver to onMouseDown for the Events in the Behaviors Window.

▲ *Selecting screen.gif for Set Source to.*

effective slicing

Using Guides: The Guides (View⇨ Show Rules) is an effective and convenient tool for precise slicing. After dividing the frame using Guides, use Slices⇨Create Slices from Guides to convert it to slices. The slices created in this way are erased or combined to complete the slicing step.

Using Divide Slice: In order to slice an equilateral and precisely arranged image, like menu navigation buttons, first organize the entire frame into one slice and then choose Slices⇨Divide Slice to divide the slice into several frames.

Using Auto-Slice: Auto-Slice, a derivation of the User-Slice, has the advantage that file names and optimization configurations are automatically applied. If the optimization is applied before slicing the frame, the file name

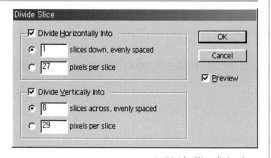

▲ *Divide Slice dialog box.*

conditions, specified beforehand under Output Settings, are applied.

Inserting a Background Image and Completing the HTML Page

Finally, you'll complete the HTML page by saving a portion of the image as an image file and applying it as the background.

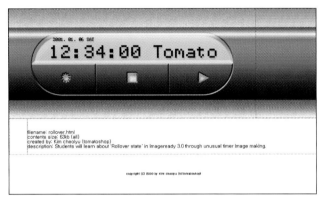

▲ *The final result as seen in Dreamweaver.*

1.

In the History Palette of ImageReady, convert to the state right before the Crop command was applied in the GIF animation.

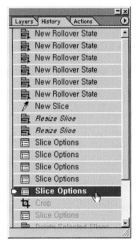

▶ *Retrieving the image from the History Palette.*

copying the HTML source in the slice

The HTML file, created in ImageReady, is divided into the ⟨IMG⟩ tag, which loads the image, the ⟨TABLE⟩ tag, which arranges the loaded image, the script for the operation of the Rollover image, and ⟨MAP⟩.

The Edit⇨Copy HTML Code command is used to copy portions of these codes and then load them into the HTML editor.

For All Slices: Copy the ⟨TABLE⟩ tag to arrange all the slices. When the Rollover function is added in ImageReady, it loads all unnecessary slices at the same time. Therefore, this is used only to copy non-JavaScript sources.

For Selected Slices: Copy the ⟨TABLE⟩ tag to arrange only selected slices. Generally, several ⟨TABLE⟩ tags are used when making an HTML page. Because ImageReady uses one ⟨TABLE⟩ tag to slice all other frames, it is an effective means of managing the sliced frames. To create a separate, internal ⟨TABLE⟩, use For Selected Slices.

For Preloads: This script is copied to preload a rollover image when the browser page is downloaded.

2.

Use the Slice Tool from the Toolbox to select and slice a portion on the right side of the image that will be used as the background. Then enter the name backimage in the Slice Palette.

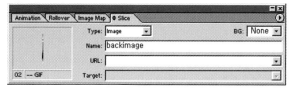 

▲ Entering the file name in the Slice Palette.   ▲ Selecting the background with the Slice Tool.

3.

Choose File⇨Save Optimized As. In the dialog box, set the File Format to Images Only and, with the Selected Slices option selected, specify the backimage file from the Images folder.

▲ Save Optimized As dialog box.

4.

Open Dreamweaver and choose Page Properties from the Modify menu. In the dialog box, set the values for Left Margin, Top Margin, and Margin Height all to 0 and apply it to the image.

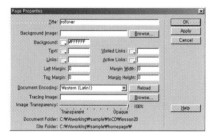

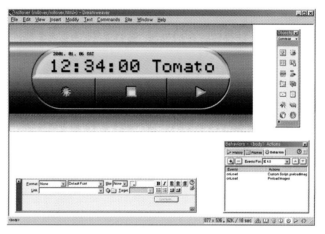

▲ *Configuring Page Properties.*

▲ *Setting the margins to 0 removes the empty spaces on the sides and at the top.*

5.

Select the entire table by clicking the edges of the table. Cut out the table by choosing Edit⇨Cut or by using the shortcut keys Ctrl (Cmd) + X.

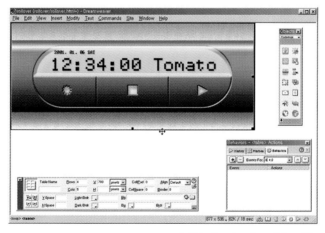

▲ *Selecting the edges of the table.*

Linking to another software product

The File⟂Jump To feature allows you to view your work in other software programs, much like a network. The basic Jump To function between ImageReady and Photoshop allows the results of the work in progress to be shared between the two programs, and the HTML file saved in Notepad or some other HTML editor can also be shared. In addition, the File⟂ Preview in command allows the work to be viewed in the Internet Explorer or Netscape browser. A similar function exists in Dreamweaver, Properties Window⟂Edit, and it allows Dreamweaver to send information to ImageReady or Photoshop.

The special field of Web design gave birth to the simultaneous use of image software and HTML editors. For image files, before they culminate in the final HTML page, they undergo much editing as you transverse between the two programs. The Jump To feature was created to lessen the work time and allow users to conveniently utilize the two programs.

6.

Select Insert Table from the Objects Window to create a new table in which to insert the background image.
In the Insert Table dialog box, set Rows to 1, Columns to 1, Cell Padding to 0, Cell Spacing to 0, and Width to 100 Percent to create the table.

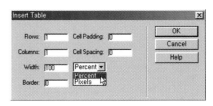

▲ *Insert Table dialog box.*

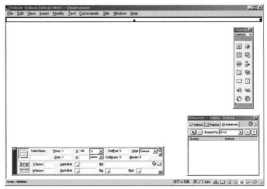

▲ *The new table with a width of 100%.*

7.

Select the interior of the newly created table and paste the table that was cut out in Step 5 (Ctrl + v).

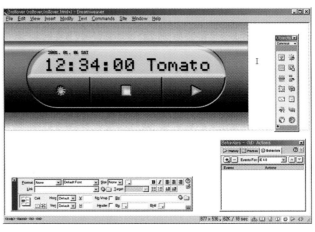

▲ *The table that was cut out is pasted into the new table.*

8.

After clicking the edges of the new table (width: 100%) to select the entire table, go to the Properties Window and look for backimage.gif for the table background image (Bg).

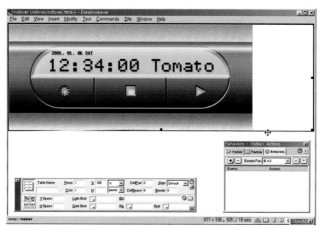

▲ *Selecting the table with a width of 100%.*

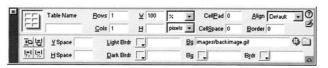

▲ *Entering the table background image.*

9.

Due to the addition of the JavaScript configuration, the button on the left now controls the background lighting, the button in the middle stops the animation, and the button on the right plays the animation. You can load the HTML file into the browser and verify it.

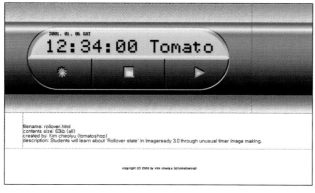

▲ *The final result as seen in Dreamweaver.*

273

Lesson 34

Using Image Map

The Image Map refers to areas that are configured to contain hyperlinks, which allow for movement between Web pages. In this lesson, you'll learn how to configure the Image Map in ImageReady.

LESSON HIGHLIGHTS

The Image Map Area is created using the Image Map Tool in the Toolbox, and you can configure this area using Layer : New Layer Based Image Map Area.

This frame configured using New Layer Based Image Map Area contains a rectangular tag and can be switched to a circle or polygon in the Image Map Palette. The function sequence is Layer : New Layer Based Image Map Area, File : Preview In, Image Map Palette, and Optimize Palette.

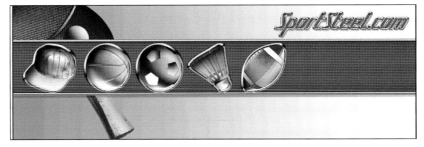

▲ The image for the Image Map.

Image Map applies individual hyperlinks to sections of an image and is used when slicing is difficult or when rollover or other special effects have not been added.

In ImageReady, you can configure Image Map by using the Image Map Tool in the Toolbox or by converting the image frame into an Image Map frame directly in the layer.

The hyperlink is applied from within the Image Map Palette and the result, saved using Save Optimized, is verified.

Applying New Layer Based Image Map Area

Layer⇨New Layer Based Image Map Area converts the image within a layer into an Image Map.

1.

Activate the baseball cap layer.

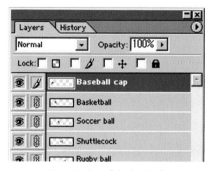

▲ *Activation of the baseball cap layer.*

2.

*Choose Layer⇨New Layer Based Image Map
Area to create a rectangular image map frame
around the baseball cap.*

▲ *The configured image map area.*

Image Map Frame

You can hide or display the image map frame by using the Toggle Image Maps Visibility function in the Toolbox.

▲ *The toggle button used to control the
image map's visibility.*

3.

*As a default, the New Layer Based Image Map Area command configures rectangular
image map areas. In order to select an image map frame that fits the image frame in
the layer completely, change the default shape using the Shape option in the Image
Map Palette.*

converting to the select tool

Pressing the Ctrl (Cmd on Mac) key while using the Image Map Tool allows you to switch to the Select Tool.

Applying Circle, Polygon Image Map

1.

Select the Circle Image Map Tool in the Toolbox and create a frame around the basketball and soccer balls.

For an exact frame, use the Image Map Select to adjust the size and position of the frame.

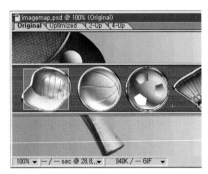

▲ Creating the circle image map.

2.

Use the Polygon Image Map Tool to configure the frames for the remaining images.

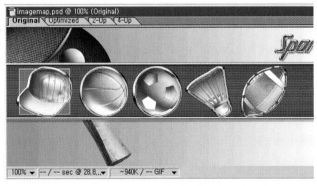

▲ Creating the polygon image map.

Configuring the Image Map Palette

You'll adjust the rectangular frame around the baseball cap to fit the image.

1.

Use the Image Map Select Tool to select the image map frame surrounding the baseball cap.

spacer.gif

When HTML is used to create a homepage, the `<TABLE>` tag is used quite frequently. When making a 1x1 pixel cell for a table, the image needs to be inserted between the `<TD>` tag and the `</TD>` tag defining that cell. Image frames set up as No Image are replaced with expandable Spacer.Gif files. ImageReady tries to facilitate the creation of HTML by automatically filling in transparent frames with Spacer.Gif files. In addition, when tables are inserted in HTML files created using ImageReady, there is an invisible Spacer frame at the top of the table. This frame is used to prevent the warping of complex tables that may be created.

2.

In the Image Map Palette, select the Polygon shape in the Layer Image Map and set the Quality to 100 to create a detailed frame.

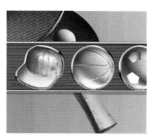

▲ *The Polygon Image Map drawn to fit the baseball cap.*

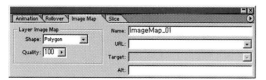

▲ *Configuring the Image Map Palette.*

HTML Preview

Use the File⇨Preview In command to select the general browser and verify the application of the image map.

Save the image and the HTML file using the File⇨Save Optimized command.

▲ *Previewing the HTML file in the browser.*

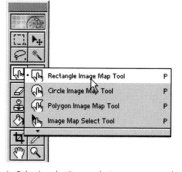
277

Reducing the size of the HTML file

You'll use the image that you used here in this example to see how you can reduce the size of the overall image in HTML. When the image in this example is set to GIF 32 Dithered, the file size is 40.45KB. If you add the 2.75KB HTML file, the total size comes to 43.2KB. However, because the image uses the optimized GIF 32-color, there is a problem in the stepwise gradation in the background.

Step 1: An image frame with a detailed pattern uses the background tag. There are two types of patterns in this image. One is the gradation seen in the background, and the other is the stripe pattern of the buttons. HTML has a Background subtag that applies a small capacity pattern to the background of the overall image.

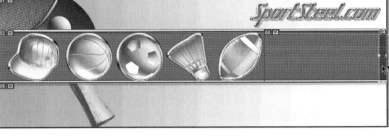

1. First, you'll use the stripe pattern of the buttons as the background of the entire image.

▲ *Slicing the stripe pattern to use it as the background.*

2. Use the Slice Tool to divide the image into top, middle, and bottom sections and divide the button image in the center into the actual Slice 02, the blank space, Slice 03, and the background pattern, Slice 04.

4. Set Slices 02 and 04 to GIF 32 Dithered in the Optimize Palette.

3. In the Slice Palette, set the Type of Slice 03 to No Image.

▲ *Slice 03, which is used as the blank space.*

▲ *Optimizing the image.*

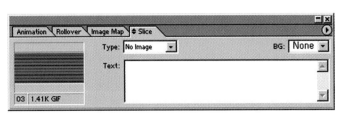

▲ *Setting Slice 03 to Type: No Image.*

Reducing the size of the HTML file (cont.)

Step 2: Use a transparent background to reduce the image color.

The overall gradation frame of the image is saved as the background pattern, and the actual image is made transparent to reduce the file size.

1. Use the Slice Tool to divide up the top and bottom image frames.

   Of all 12 slices, Slice 02 at the top and Slices 08 and 10 at the bottom correspond to empty spaces in the image.

   First of all, create a new slice in the bottom frame for the gradation background pattern and save it.

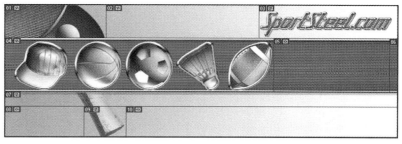

▲ *The divided slice frame.*

2. Hide the layer of the ping-pong paddle in the background and convert all slices to User-Slice so that they are not affected by the new slice.

▲ *The creation of the new slice frame for the background gradation pattern.*

3. Optimize the newly created slice, Slice 11, by setting it to JPEG High and name it gradient.

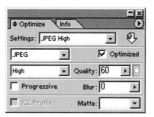

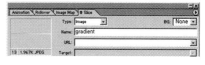

▲ *Entering the name, gradient.*

▲ *Optimization of the background image.*

4. With Slice 13 selected, choose File⇨Save Optimized and set the File Format to Images Only and choose the Selected Slices option. Save this slice in the Images folder. (The file name that is entered is ignored due to the name entered in the Slice Palette.)

Reducing the size of the HTML file (cont.)

5. After making the Gradient.Jpg file, either delete Slice 11 or hide it by selecting the Send Slices To Back button in the Slice Option Palette.

▲ The Send Slices To Back button in the Slice Option Palette.

6. Use the Matte option to blend the outline of the transparent background image with the background image. First, use the Eyedropper Tool to specify the color in the center of the gradation as the foreground color.

▲ Selecting the color in the middle of the gradation with the Eyedropper Tool.

Hide the background gradation layer in the Layers Palette.

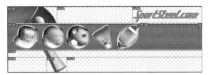

▲ Hiding the background gradation.

▲ The color in the middle of the gradation is specified as the foreground color.

7. In the Slice Palette, set the Type of Slices 02, 08, and 10 to No Image.

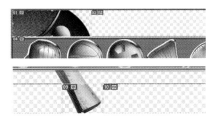

▲ Setting Slices 02, 08, and 10 to No Image.

8. Apply GIF 16 Transparency to Slices 01 and 09 and select the foreground color from Matte.

▲ Selecting the foreground color from Matte.

Reducing the size of the HTML file (cont.)

9. Optimize Slices 03 and 07 by selecting GIF 32 Transparency and the foreground color under Matte.

▲ *Slices 03 and 07.*

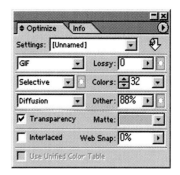

▲ *Optimization of slices 03 and 07.*

10. Choose File⇨Save Optimized As and change the File Format to HTML and Images. Then select the All Slices option and save the HTML and image files again.

◀ *Save Optimized As dialog box (Windows).*

Step 3: Edit the HTML tag to fill in the empty spaces with the background image.

1. Open Dreamweaver 4 and load the Imagemap.Html file.

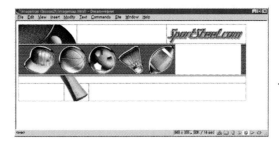

◀ *Opening the Imagemap.Html file in Dreamweaver.*

2. Choose Modify⇨Page Properties and set Background Image to Gradient.Jpg. Set the values for Left Margin, Top Margin, Margin Width, and Margin Height to remove the empty spaces from the HTML file.

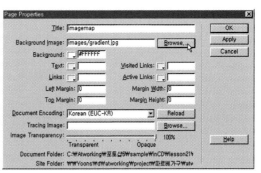

◀ *Configuring Page Properties.*

Reducing the size of the HTML file (cont.)

3. Select the Spacer.Gif image that was applied to Slices 02, 05, 08, and 10 and that were set to No Image and delete it.

   Note that slices that are set to No Image will appear with a Spacer.Gif file when the HTML file is created.

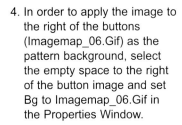

▲ *The 1 x 1 pixel Spacer.Gif file expands to fill in the frames that were set to No Image.*

4. In order to apply the image to the right of the buttons (Imagemap_06.Gif) as the pattern background, select the empty space to the right of the button image and set Bg to Imagemap_06.Gif in the Properties Window.

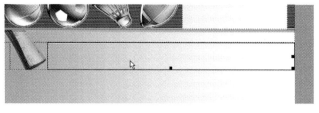

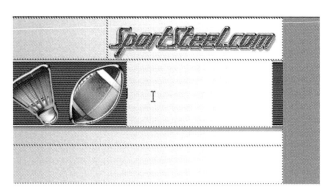

▲ *Selecting the empty space to the right.*

◀ *Applying the background image in the Properties Window.*

5. After optimizing the HTML file and the image, the total size comes to 37.02KB (image: 33.2KB; HTML file: 3.82KB). This is 6KB less than the previous size of 43.2KB.

▲ *The final HTML page as seen in Dreamweaver.*

:: :

chapter 5

Web Site Design

You'll look at how you can use Photoshop and ImageReady to create a Web site and discover helpful hints on Web design.

Lesson 35

What You Need to Know for Web Site Design

LESSON HIGHLIGHTS

This lesson covers the important, need-to-know details behind Web site design and creation.

The Web sites that you've seen on your PC monitor are composed of pages written in HTML (HyperText Markup Language). Web browsers then take this information and display it as images, audio/visual files, or text. Everything that you need to know about Web site design is based on the monitor, HTML, and the Web browser. You'll look at each one in turn.

The Importance of HTML

Basically, a Web site is based upon a language known as HTML. No matter how complex a site is, it still has HTML as a fundamental basis. In other words, once you understand HTML, you'll have little problem understanding the makeup of any Web site. If something is wrong with your homepage, you're going to have to look through the HTML source to find out what's wrong. If you have a good understanding of HTML, you should have no problem finding the source of the problem. HTML is easy enough that sites teaching it are abundant on the Web, which is one reason the World Wide Web has been so successful.

▲ A Web site seen in a browser.

▶ An HTML source file.

Managing Image Folders

HTML sources are made up of
collections of text, JavaScript, and
other miscellaneous source files.
Images, Flash animation, and
program source files are saved in
special folders and are called upon
by HTML interpreters. When they
are called upon and the results
assembled, the Web browser displays
a readable page. When the respective
page is read again, it calls the page
saved (cached) on the hard disk to
save the time that it takes to load
the page elements of the first page
that was loaded. This is the reason
why images that are used several

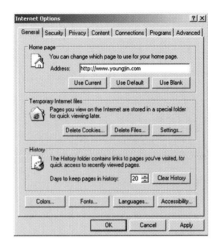

▲ *The Temporary Internet files preference
located within the Internet Explorer Web
browser's (General) Internet options.*

times on a site are saved together in one folder. Once an image has been
loaded, it's cached on the hard disk, thereby reducing the time that it takes
to load a second time. This method is used frequently for linking logos and
main menu navigators.

Web Color

The Web site design is the final result that is generated onto the monitor.
The monitors that you use display RGB colors and (typically) a resolution
of 800 x 600 or 1,024 x 768, although other resolutions, such as 640 x
480, 1,280 x 1,024, and 1,600 x 1,200 are not uncommon. However,
depending on the installation of a video card or the manufacturer of the
monitor, there can be anywhere from very small to very large differences
in monitor color. As a result, the color of a Web site can be far from perfect.
At times, only the designer of the Web site will be able to see the color as
it was meant to be seen. Depending on the user's monitor type, the Web
site seen on the system can be very different from what was intended by
the designer. Web-safe colors are an attempt to alleviate some of this problem.
Macintosh and Windows operating systems officially present to the world
216 colors, after removing the differences in the presentation of the 256
colors that are found on the system palette, that are safe to use on the Web.

These 216 colors, otherwise known as the Web-safe Color Palette, Netscape Color Cube, or the 6x6x6 palette, is now a Web standard. To ensure consistent results, the Web site must be created using these 216 Web-safe colors. These Web-safe colors also eliminate the problem that was seen in the ugly representation of a 16-bit Web site on an 8-bit color monitor.

◀ An image using Web-safe colors.
Background: R: 255, G: 51, B: 51.
Text: R: 51, G: 51, B: 153.

◀ Viewing a slightly color-modified image on an 8-bit color monitor.
Background: R: 237, G: 62, B: 62.
Text: R: 35, G: 75, B: 156.

Although Web-safe colors ensure consistent results across different platforms, you have a limited choice of color. This is more of a problem in this day and age when more splendid and extravagant images are finding their way onto the Web every day. In the end, it comes down to your audience. How far you intend to take your Web site in terms of color depends largely on who you expect your audience to be. If you're presenting your site to the more than 400 million users around the world, then practicality and efficiency should be key. However, if you're focusing on only a small audience, you can afford to be more daring and adventurous in terms of color and design.

web-safe color

#336600	#99FF00	#99FF33		#000099	#3366FF	#000066	
#99CC66	#99CC00	#99CC33		#0066FF	#0033CC	#0000CC	
#669900	#CCFF66	#CCFF00		#0000CC	#0018CC	#0000CC	
#CCFF33	#666600	#666633		#0033FF	#0018CC	#003366	#99CCFF
#CCCC99	#CCCC66	#CCCC33		#0033FF	#0033FF	#0033FF	#66CCFF
#999966	#999933	#999900		#3366FF	#0033CC	#0066CC	#3399CC
#333300	#FFFFFF	#CCCCCC		#33CCFF	#00CCFF	#3399CC	#99CCCC
#999999	#666666	#333333		#0099CC	#0033333	#669999	
#000000	#000000	#000000		#66CCCC	#339909	#CCFFFF	
#FF0000	#CC0000	#FF6666		#00FFFF	#66FFFF	#33FFFF	
#FFCCCC	#FF9999	#FF6666		#00FFFF	#00CCCC	#99FFCC	
#FF3333	#FF0033	#CC0033		#66FFCC	#33FFCC	#00FFCC	
#CC9999	#CC6666	#330000		#33CCCC	#009999	#66CC99	
#FF0699	#FF3366	#FF0066		#33CC99	#00CC99	#339999	
#CC3366	#999666	#663333		#0099CC	#0066CC	#66FF99	
#FF99CC	#FF3399	#FF0099		#33FF99	#00FF99	#33CC66	
#CC0066	#993366	#660033		#00CC66	#009933	#99FF99	
#FF66CC	#FF00CC	#FF33CC		#66FF66	#33FF66	#00FF66	
#CC6699	#CC0099			#339933	#006699	#CCFFCC	
#FFCCFF	#FF99FF	#FF66FF		#996699	#66CC66	#669966	
#FF33FF	#FF00FF	#CC3399		#006600	#003300	#33FF33	
#CC99CC	#CC66CC	#CC00CC		#00FF33	#00CC00	#33CC33	
#CC33CC	#996699	#993399		#00CC33	#66FF00	#66FF33	
#CC66FF	#CC33FF	#CC99FF		#33FF00	#33CC00	#339900	
#9900FF	#9900CC	#660066		#009900	#CCFF99	#99FF66	
#CC99FF	#9933CC	#9933FF		#66CC00	#66CC33	#669933	
#9900FF	#660099	#663366		#FFFFCC	#FFFF99	#FFFF66	
#9966CC	#9966FF	#330033		#FFFF33	#FFFF00	#CCCC00	
#CCCCFF	#9999FF	#663399		#FFCC66	#FFCC00	#FFCC33	
#330099	#330066			#CC9900	#CC9933	#999900	
#9999CC	#6666CC			#FF9900	#FF9933	#CC9966	
#9999CC	#6666FF			#CC9900	#996633	#FF6600	
#3333FF	#3333FF	#333366		#FFCC99	#FF9966	#FF6600	
				#CC6633	#993300	#660000	
				#FF9933	#CC3300	#FF3300	

Connection Speed

One of the basic things you must consider when designing a Web site, along with color, is connection speed. Connection speed refers to how many KB per second users can download, depending on whether they use a modem or high-speed connection (such as ADSL or cable-modem). Users connect to the Web at speeds ranging anywhere from a very slow 9,600 Kbits per second to a very fast few Mbytes per second.

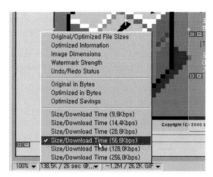

▲ *Size/Download Time information in ImageReady 3.0.*

In order to cater to such a various audience, a Web site must be created that is accessible to all these people. If it takes longer than just a few (some say eight is a good break point) seconds for a page to download, the visitor will surely move onto another site. For this reason, Web sites should maintain a file size of 40 to 70 Kbytes. However, this is only a general rule. Sites that contain a lot of multimedia will exceed this capacity.

Most software programs designed for Web design contain a feature that tells users how long it takes to download images and HTML files. The Optimized image window in ImageReady 3.0 shows, at the bottom left, how big the entire, optimized image file is and how long it will take to download

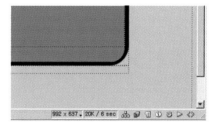

▲ *The download time information shown in Dreamweaver 4.*

it for different modem speeds. The HTML editor, Dreamweaver 4, also displays the size of the entire page (image + HTML source file) and how long it will take to download.

It is not uncommon to see many Web sites that stick to simple designs because of such limitations in size and download speed. Search engines are examples of such sites.

The standard search engine page design was first introduced by Yahoo, and many domestic search engines have followed its lead. This simple design includes a simple logo at the top, a search window, and search classifications. Apart from the title, the search engines do not use any images. Search engines cater to a very wide variety of audiences. Therefore, in order to maintain an adequate download time, extraneous image files, which can slow down the page, are avoided.

▲ kr.yahoo.com

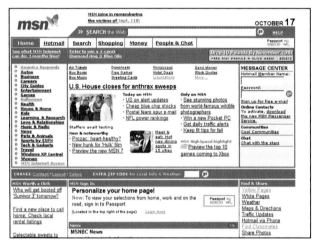

▲ www.msn.com

Organization of the Web Site

In order to form a Web page, images, be they static or dynamic, need to follow a standard order. Like the roots of a tree that branch out in all different directions from the base, there is sense of order in how text and pages are linked. The many pages of a Web site are linked to one central page. When users enter the URL, the first page that they see is this main page, the root of the entire site. Linked to this main page are the subpages, the branches of the tree, and contained within these subpages are the respective contents, which are like the leaves and berries on a tree. These are the three basic elements of a Web site. In order to disperse the wealth of information held in the subpages, several main pages are made, and portal pages, sort of like gigantic main pages, act as intermediaries between these main pages or are applied as gigantic main pages. However, this is just an extension of the basic, three-step Web page construction.

This basic, three-step Web page construction contains a whole system of links that allow users to move between the many pages using menu navigation. This menu navigation is actually made up of hyperlink HTML tags that move to the page that the user clicks on. However, hyperlinks have the disadvantage that pages need to be moved through in stepwise fashion before coming to the page desired by the user. In answer to this problem, many sites now contain a site map, which gives users a bird's eye view of the entire site, and a search engine.

▲ *The portal page at www.ford.com.*

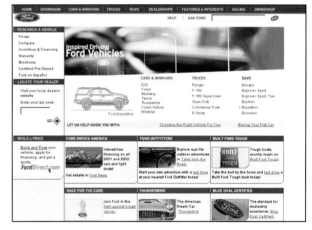

▲ *The Ford Vehicles main page at www.fordvehicles.com.*

▲ *The Mustang subpage of the Ford Vehicles site (www.dm.co).*

▲ *The V6 convertible page.*

Organization of the Web Page

After constructing the Web contents structure table and menu navigation, you must construct the Web page layout, which is the foundation of the Web site. Starting with the main page, which should be used to fully present the identity of the Web site, the subpages and contents page must strike a balance between being consistent with the main page and maintaining its own uniqueness.

The structure of the Web page is largely divided into a menu navigation frame and a contents frame. The menu navigation is like the remote control for a television set that is used to move between pages and is also the aspect of the Web site that gains the most attention from visitors. It also acts as a scaled-down version of a site map so that visitors can see the entire contents of the Web site at a glance. Therefore, many navigations are clear and concise and are always in the same location, despite the movement between the pages, so as to minimize the confusion of visitors as they become accustomed to its use, and are simple in design.

▲ www.fordvehicles.com.

▲ Menu navigation frame.

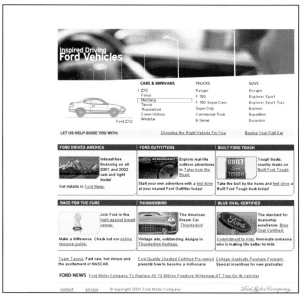

▲ Contents frame.

The contents frame of the pages or subpages require detailed descriptions of highlight contents, news, and other detailed elements where menu navigation alone is not enough to encompass all the possible contents. They usually contain a title and a brief summary of the page, some even with pictures to capture the users attention, arranged in decreasing order of relevance. GIF and Flash animations are also used as attention-grabbers. The two-step layout is the most common; however, one-step and combinations of various layout styles (for a more informal style) are also used.

two-step layout of the contents

▲ *www.msn.com.*

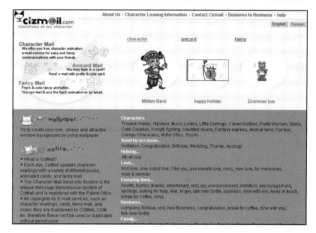

▲ *www.cizmail.com.*

combination of the one-step and two-step layouts

◀ *www.kagi.com.*

Menu Navigation Design

LESSON HIGHLIGHTS

You'll look at the organization and use of menu navigation and, through examples, see how menu navigation is implemented.

Suppose that you are visiting a high-rise building. Generally, on the ground floor, some sort of information panel tells you what is located on each floor of the building. If you're a first-time visitor, you will, undoubtedly, need to refer to this panel so that you know where to go. Of course, you can also ask someone at an information desk or a security guard. Here, the information panel is categorized under Global Navigation, the ultimate constituent element of menu navigation.

▲ An example of menu navigation elements.

Global Navigation

Global navigation is the navigation method that is applied to the entire site and allows for horizontal and vertical movement between pages. It usually contains the main category menu.

In accordance with the first general rule for anything that is applied to an entire site, global navigation is designed simply, without any visual obstructions, and doesn't contain any embellishments that might distract from the text.

Next, information appears at each level. Users will be able to find where they need to go by seeing where and how the information is categorized on the page. This information is categorized under the second menu category, Local Navigation.

Local Navigation

You can use local navigation whenever you have an excessive amount of global navigation or whenever you need subnavigation. The design of local navigation can take on many forms. It can borrow the design of the global navigation, act as an extension of global navigation, or change subtly to fit the design of the subpage. Now that you have covered these basic concepts, you'll look at how to draw up a simple menu navigator and how to design a simple HTML page using ImageReady.

In this example, you'll design a simple page that introduces Photoshop 6.0. This small-scale information site will focus on introducing the software and will include the latest news on the software, a Photoshop image gallery, and a Techniques/Tips page.

The basic concept of the design is Easy to Read. Containing only the menu, title, submenus, and important information, unnecessary embellishments are avoided and the focus is placed on relaying information. In order to keep the images somewhat planar and yet make them stand out a bit, they're designed in 2.5D, and the Rollover function was applied to add a touch of fun to the page.

> ### 2.5D (2.5 dimension)
>
> The term 2.5 dimension is used to refer to a type of protruding effect (an effect that isn't exactly 2-dimension and yet isn't really 3-dimension either) that is used frequently on Web sites.

Understanding the Vertical Menu Organization

A: Main Menu; Current Location
B: Category Headings and Subheadings
C: Page Menus; Go to First Page; Search Results

▲ *Page organization.*

using the polygon tool to draw various shapes

The Polygon Tool adjusts the vertices and curvature to draw various shapes. The following examples are shapes that were drawn after adjusting Sides and Geometry Options in the Options Bar of the Polygon Tool.

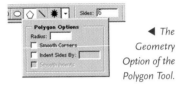

◀ The Geometry Option of the Polygon Tool.

Sides: 5

Indent Sides By: 60%

Smooth Indents

Sides: 12

Indent Sides By: 80%

Smooth Indents

Sides: 3

Smooth Corners

Sides: 18

Smooth Corners

Indent Sides By: 80%

Sides: 6

Indent Sides By: 50%

After moving the outline of the configured shape.

Drawing the External Form

To create a rounded rectangular page, you'll work with the Rounded Rectangle Tool from the Toolbox. The Shape Tool is also a useful tool for creating an image in a new layer and for creating a variable form in which you can apply Layer Style.

1.

You'll use a blue background color (R: 52, G: 119, B: 254) for this site. Turn your attention for a moment to the Color Picker function.

Open the Color Picker by clicking the foreground or background color in the Toolbox and enter the values for the RGB colors that will be applied to the site.

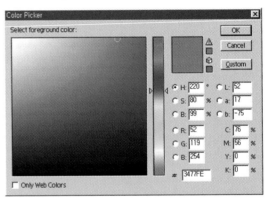

▲ Color Picker dialog box.

2.

To find the closest Web-safe colors for the color that you chose, click the color button under the picture of the cube. Remember that Web-safe colors prevent the distortion of your site when it's viewed on 256-color monitors of other operating systems.

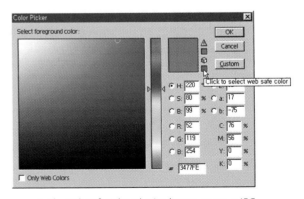

▲ The Web-Safe Color selection button. 05-271~3.JPG.

3.

Now, after specifying the color, use the Rounded Rectangle Tool to draw the image of the desired size. If you already know the size information for the image, you can use the Geometry Options in the Options Bar.

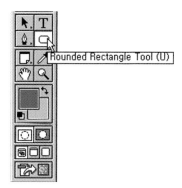

▲ *Selecting the Rounded Rectangle Tool.*

4.

Set the Radius to 30 px and the Fixed Size, in Geometry Options, to 700 x 500 px to draw a rounded rectangle of that size.

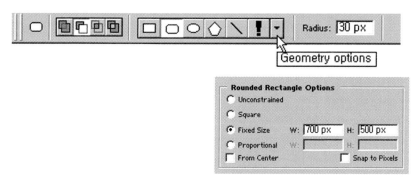

▲ *The dialog box that appears after clicking*
Geometry Options.

5.

The shape that appears will be the size that you specified. Now all you have to do is position it.

You can add a blue contour by using the Stroke command in Layer Style. After specifying the size of the contour, set the Position to Inside for the Stroke command so that the contour doesn't go outside the lines of the shape.

▲ Positioning the rounded rectangle shape.

Modifying the Shape

Make another shape of the same size in a layer below. You can use the Shape Tool to adjust Path and the size of the shape.

Use the Path Component Selection Tool to move the shape or to apply Transform.

Use the Direct Selection Tool to move or delete vertices of a shape.

Using Transform to adjust the size of the shape will cause distortion. Therefore, use the Direct Selection Tool to select and move a portion of the shape to adjust the size.

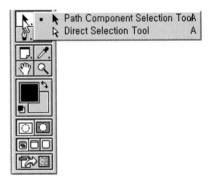

▲ Using the Direct Selection Tool.

▲ Selecting a portion of the shape.

Drawing Menu Images

1.

A convenient way to add images to existing layers is to take advantage of the steps in the layers to create a hidden form.

▲ *Drawing the menu image.*

As you can see here, the rounded rectangular shape of the main menu is partially hidden by the external shape.

2.

You'll draw the shape for the layer below and adjust the position to create the desired shape.

▲ *Entering the text.*

It is best to adjust the size and spacing of the buttons based on the text. This reduces unnecessary frames and ensures even spacing.

3.

First, enter the text and create even spacing. Then draw in the background button based on the text spacing that you created.

▲ *Text font and size information.*

▲ *Creating the background image based on the text spacing.*

---

vertically oriented text

You can use the Type Tool to enter vertically oriented text. One way is to select Vertically Orient Text in the Type Options Bar before entering the text and then selecting Rotate Character from the pop-up menu that appears by clicking the arrow button at the top right in the Character Palette to rotate the entered text.

Another method is to enter the text and then use the Transform command to rotate the text 90°.

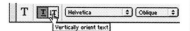

▲ *The Vertically Orient Text option of the Type Tool.*

---

small fonts

Looking at the Options Bar for the button text, you can see that a 12 pt Arial font, with Antialias set to None, is used. The smallest font size for a Web image that doesn't use Antialiasing is 8 pt for Roman characters. Fonts smaller than this will cause the text to run into each other.

▲ *Text with (below) and without (above) Antialiasing*

297

Slicing the Frame Using ImageReady

The Jump to ImageReady icon in the Toolbox loads the current image file in ImageReady. However, for slower computers, I suggest that you use the File⟶Open command to prevent the work from being slowed down. It's also possible to open both ImageReady and Photoshop on the desktop and work on the same image simultaneously in both programs. Making changes to the image in one program will cause the same changes to take place in the image in the other program, thereby preventing the need to jump from one program to another. However, this again can drastically slow down the work speed and is, therefore, not recommended.

▲ *The Jump to ImageReady icon.*

1.

First of all, copy a gray button image, for the Rollover button, in a new layer.

In order to add color to grayscale images, access the Colorize option in the Image⟶Adjust⟶ Hue/Saturation dialog box.

▲ *Applying a purple color (R: 143, G: 126, B: 207) to the buttons.*

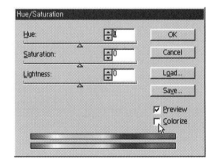

▲ *Checking the Colorize button in the Hue/Saturation dialog box.*

2.

Before configuring the Slice frame, changing the Optimize Palette options to the defaults will make the work easier. Just as you first set the time interval in the Animation Palette before making the animation, configuring the options before working on the Slice frame will allow the same options to be applied to all the slices that are created from this point on. This prevents you from having to go back and configure the options for each slice that you create.

Other than appearing rounded in shape, it's not necessary for the slice images to be different in color. Therefore, in the Optimize Palette, you select GIF 16 color.

Check the Interlaced option so that all the image files will appear in stepwise fashion when generated in the browser.

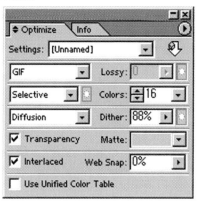

▲ *Optimize Palette properties.*

Entering Slice Information and Rollover Images

In order for slice frames created in ImageReady to become one image file, they must bypass the Optimize and Slice Palettes and, as needed, the Animation and Rollover Palettes.

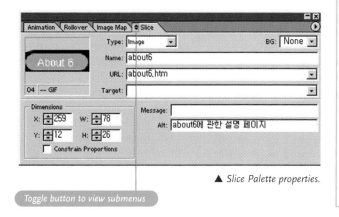

Toggle button to view submenus

▲ *Slice Palette properties.*

---

matte

Discrepancies in color can appear between the outlines of images with Transparency applied and the background. Matte is the function that removes this discrepancy.

---

use magnify

When creating slice frames, you must magnify the work window so that you can see the entire image and create minute frame divisions. Creating precise frames is difficult even with the Snap option in place because incorrect frame divisions can occur due to the invisible Antialias frames. Therefore, to avoid such errors, it's a good idea to get into the habit of working in a magnified work window.

The Slice menu contains the Divide Slice choice. When this function is used to create menu images, as you are doing here, it keeps you from having to create each slice one at a time. First one big slice is made that encompasses the entire menu, and then you magnify the window and use this function to create precisely divided slices.

You can move between the Slice Tool and the Slice Select Tool by pressing Shift+K.

Entering Information in the Slice Palette

The Slice Palette contains information on the file name and is used to specify the Slice type and background color. For the various subtags applied to the images in HTML, enter the file name, configure the links within the image tag, add additional information, and control the slice size using appropriate values.

These configurations are not really for the entire image but are the configurations of supplementary functions. This is extremely helpful after the creation of the actual HTML file or when rules exist for naming the files in the previously made folder. Even without making the configurations for the supplementary functions, you can still proceed with the work and specify the basic file name + slice number rule to apply to the slice while ignoring, to some degree, the properties of the Slice Palette. You'll look more closely at these standard application rules.

Configuring the Rollover Image

When Rollover image properties are applied to the slice, the image file is created and named according to the rule, file name + rollover status.ext. This is applied automatically. You can specify their own file-naming rules by choosing File⇨Output Settings⇨Saving Files.

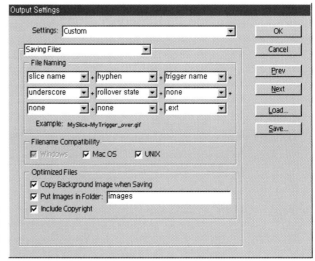

▶ *Configuring the Saving Files option in the Output Settings dialog box.*

You can specify the file name and the corresponding rules in the Output Settings dialog box by choosing Saving Files⇨File Naming.

The nine selection bars are used to determine the eight-step file name and extension rule. The default setting is set to slice name + hyphen + trigger name + underscore + rollover state.ext in this order. This default rule is selectively applied on a case by case basis. For example, when the Rollover effect is applied to several image slices, due to one slice, the trigger name is not applicable and is not applied.

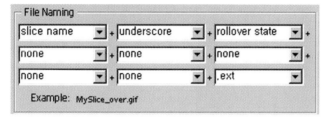

▲ *Simplification of file naming.*

FYI

Slightly different from previous versions, you can now move between tools in the same categories in Photoshop 6 and ImageReady 3 by using the Shift key plus the corresponding shortcut key.

Execute Slices⇨Divide Slice to create eight horizontal frames. Use the Slice Select Tool to adjust each slice to fit the size of the respective menus.

Removing the slice numbers and symbols: For experienced users of Photoshop, the slice numbers and the nontransparent frame divisions will appear very strange. These numbers and frames will appear on top of the image creating a cluttered workspace. You can fix this, however, by using Slice Preferences.

Edit⇨Preferences contains functions used to adjust the slice outline and numbers and the color, size, and opacity of the symbols. Setting the Numbers and Symbols options to None will remove the slice numbers that appear in the image window.

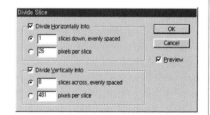

▲ *Divide Slice dialog box.*

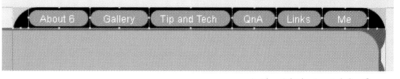

▲ *The eight horizontal slice frames.*

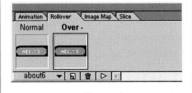
Although you can use several of the selection bars at a time to create complex naming regulations, you may have a hard time recognizing your own rules if they're too complex. It is not the purpose of these regulations to create long names but to add the convenience of creating automatic file names.

A file name of the form slice name + underscore + rollover state.ext is created automatically for the rollover and slice image files.

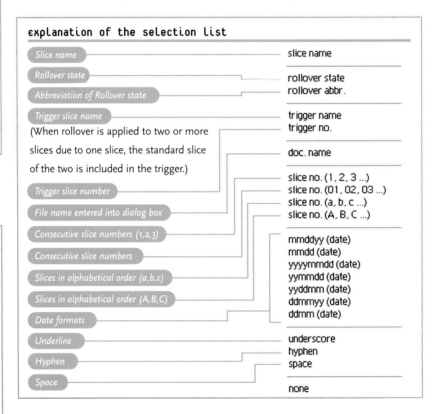

Saving the Optimized Image

Speaking from my own experience, I think ImageReady is extremely useful and convenient for slicing/optimizing slice frames, creating Rollover images, and making GIF animations. However, problems arise when these files are made into HTML files.

There is no problem when ImageReady is used to create simple HTML files. The problems only arise when Rollover images are attempted. When several menu images are made on one layer and sliced and then Rollover is substituted into each slice, the Rollover buttons that are created respond simultaneously. To prevent this from happening, each menu image must be made on a separate layer. However, a Web site already contains numerous layers, even without the additional layers that need to be devoted to just the menu. This is why many users prefer to complete the menu in one layer. To resolve this dilemma, Rollover-applied HTML files are created in HTML editors.

TIP

When several slices are selected to be optimized at the same time, such as menu navigation buttons, or when File Save commands are applied or modified, it is much more efficient to use Slice⇨Save Slice Selection to save the slice, with it selected in its entirety, and to load it as needed.

1.

Save the slices that are set up as menu images.

First, select all the slices of the menu image using the Slice Select Tool while pressing the Shift key.

2.

In the File⇨Save Optimized As dialog box, set the File Format to Images Only and restrict the saved slice frames by selecting Selected Slices at the bottom.

The file name of the small image indicated in the File Name line is applicable only when the Doc.name has been specified under Saving Files in the Output Settings dialog box.

▲ *Selecting Select Slices.*

Creating Icons Using Microangelo 5 (Windows-Only)

LESSON HIGHLIGHTS

Learning how to create icon files to add icons and animated cursors that match your desktop can be quite an enjoyable experience.

The function sequence is Straight Line Tool, Color Blend, and Flood Tool.

In this lesson, you'll learn how to use another software program used to create icons inside a 32 x 32 pixel square. You'll then use this program to create and magnify an icon image that will be used as the main image on a unique homepage.

Understanding Icon Images

When a bitmap image is magnified, it looks like a rough image that is made up of rectangular pixels. This effect will be applied to an image of actual size to create some differentiation.

Icons or Web site images on Windows or Macintosh operating systems that utilize GUIs (Graphic User Interfaces) mostly use 16 or 256 colors. Therefore, they can be made quite easily using most icon-creation software programs.

You'll use one such Windows software program, Microangelo 5, to make simple icons and then complete the image by capturing a still of the enlarged image.

▲ *An image used at a homepage.*

Understanding Microangelo 5

1.

Five small programs, Animator, Explorer, Librarian, On Display, and Studio, are installed with the installation of Microangelo 5.

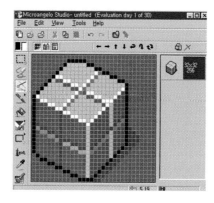

2.

Select Studio by choosing Start⇨Program⇨Microangelo.

This program is very easy to use. You use the tools on the left of the central image window to draw the desired shapes. This Toolbox contains very simple tools, including those used to draw or erase basic 2D figures and lines. The size and color information of the current image is shown on the right. The default setting is 32 x 32 pixel, 256-color image.

▲ *Running Microangelo Studio.*

Microangelo 5 Folders

Animator is a program used to create icons and GIF animations, and Explorer brings up the explorer. Librarian is a program that ties together and saves 16 x 16, 32 x 32, and 48 x 48 size icons, and On Display exchanges the Windows icons with the icons that are created in this program. Studio is an easy and convenient tool for creating simple icons.

Drawing the Outer Line

1.

Select Straight Line from the toolbar.

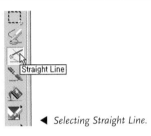

◀ *Selecting Straight Line.*

2.

Draw in the outline of the image in black. Because Microangelo cannot display Antialiased images, there are many restrictions on the shapes that you can draw.

You need spatial and depth perception to create a 3D image on a planar surface. This is not that difficult to do given some basic rules.

You'll also be able to create the 3D image seen here by drawing your image in the same way.

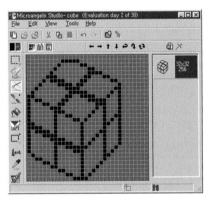

▲ *Drawing in the outline.*

Coloring

1.

You'll add a very bright color to the top, a neutral color to the lower left, and a very dark color to the right. To create this color gradation, you use the Color Blend tool. This tool displays the ten color gradations between two colors and shows you which one will be used.

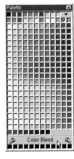

◀ *Color Blend.*

2.

Choose a bright blue color for the bright area and a dark blue color for the darkened area and pour them into the icons shaped like cones on either end of Color Blend to display the ten midtones between these two colors.

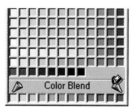 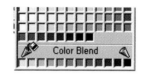

▲ *Entering the colors on either end.*

3.

Choose five color gradations from the ten shown and drag them into place in the palette.

▲ *The contents of the palette that allows the colors entered into Color Blend to be used.*

4.

The colors use the Flood and Straight Line tools from the Toolbox.

▲ *Flood Tool.*

5.

First color the bright, neutral, and dark regions using the Flood Tool and add beveling to create dimensionality.

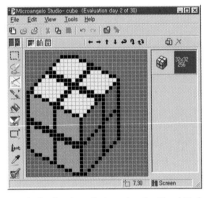

▲ *Application of color using the Flood Tool.*

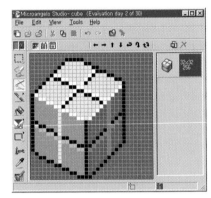

▲ *Adding beveling.*

6.

You can verify the actual size of the image in the Actual Size and Preview windows. The only difference between the two is that the Preview window displays the entire work process. Therefore, you can use either window to check the size of the image.

▲ *Preview window.*

7.

The blue-green color of the background will not be applied to the actual image. Rather, the Screen color will be used. This Screen color is selected in the Color Palette and acts just like an eraser.

Right-clicking the mouse in Microangelo causes the selected color to be applied. Right-click the mouse to apply the Screen color. Screen color is also useful for covering up mistakes.

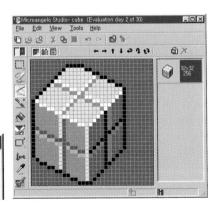

▲ *Selecting the Screen color.*

Saving the icon with Icon Restore selected allows it to be used as a background or software icon.

Capturing the Magnified Image

1.

When finished, save the image in GIF format using the File⊅Save command and then load it into Photoshop.

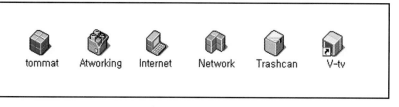

▲ *The icons created in this example are used as desktop icons.*

2.

Use the Zoom Tool in the Toolbox to magnify the image to a fixed size and save this image using the Print Screen key or image capture software.

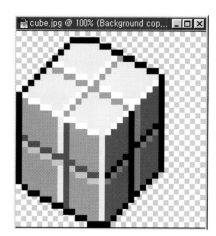

▲ *Completed image.*

> **using numerical values to magnify the screen**
>
> Magnifying the screen using numerical values is done in the Navigator window. When Image⊅Image Size is used to adjust the image size or when Transform is applied to the image, the Antialias effect is also applied causing a totally different result to occur. Therefore, it's a good idea to use screen capture techniques when adjusting the size of images with exact shapes, as in this example.

Completing the Homepage Using Dreamweaver 4

LESSON HIGHLIGHTS

You'll learn how to use a
<TABLE> tag so that the
homepage always remains
centered on the page despite
the changing size of the
browser.

In this lesson, you'll learn how to use Dreamweaver 4 to add Rollover effects, how to set up tags to create centered homepages, and how to make and use tables that fit the shape of the image.

Images and text are arranged on background images and text. In arranging the foreground images and text, you need to keep in mind the slicing of other images. Users with less experience in Web design tend to make more mistakes doing this. After making a graphic centered around an image, they do not know how to cut out the area where the text will be inserted and they also have difficulty using the HTML <TABLE> tag.

A homepage that completely surrounds an image is, in terms of file capacity, not useful. However, it's a good idea to practice creating homepages with complex images in order to increase an understanding of HTML. Therefore, I chose such a homepage for the example in this lesson.

You'll learn how to use a <TABLE> tag that allows for expansion of the page height in creating the HTML. This is the common method used for creating homepages that completely envelope the image and is also good practice for using the <TABLE> tag.

Slicing the Image Slice Frame

1.

The image on the right shows, in different colors, how the text and image frames are divided for HTML coding. Once you become more comfortable with homepage image slicing, try experimenting with smaller slices that will reduce the size of the image. Here, you simplified the slices to make things a little easier.

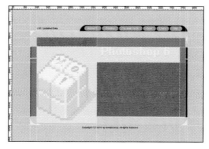

▲ *Yellow: Image frame; Red: Text frame; Blue: Empty space.*

2.

Load the file into ImageReady to see how the slices are set up. Open the Slice and Rollover Palettes to observe the properties of the image and empty space frames and the setup of the Rollover button.

The outer areas of the homepage that are shown here in gray (these are the slice frames that do not include any images or text) are set

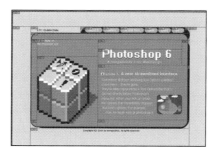

▲ *The slice frames configured for the homepage.*

up as No Image in the Slice Palette. The images on either side of the center are also set to No Image so that they can be applied as the background image for the <TABLE> tag. The Optimize properties are set to GIF format with a maximum of 32 colors.

311

Suppose that a certain piece of software is divided into beginning, intermediary, and advanced levels. What do you do? In order to prevent taking up a lot of disk space, as you are now, it's a good idea to obtain the beginning level, which reviews the most basic tools, and then, when you are ready to move on, to obtain the patch for the intermediary level, which will add additional tools and features. What this means in real life is that HTML's several hundred tools and functions do not all need to be mastered at the beginning level. All you really need to know to create a homepage is how to enter text and images on an HTML page and how to create a table for the arrangement of these elements. In other words, the tools and functions that you'll learn in a beginner program are more than enough to create an adequate homepage.

This holds true for HTML editors as well. Everything you need to know to create a basic homepage is contained in a beginning level HTML editor program. In this lesson, you'll be looking at one type of HTML editor program, Dreamweaver 4. This program covers the basics, such as table creation and use, and therefore, the beginner should have no problem following along with this example.

3.

Save all the images to a folder by choosing File⟶Save Optimized. When saving, make sure that only the images, and not the HTML files, are saved. When HTML files are saved along with the images, an image folder will not be created. Make a separate folder for the HTML and create the image folder beneath it as a subfolder and save the images here.

You create the image folder through the Custom dialog box after clicking the Output Settings button in the Save dialog box.

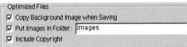

▲ *Selecting Put Images in Folder to create the image folder.*

Making the Table Frame

1.

Load Dreamweaver 4 and create a new index.html file using the File⟶Save command. Then click Insert Table in the Objects window.

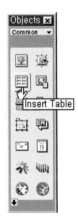

▶ *Selecting Insert Table.*

2.

In the Insert Table dialog box, set Rows to 1, Columns to 1, and Width to 100 Percent. Set the remaining values to 0.

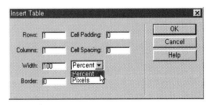

▲ *Insert Table dialog box.*

3.

The table must be selected while it's being created. In the Properties window, enter 100% for the Height value.

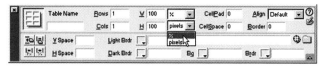

▲ *Entering 100% for the Height.*

4.

Clicking the inside of the table with the mouse allows you to configure Properties for the TD tag. In the Properties window, set the Horizontal value to Center so that the homepage is always aligned in the center of the screen whenever it is loaded.

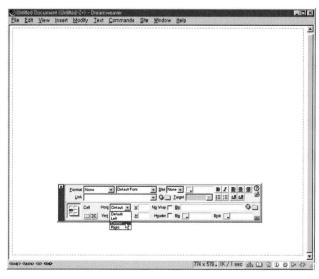

▲ *Setting up center alignment.*

creating a homepage

You can create a homepage where the position of the elements and the horizontal alignments change with the size of the browser. The width and height of tables, images, and frames for the HTML tag are entered in units of pixels or percents (%). The percent value here is in proportion to the size of the browser window. Therefore, when the <TABLE> tag of the sliced page is set to 100%, the width and the height of the page are used as the outer edge of the browser window and will adjust and realign itself as the size of the browser window changes.

5.

Make a new table inside the previously created table.

Set the Rows to 3 and the Width to 700 Pixels to create a three-row (TR) column 700 pixels wide. The top row (table) is for the menu, the middle table is for the image and text, and the bottom table is for the copyright information.

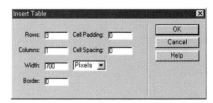

▲ *Insert Table properties.*

▲ *The newly created table.*

Inserting a Rollover Image

1.

First, click the top row, where the menu images will be placed, with the mouse so that text, images, and tables can be entered.

Divide the table row into nine columns (TD) for the menu images and the location indicator that will be placed on the left.

▲ *The table cells created in the top row.*

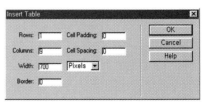

▲ *Configuring the row where the menu images will be entered.*

2.

To adjust the
width of the first
box on the left,
where text will be
entered, open the
Slice Palette
extension menu
in ImageReady
and verify the
Width value
under Dimensions.

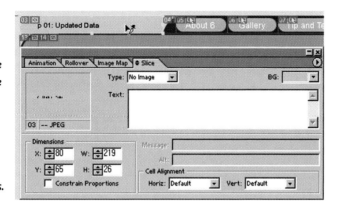

3.

Go back to Dreamweaver and, selecting the interior of the first box, enter 219 for the
Width value in the Properties window.

▶ Setting the
width of the first
box to 219 Pixels.

4.

Select the second box and choose Insert Image from
the Objects window. Look for the Menu_l.Gif file in
the Images folder and load it into the second box.

▲ The image file entered into the second box.

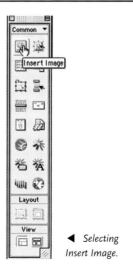

◀ Selecting
Insert Image.

315

5.

Select the third box with the mouse. Click Insert Rollover Image and load the rollover image.

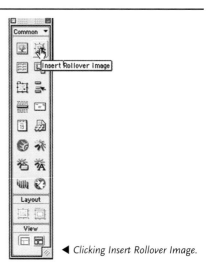

◀ *Clicking Insert Rollover Image.*

6.

In the Insert Rollover Image dialog box, enter the Image Name and then load the Original and Rollover images. The images that will be loaded are as follows: Original image (top); Rollover image (bottom).

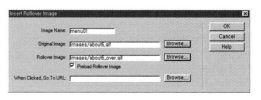

▲ *Insert Rollover Image dialog box.*

7.

Insert one Rollover image for each box. The menu is complete when the Menu_r.Gif image is inserted into the final box.

▲ *Each of the eight image files are loaded into each of the eight boxes.*

Inserting the Main Image and Text

1.

Divide the middle row into three segments and, after selecting the entire row with the mouse, load the Border_top.Gif file from the Images folder.

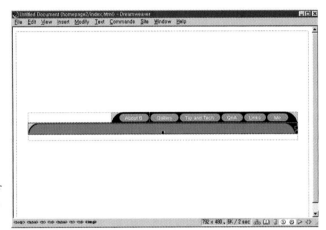

▶ *The Border_top.Gif file loaded into the second row.*

2.

Next, you'll create the table where the main images and text will be entered. Insert the table row divided into three cells (TD) below the image. (The interior of the table will adjust to fit the size of the image that is inserted. Therefore, the arrow keys on the keyboard are convenient for inserting a new element into the same segment.)

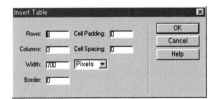

▲ *Creating the table for the insertion of the main images and text.*

3.

Starting with the segment on the left, set the width of each to 28, 269, and 403 pixels, respectively.

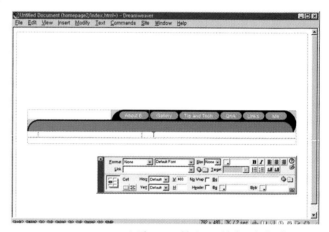

▲ *The new table inserted below the border image.*

4.

Set the height of the segment on the far left to 378.

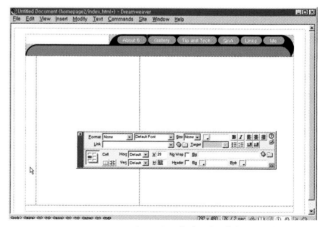

▲ *Setting the height of the new table to 378.*

5.

Load the Border_left2.Gif file and set the alignment of the segment on the left to Bottom in the Properties window.

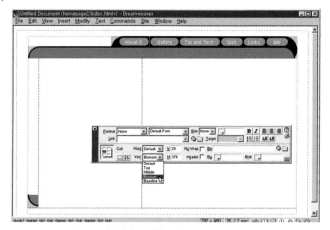

▲ *The Border_left2.Gif file is loaded and aligned at the bottom.*

6.

Return to the Properties window and click the Background URL of cell button under Bg so that the Border_left_c.Gif file is used as the background image.

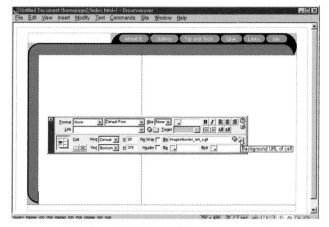

▲ *Setting up the background image in the segment on the left.*

creating tables

When the table is created, each of the cells are displayed with a <TD> tag. When the images are used as backgrounds for the <TD> tags, the table adjusts to fit the desired size and prevents the distortion of the page that can otherwise occur.

This method is used on a lot of sites and is an extremely useful procedure for maintaining the size of the page.

7.

Next, insert a table with a width of 269 pixels and that encompasses two rows into the second cell of the already existing table, for the main image and the title.

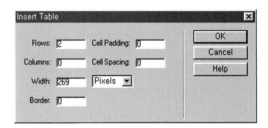

▲ *Creating the table for the main image.*

8.

In the Properties window, set the height of the table to 378 and load the Image_feature.Gif file into the bottom cell.

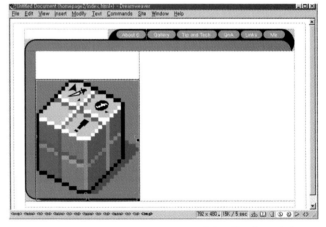

▲ *Inserting the main image.*

9.

Select the third cell and create a table that encompasses three rows of and has a width of 403 pixels.

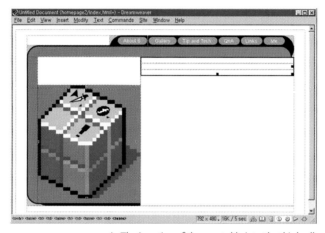

▲ *The insertion of the new table into the third cell.*

10.

Make a table that encompasses two rows and has a width of 403 pixels in the top-most cell and load the Title.gif and Border_right.Gif files into each cell starting with the cell on the left.

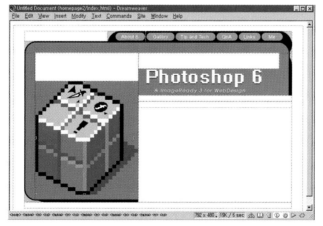

▲ *Creating the table for the title.*

Applying the Background Color

Selecting the table that was created for the main image and text, specify the background color in the Properties window.

▲ Selecting the table.

▲ The button used to specify the background color of the table.

1.

In the window used to specify the background color, deselect the Snap To Web Safe option in the pop-up menu at the top right and then select the background color in the work window using the eyedropper.

When the Safe-Color option is selected, it replaces the colors that you used with the closest Web-safe colors.

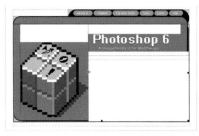

▲ After applying the background color.

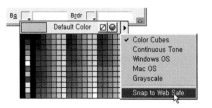

▲ The color selection (work) window.

▲ Selecting the color of the work window as the background color.

2.

Next, create a table, with a width of 403 pixels and that encompasses one row of two columns, for the contents and the image of the borderline that will be placed on the right.

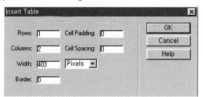

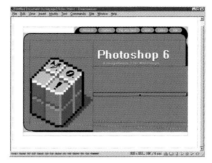

▲ Creating the table for the contents and the right borderline.

3.

In the Properties window, set the height of the table to 235 pixels.

▲ Specifying the height of the table.

4.

Set the width of the two cells to 394 and 9 pixels, respectively.

Select the segment on the right with the mouse and set the background color to black.

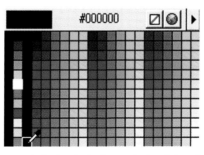

▲ Setting the background color of the cell on the right (the cell with a width of 9 pixels) to black.

5.

Finally, load the Border_Bottom.Gif file into the segment on the bottom.

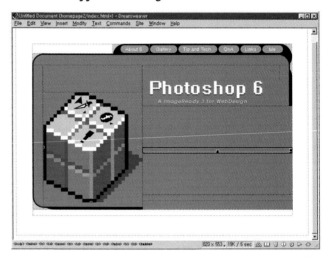

▲ Inserting the Border_Bottom.Gif file.

6.

The overall background color can be changed in Modify⇨Page Properties⇨ Background. Again you select the color with the Safe-Color option deselected.

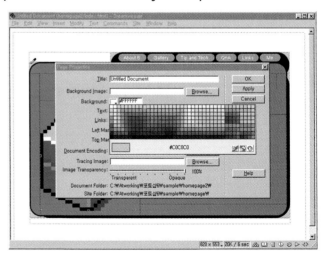

▲ Choosing Page Properties to modify the entire background color.

Verifying the Result

Load the completed page into the browser to verify the results.

Due to the table that is inserted below the Border_top.Gif file, a space will appear between the image and the table. This occurs because a space is inserted between the image and table tags and can be fixed by modifying the tags themselves. Click Show Code Inspector at the lower left corner of the Dreamweaver work window to load the HTML source window and, selecting the Border_top.Gif image, look for the position of the corresponding HTML source code.

Remove the space between the two tables by moving the table tag following the image tag in the HTML source window.

Save the HTML file again and go back to the browser to see that the problem has been fixed. You might need to press the browser's Refresh button to make certain that the modified page is loaded.

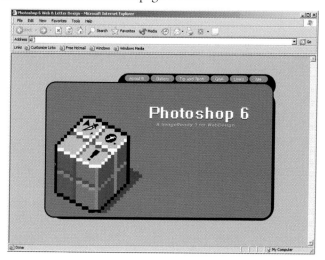

▲ *The completed homepage.*

▲ *Selecting Show Code Inspector.*

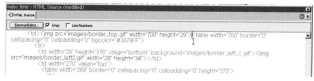

▲ *Modifying the contents in the HTML source window.*

325

::

Reference Sites

In this section, I've compiled a collection of superior Web sites that you can use as references when creating your own Web sites.

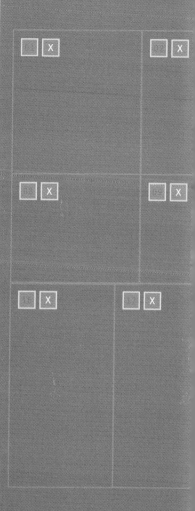

Christian Dior

www.dior.com

In keeping with its purpose as a site devoted to cosmetics, this site uses a glossy finish that makes the site appear glamorous and very feminine.

▲ *www.dior.com*

▲ *The Christian Dior site (www.dior.com/beauty-dior.as/)*

▲ *The product, Tendre Poison, shown under the Fragrance Universe menu. (www.dior.com/beauty-dior.as/)*

WDDG Web Architecture and Design Group
www.wddg.com

Here is the homepage of a Web design agency and several portfolio sites that really utilize dynamic animations to their full effect. They make excellent use of animation to fully capture the attention of the visitor.

This is a personal homepage that contains a portfolio of fashion photographs. The thing to take note of here on this site is that the designer uses a Photoview in the gallery. The addition of this feature prevents the potential tediousness that is seen on other portfolio sites.

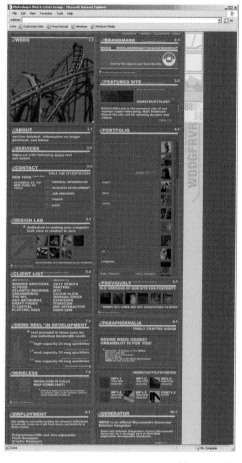

▲ www.wddg.com/wddg

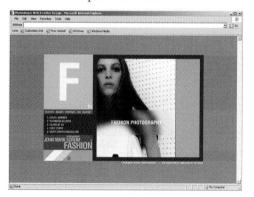

▲ www.johnmarksorum.com

▲ www.terryschocolate.com

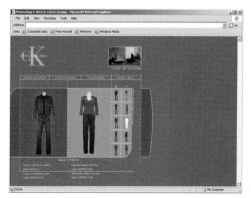

◀ www.mtv.com/mtv/ marketing /ckjnetwork/ prelaunch/index_dressing.html

Kaliber10000

www.k1ok.net

A designer's sensitivity, an author's mindset, an opportunity to witness new graphic identities. . . . This site contains a collection of project sites and personal homepages through which you can truly observe and experience utterly unique designs. Kaliber10000 is a landmark in the design community, and you'll be able to obtain many ideas while browsing through the projects of many designers that are on this site.

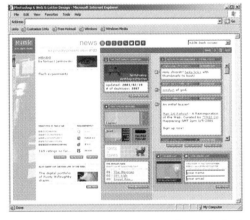

▲ *www.k1ok.net*

▲ *issu*

▲ *the [on] display exhibition*

Linkdup

www.linkdup.com

Like Kaliber10000 and Moluv's Picks, this is a site that contains a collection
of superior Web site designs.

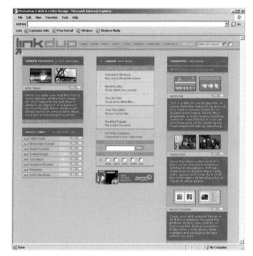

▲ *www.linkdup.com*

Moluv's Picks

www.moluv.com

This new site frequently updates its
list of well-designed sites. Managed
by an individual by the name of
Maurice Wright, this site was originally started as a means of publicly
sharing site addresses and now contains more than 800 sites.

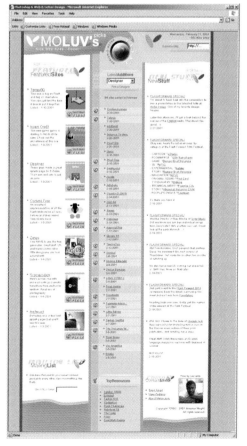

▲ *www.moluv.com*

Pre>loaded Web Agency
www.preloaded.com

Do you remember how old television sets used to run? This site uses old TV sets as its main concept as it uses the dials as a method of navigation. With the concept of Internet in TV and TV in the Internet, this site successfully combines two, almost contradictory, mediums.

▲ *www.preloaded.com/v2/indexplus.html*

▲ *www.preloaded.com*

Me company

www.mecompany.com

This is the homepage of a design company located in London, England. The menu navigation buttons are hidden in the swirling vortex of circles on its main page, and these buttons must be found in order to view the desktop. The site adds a new twist in the form of an amusing seek-and-find kind of game.

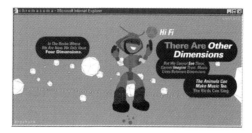

▲ *cromasoma*

▲ *www.mecompany.com*

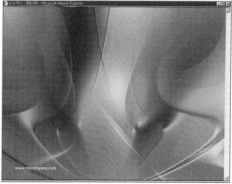

▲ *Desktop image*

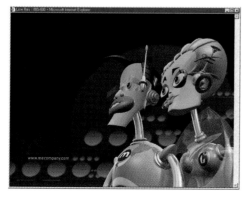

▲ *Desktop image*

▲ *Desktop image*

Bang & Olufsen
www.bang-olufsen.com

This is the homepage of the top audio designers, Bang & Olufsen.

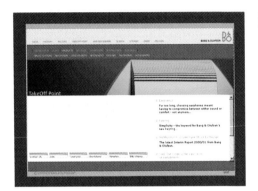 

▲ *www.bang-olufsen.com*   ▲ *product*

Andi's Skizzenblock
www.andi.com

This is the homepage of the freelance designer Andi Kuhn, from Munich, Germany. A collection of amusing, lifelike photographs make you feel as if you're browsing through a photo album or a scrapbook.

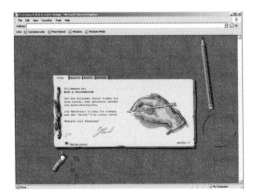 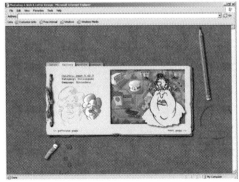

▲ *www.andi.com*   ▲ *portfolio*

Kodak Digital Innovators

www.kodak.com/US/en/corp/features/digitalinnovators

This Web site utilizes an innovative idea of color-coding its site into four colors so that visitors can find where they need to go. This site allows you to observe the brilliant design of the Web design agency, Second Story.

▶ *www.kodak.com/US/en/corp/features/*
digitalinnovator

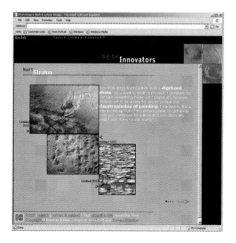

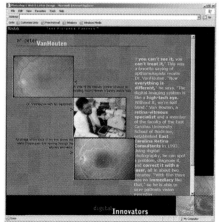

2advanced Web Agency
www.2advanced.com

This is the homepage of the Web design agency 2advanced Web Agency, located in California. Created by the designer Eric Jordan, this site allows you to glimpse a mechanistic Flash Web site.

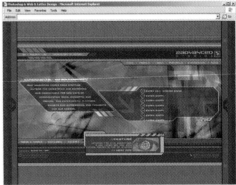

▲ *www.2advanced.com/flashindex.htm*

Blastradius Web Agency
www.blastradius.com

This is the Blastradius homepage, famous for its use of dynamic G-Shock Web animation.

▲ *www.blastradius.com*

Gabocorp studio

www.gabocorp.com

This site uses Flash animation to create the dynamic site. One of the leaders in Flash animation techniques, this site started the whole Flash animation frenzy.

▲ *www.gabocorp.com*

Hillmancurtis

www.hillmancurtis.com

This is the marketing site of Hillman Curtis, known as the leader of the Macromedia Flash site.

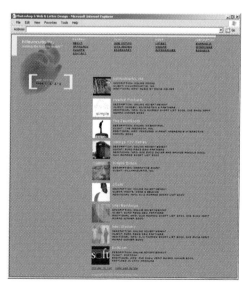

▲ *www.hillmancurtis.com*

337

Juxt Interactive Media
www.juxtinteractive.com

This is the homepage of Juxt Interactive Media, where Todd Purgason, one of the famous creators of Flash animation, along with Hillman Curtis, is Creative Director.

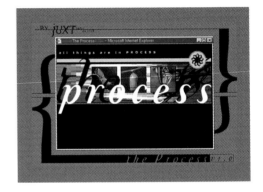

▲ *www.juxtinteractive.com*

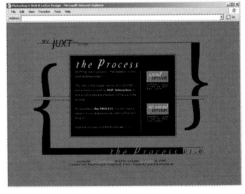

▲ *www.juxtinteractive.com/theprocess/index.html*

Workbook

www.workbook.com

This is the famous Workbook site that contains the ShowCase of photographers along with an immense collection of images and illustrations.

▲ *www.workbook.com*

▲ *photographer*

▲ *view image*

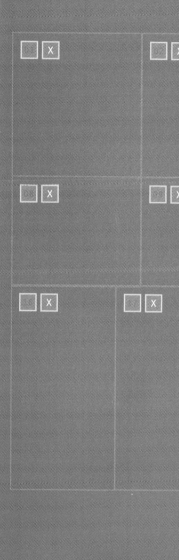

Appendix B

::

About the CD

This appendix provides you with information on the contents of the CD that accompanies this book. For the latest and greatest information, please refer to the ReadMe file located at the root of the CD. Here is what you will find:

- *System Requirements*

- *Using the CD with Windows and Macintosh*

- *What's on the CD*

- *Troubleshooting*

Minimum Recommended System Requirements

For Windows 9x, 2000, NT4 (with SP 4 or later), Me, or XP: a PC with a 120-Mhz or faster Pentium processor; at least 32 MB of RAM (we recommend at least 64 MB); an Ethernet network interface card (NIC) or modem with a speed of at least 28,800 bps; and a CD-ROM drive.

For Macintosh: a Mac OS computer with a 68040 or faster processor running OS 7.6 or later; and at least 32 MB of RAM (we recommend at least 64 MB).

Using the CD with Windows

To install the items from the CD to your hard drive, follow these steps:

1.

Insert the CD into your computer's CD-ROM drive.

If you do not have autorun enabled or if the autorun window does not appear, follow the steps below to access the CD; otherwise, skip to step 4.

2.

Click Start↷Run.

3.

In the dialog box that appears, type d:\setup.exe, where d is the letter of your CD-ROM drive. This will bring up the autorun window described above.

4.

Click Install.

Using the CD with the Mac OS

To install the items from the CD to your hard drive, follow these steps:

1.

Insert the CD into your CD-ROM drive.

2.

Double-click the icon for the CD after it appears on the desktop.

3.

Most programs come with installers; for those, simply open the program's folder on the CD and double-click the Install or Installer icon. Note: To install some programs, just drag the program's folder from the CD window and drop it on your hard drive icon.

What's on the CD

Here's a summary of the software and other materials on the CD.

Author Samples

All the samples and examples seen in the book are included on the CD in a folder called Author. The complete works are also included so that users can verify and compare their results.

Applications

You'll find three different kinds of applications are on the CD. *Shareware programs* are fully functional, trial versions of copyrighted programs. If you like particular programs, register with their authors for a nominal fee and receive licenses, enhanced versions, and technical support. *Freeware programs* are copyrighted games, applications, and utilities that are free for personal use. Unlike shareware, these programs do not require a fee or provide technical support. *Trial, demo, or evaluation versions* are usually limited either by time or functionality (such as being unable to save projects). Some trial versions are very sensitive to system date changes. If you alter your computer's date, the programs will "time out" and will no longer be functional.

100 Styles for Web Graphics

For Windows and Macintosh. The 100Styles.Asl file, located in the 100Styles folder in the CD-ROM, is copied into the Styles folder after installing Photoshop (Photoshop 6.0/Presets/Styles), and then, after executing Photoshop, the 100Styles.Asl file is found in Styles Palette or Preset Manager.

Photoshop

Trial version. For Windows and Macintosh. Check out this graphics programs from Adobe Systems. Also included is Adobe's Image Ready. For more information, check out www.adobe.com.

Illustrator

Trial version. For Windows and Macintosh. Use Adobe Systems' Illustrator to create professional looking graphics for your Web site. For more information, check out www.adobe.com.

Dreamweaver

Trial version. For Windows and Macintosh. Create top-notch looking Web sites with this easy-to-use HTML editor program from Macromedia. For more information, check out www.macromedia.com.

Flash

Trial version. For Windows and Macintosh. A Web animation tool from Macromedia you can use to create content for your Web site. For more information, check out www.macromedia.com.

MicroAngelo

Trial version. For Windows. Create icons, GIF animations, and clipart with MicroAngelo from Impact Software. For more information, check out www.impactsoft.com.

Troubleshooting

If you have difficulty installing or using any of the materials on the companion CD, try the following solutions:

- Turn off any antivirus software that you may have running. (Be sure to turn the antivirus software back on later.)
- Close all running programs. The more programs you're running, the less memory is available to other programs.
- Reference the ReadMe file located at the root of the CD-ROM, which has the latest product information at the time of publication.

If you still have trouble with the CD, please call the Hungry Minds Customer Care phone number: (800) 762-2974. Outside the United States, call 1 (317) 572-3994. You can also contact Hungry Minds Customer Service by e-mail at techsupdum@wiley.com. Hungry Minds will provide technical support only for installation and other general quality control items; for technical support on the applications themselves, consult the program's vendor or author.

A

accessing files, on the CD, 343

Acrobat Reader (Adobe), 56

actions, applying, to images, 36, 253

active links, color of, 37

Add a Layer Style command, 11, 81, 91

Add to Favorite command, 12

Adjust command, 134, 152

Adjust menu

  Hue/Saturation command, 93

  Posterize command, 152

  Threshold command, 152

Adjustment Layer

  adding, 22

  adding color with, 66-68

  described, 3

  selecting, 57

  simplifying images and, 152

  3-D text and, 93

Alpha Channels, 107, 110.
  See also channels

Amethyst-after.Psd, 121

Amethyst.Psd, 114

Animation Palette, 235, 244, 249, 252, 264. *See also* animations

  duplicating frames in, 30

  Tween function and, 29

  Reverse Frames feature in, 32

animations, 234-236, 244-255.
  See also Animation Palette

  actions and, 251-252

  basic description of, 255

  file size issues and, 31, 246, 253-254

  layer masks and, 250-251

loading speed of, 252

optimizing, 246, 253-254

Rollover buttons and, 264-268, 299

Tween function and, 29, 31, 247

Annotations, 27, 55-56

anti-aliasing, 149, 186, 309

Append command, 69

Aquarium-after.Psd, 184

Aquarium.Psd, 179

Arc option, 94, 95, 96

arrowheads, 155

Audio Annotation Tool, 27, 55

Automate command, 34, 35

Auto-Slice feature, 5, 259, 268

B

background color, 37, 44-45, 52.
  See also backgrounds; color

  Background layers and, 191

  tables and, 322, 323

Background layer, 190-191.
  See also layers

backgrounds. *See also* background color; Background layer

  applying patterns to, 179, 180

  gradations in, 44-45

  for icons, 308

  for Image Gallery Web sites, 41-51

  metallic text effects and, 135

  optimizing, 57-51

  protruding, 127-128

  for Rollover buttons, 269

  saving, 50-51

  slicing, 42-45

  for text, 142-144, 181-182

tiling, 14

transparent, 47-51

Ball.Psd, 75

banners, 36, 37

Basketball.jpg, 133

Batch feature, 36

Bend option, 94, 95

Bevel effect, 11-12, 14, 112-115

  Contour Editor and, 117

  Global Light option and, 81

  metallic text effects and, 137-138

  patterns and, 81, 83, 86, 180, 183

  plastic buttons and, 147

  protruding backgrounds and, 127-128

  Quartz effect and, 114-115, 123-124

Blur command, 170, 177

Blurredtext.Psd, 109, 110

boldface font, 52. *See also* fonts

bowl shapes, 154-155

browsers, 38, 53

Brushed Metal effect, 71, 91, 99

brushes

  files for, loading, 72

  selecting, 17-18

  sets of, 18

  types of, 72

Bulge effect, 96

Button_plastic-after.Psd, 152

Button_plastic.Psd, 145

buttons. See also Rollover buttons

  adding shapes to, 61

  adding slice frames to, 43

  adding styles to, 65

  color for, 66-68, 146-147, 151-152

  creating, 59-68, 145-152, 230-231

J

Jade-after. Psd, 126
Jade.Psd, 123
JASC Paint Shop Pro, 18, 72
.JBR file extension, 72
Join-after.Psd, 191
Join.Psd, 185
Joint Photographic Experts Group
(JPEG), 27, 36, 50, 74
    compression, 240
    optimizing, 231, 233-234,
        240-243
    slice frames and, 232, 238-239
Jump To feature, 76, 230, 271

K

Kai's Power Goo (Metatools), 26

L

Layer Based Slice feature, 32, 74-76
Layer Properties dialog box, 172
Layer Style command, 79
Layer Style dialog box, 11-12, 14,
    116-117, 137
Layer Style Palette, 9, 44-45, 66, 81,
    126, 141
Layer Styles, 7, 9-14, 18, 44-45,
    116-117. See also Layer Style Palette
    applying, 10-14, 183
    background images and, 44
layers. See also Layer Styles; Layers
    Palette
    converting, 187
    copying, 189
    creating, 60-61
    deleting, 188
    hiding, 47, 186

managing, with Layer Sets, 7
merging, 189
properties of, 7
rasterized, 95, 187
slicing, 16
Layers Palette, 60, 67, 75, 91, 93
    adjusting presets in, 18
    disabling thumbnails in, 29
    hiding layers in, 47
    Lock function in, 150
    merging layers with, 189
    new features in, 8
layouts, 35, 230-231
Lighting effects, 81, 109, 113, 124,
    168-177
Lighting Effects command, 109, 113
Lighting Effects Filter, 124
Line Tool, 186
links
    color of, 37
    entering frames as, in the Image
Liquify command, 26
Load button, 69, 70
Load Path As A Selection option,
    170
Lock feature, 78, 150

M

Macromedia Dreamweaver.
    See Dreamweaver (Macromedia)
Macromedia Flash. See Flash
    (Macromedia)
Maintain Aspect Ratio option, 170,
    302
Map Palette, 28
<MAP> tag, 236, 270
Marquee Tool, 5, 76

masks, 180-182, 250-251
Matte options, 48, 241, 242, 299,
    280
Measure Tool, 43
Memo Pads, 52
memory, 71
menus. See also specific menus
    drawing images for, 297
    vertical, organization of, 293
Merge Linked command, 189
metallic textures, 133-144
MicroAngelo, 304-309, 345
Midtones, 134
Move Tool, 76, 150

N

navigation schemes
    described, 288-289
    global, 292-293
    local, 292, 293
    Rollover buttons and, 298-303
    vertical menu organization and,
        293
Navigator window, 309
New command, 103
New Layer Based Image Map
    feature, 32
New Layer Based Slice feature, 16,
    32, 42-43, 75, 32
New Style dialog box, 84, 121, 149
No Dither option, 48
Notes Tool, 26, 27, 54-56
Notes Tool command, 54

O

Offset Filter, 79, 85
Open dialog box, 12

352

Hungry Minds, Inc.
End-User License Agreement

READ THIS. You should carefully read these terms and conditions before opening the software packet(s) included with this book ("Book"). This is a license agreement ("Agreement") between you and Hungry Minds, Inc. ("HMI"). By opening the accompanying software packet(s), you acknowledge that you have read and accept the following terms and conditions. If you do not agree and do not want to be bound by such terms and conditions, promptly return the Book and the unopened software packet(s) to the place you obtained them for a full refund.

1. **License Grant.** HMI grants to you (either an individual or entity) a nonexclusive license to use one copy of the enclosed software program(s) (collectively, the "Software") solely for your own personal or business purposes on a single computer (whether a standard computer or a workstation component of a multi-user network). The Software is in use on a computer when it is loaded into temporary memory (RAM) or installed into permanent memory (hard disk, CD-ROM, or other storage device). HMI reserves all rights not expressly granted herein.

2. **Ownership.** HMI is the owner of all right, title, and interest, including copyright, in and to the compilation of the Software recorded on the disk(s) or CD-ROM ("Software Media"). Copyright to the individual programs recorded on the Software Media is owned by the author or other authorized copyright owner of each program. Ownership of the Software and all proprietary rights relating thereto remain with HMI and its licensers.

3. **Restrictions On Use and Transfer.**

   (a) You may only (i) make one copy of the Software for backup or archival purposes, or (ii) transfer the Software to a single hard disk, provided that you keep the original for backup or archival purposes. You may not (i) rent or lease the Software, (ii) copy or reproduce the Software through a LAN or other network system or through any computer subscriber system or bulletin-board system, or (iii) modify, adapt, or create derivative works based on the Software.

   (b) You may not reverse engineer, decompile, or disassemble the Software. You may transfer the Software and user documentation on a permanent basis, provided that the transferee agrees to accept the terms and conditions of this Agreement and you retain no copies. If the Software is an update or has been updated, any transfer must include the most recent update and all prior versions.

4. **Restrictions on Use of Individual Programs.** You must follow the individual requirements and restrictions detailed for each individual program in Appendix B of this Book. These limitations are also contained in the individual license agreements recorded on the Software Media. These limitations may include a requirement that after using the program for a specified period of time, the user must pay a registration fee or discontinue use. By opening the Software packet(s), you will be agreeing to abide by the licenses and restrictions for these individual programs that are detailed in Appendix B and on the Software Media. None of the material on this Software Media or listed in this Book may ever be redistributed, in original or modified form, for commercial purposes.

5. Limited Warranty.

(a) HMI warrants that the Software and Software Media are free from defects in materials and workmanship under normal use for a period of sixty (60) days from the date of purchase of this Book. If HMI receives notification within the warranty period of defects in materials or workmanship, HMI will replace the defective Software Media.

(b) HMI AND THE AUTHOR OF THE BOOK DISCLAIM ALL OTHER WARRANTIES, EXPRESS OR IMPLIED, INCLUDING WITHOUT LIMITATION IMPLIED WARRANTIES OF MERCHANTABILITY AND FITNESS FOR A PARTICULAR PURPOSE, WITH RESPECT TO THE SOFTWARE, THE PROGRAMS, THE SOURCE CODE CONTAINED THEREIN, AND/OR THE TECHNIQUES DESCRIBED IN THIS BOOK. HMI DOES NOT WARRANT THAT THE FUNCTIONS CONTAINED IN THE SOFTWARE WILL MEET YOUR REQUIREMENTS OR THAT THE OPERATION OF THE SOFTWARE WILL BE ERROR FREE.

(c) This limited warranty gives you specific legal rights, and you may have other rights that vary from jurisdiction to jurisdiction.

6. Remedies.

(a) HMI's entire liability and your exclusive remedy for defects in materials and workmanship shall be limited to replacement of the Software Media, which may be returned to HMI with a copy of your receipt at the following address: Software Media Fulfillment Department, Attn.: *Photoshop Design for the Web*, Hungry Minds, Inc., 10475 Crosspoint Blvd., Indianapolis, IN 46256, or call 1-800-762-2974. Please allow four to six weeks for delivery. This Limited Warranty is void if failure of the Software Media has resulted from accident, abuse, or misapplication. Any replacement Software Media will be warranted for the remainder of the original warranty period or thirty (30) days, whichever is longer.

(b) In no event shall HMI or the author be liable for any damages whatsoever (including without limitation damages for loss of business profits, business interruption, loss of business information, or any other pecuniary loss) arising from the use of or inability to use the Book or the Software, even if HMI has been advised of the possibility of such damages.

(c) Because some jurisdictions do not allow the exclusion or limitation of liability for consequential or incidental damages, the above limitation or exclusion may not apply to you.

7. U.S. Government Restricted Rights. Use, duplication, or disclosure of the Software for or on behalf of the United States of America, its agencies and/or instrumentalities (the "U.S. Government") is subject to restrictions as stated in paragraph (c)(1)(ii) of the Rights in Technical Data and Computer Software clause of DFARS 252.227-7013, or subparagraphs (c)(1) and (2) of the Commercial Computer Software - Restricted Rights clause at FAR 52.227-19, and in similar clauses in the NASA FAR supplement, as applicable.

8. General. This Agreement constitutes the entire understanding of the parties and revokes and supersedes all prior agreements, oral or written, between them and may not be modified or amended except in a writing signed by both parties hereto that specifically refers to this Agreement. This Agreement shall take precedence over any other documents that may be in conflict herewith. If any one or more provisions contained in this Agreement are held by any court or tribunal to be invalid, illegal, or otherwise unenforceable, each and every other provision shall remain in full force and effect.